George B. McClellan AND CIVIL WAR HISTORY

GEORGE B. McCLELLAN
and Civil War History

IN THE SHADOW OF GRANT AND SHERMAN

Thomas J. Rowland

THE KENT STATE UNIVERSITY PRESS

Kent, Ohio, and London, England

1998 by The Kent State University Press, Kent, Ohio 44242
All rights reserved
Library of Congress Catalog Card Number 98-13967
ISBN 0-87338-603-5
Manufactured in the United States of America

04 03 02 01 00 99 98   5 4 3 2 1

Library of Congress Cataloging-in-Publication Data

Rowland, Thomas J., 1952–
George B. McClellan and Civil War history : in the shadow of Grant
and Sherman / Thomas J. Rowland.
p.   cm.
Includes bibliographical references and index.
ISBN 0-87338-603-5 (alk. paper) ∞
1. McClellan, George Brinton, 1826–1885–Military leadership.
2. United States–History–Civil War, 1861–1865–Campaigns.
3. Command of troops–History–19th century.   I. Title.
E467.1.M2R69   1998
973.7'3'092–dc21   98-13967

British Library Cataloging-in-Publication data are available.

CONTENTS

Preface   vii

1.   Of Statues and Shadows   1
2.   A Foray into the Twilight Zone   16
3.   Little Mac's Peccadilloes   45
4.   The Struggle Becomes Remorseless   76
5.   Dodging the Albatross: McClellan and Grant
   and the Safety of Washington   103
6.   On to Richmond: Illusion of Easy Victory, 1861–1862   130
7.   The First Will Be Last and the Last Will Be First   165
8.   Bagging Bobby Lee   198
9.   Emerging from the Shadows   233

Note on Sources   239
Index   243

PREFACE

A PERSISTENT QUESTION THAT HAS HAUNTED ME FROM THE first day I contemplated writing about George B. McClellan, up to the very moment I write this sentence, is whether the literature really needs another book about this man. Despite some impressive evidence to the contrary, I have assured myself that it does. The first day I refer to probably goes back to my freshmen year at college in 1970. Since that time, this project has undergone many staggering, fitful starts and stops. Aiding and abetting its forward progress was the lingering puzzlement over how a general who was so talented and filled with so much promise ended up as such a miserable fizzle. The interruptions in the project were easier to understand. Throughout this period, one study after another has virtually codified the thesis that McClellan proved to be a wretched species of Civil War commander, unworthy of anything but additional condemnation. More discouragement came in the form of casual conversations with friends who possessed but a thumbnail sketch of Civil War familiarity. At the very mention of McClellan's name, a visage of contempt generally crept over their otherwise benevolent gazes, or worse, they mimed sticking their fingers down their throats. Both were clear, confirming signs of just how ingrained in the popular culture was McClellan's infamous repute. For a relative novice in the field, the commanding verdicts of acclaimed historians and the public at large made the prospect of voicing any dissenting opinions a most daunting one. At any rate, I kept coming back to the puzzle and eventually came to believe that more could be said about it.

The study of George B. McClellan that follows takes its form from my conviction that another standard biography or campaign study would serve no useful purpose. The literature is replete with such works. What was needed, in my opinion, was an analytical review of the literature itself. The format of this book, then, is many things but none of them exclusively. It contains biographical and campaign narrative elements synthesized from the excellent studies already written. In undertaking a review of the existing literature it becomes a historiographical work, thus the obvious reliance upon secondary source material. And it is revisionist to the extent that it both challenges well-established Civil War doctrine and suggests alternative mechanisms of reinterpretation. More precisely, I wanted to examine the literature that emerged in the last half century, for it is here that the consensus opinion of McClellan has taken shape. And it is here that we find the evolution of McClellan as a seriously flawed general and individual. The writers of this period, whom I will refer to as Unionist historians,[1] have thoroughly dominated the academic evaluation of McClellan's Civil War career and have directly influenced the popular perception in the process.

The complete domination of the Unionist interpretation with respect to any analysis of Civil War commanders is one of the basic assumptions of the study. The cornerstone of this interpretation is a generally unreserved approval of the efforts of Ulysses S. Grant, William T. Sherman, and Abraham Lincoln in saving the Union. The waning fortunes for rescuing the Union from utter dissolution were not reversed until the exclusive partnership of those three men was forged and made operational in the spring of 1864. Consequently, any and all efforts that preceded that climactic moment in the history of the war are deemed futile. Based upon this inviolable conviction, the Civil War leadership is ranked. And in this contextual framework, George B. McClellan is so completely overshadowed by Grant and Sherman as to practically ensure his receiving a very low grade.

I have long been uncomfortable with both the assumptions of the Unionist interpretation and the consequences it has had for the McClellan legacy. One of the sources of this discomfort has been that no account has been taken of the contextual differences that existed in fighting the war in 1861–1862, as opposed to 1864–1865. After all, it was not until Grant came east in 1864, leaving his Western command to Sherman, that both of their reputations received the acclaim that has enshrined them in the ranks of the war's greatest commanders. It seemed to me that there were material differences in the relative strengths of the Union and Confederate military machines between the time McClellan held the highest command in the North and when Grant and Sherman assumed control. The question as to why Grant's eastern predecessors found success so

---

1. For want of any better term, I have appropriated the designation "Unionist" from Joseph L. Harsh, "On the McClellan-Go-Round," *Civil War History* 19 (June 1973): 106.

elusive has never been fully answered. Was it merely, or even principally, a question of leadership, or did other factors play a more significant role?

That is the question upon which this study revolves. It is, in part, an exploration into the mythic Grant and Sherman. To a great extent, this investigation will help explain why McClellan has been discarded into the scrap heap of failed commanders, for when all is said and done, he was the most conspicuous and formidable personality in the East before Grant arrived. It offers another context for understanding why the North experienced so much disappointment in the early years of the war and how that adverse direction was reversed in the later years. In the process, it hopes to shorten the shadows Grant and Sherman have cast over McClellan without necessarily elevating the latter's stock at the expense of the other two.

This final caveat probably needs amplification and clarification. At various times, the study will appear unduly harsh in its evaluation of Grant, Sherman, and at times, Lincoln. No intentional attempt was made to create a "strawperson(s) scenario," in which Grant, Sherman, and even Lincoln are diminished in order to resurrect and elevate McClellan's career. I adopt this approach only when it seems that McClellan's critics have singled him out for flaws that were shared, and even exceeded, by many other commanders during the war. Even though I would argue that the unqualified ranking of Civil War commanders is a flawed process itself, I would still feel compelled to rank Grant and Sherman as the foremost military commanders in the North during the Civil War. If for no other reason, their success is a difficult thing to argue against. Consequently, the one thing this study does not undertake is the rehabilitation of George B. McClellan's reputation to the point of claiming he was a great commander. His lack of success militates against any such undertaking. But while I agree with those who suggest that McClellan might have been better suited for the position that Henry Halleck held during the war, I do not view him, despite his record as a field commander, as an abject failure.

Therefore, I categorically disagree with those who charge McClellan as the worst, or among the worst, Northern commanders during the war. I believe the evidence shows he was essentially a competent commander who remained reasoned in his strategic and political philosophies, which were consistent with the national policy articulated by the administration. I take particular exception to the more recent psychological profiling conducted by historians that paints McClellan as a deranged paranoic; I perceive serious problems with the methodology and a lack of perspective employed in the endeavor. At the same time, I hope I am clear in acknowledging McClellan's limitations that truly did contribute to his failure. The primary attempt being made here is to narrow the vast gulf of judgment that currently separates Grant and Sherman on one hand from McClellan on the other. Readers will decide for themselves whether or not I succeeded in restoring a balanced perspective.

A word or two about the study's organization might be helpful to readers as they traverse these pages. Although a unifying theme dominates and unites the various chapters, each of them is an equally independent essay of its own. The introductory chapter establishes the scope and direction of the historical literature on McClellan. The following two chapters review the psychological and personality issues that surround McClellan's career, as they have become the cornerstone in the literature for assessing his performance. The fourth and fifth chapters deal with specific concerns of strategic value in which many of McClellan's political and social views of the nature of the Civil War invite direct comparisons to those of Grant and Sherman. Moreover, the strategic concerns posed by planning offensive campaigns while still defending the Union capital are reviewed. The next three chapters examine McClellan's campaigns with an eye toward comparison with Grant's and Sherman's. In this process, it becomes necessary to alternate between eastern and western battlefields, and I only hope that my transitions are smooth enough so as not to confuse the reader. The last chapter serves as a conclusion in which the various themes discussed throughout the study are pulled together.

I owe several debts of gratitude to those who assisted in making this study possible. The lion's share of my thanks goes to John T. Hubbell of the Kent State University Press. In the absence of suitable professional colleagues, he filled a vacuum for me that goes beyond his general editing, and he was most responsible for guiding this work to its eventual conclusion.

Jon S. Wakelyn provided useful comments and suggestions from his reading of the manuscript. His recommendations concerning the organization and order of the essays as they appear were invaluable.

Although he is an Irish American historian, my friend, Tim Meagher, cheerfully read and offered suggestions in earlier versions of this manuscript. Another friend, Gordon Leighton, chair of the English department at Bellevue Community College in suburban Seattle, painstakingly read the entire manuscript and identified some of the more egregious grammatical and compositional deficiences. Any remaining are most assuredly of my own invention.

The nature of this study did not compel me to lean heavily on research library staffs. However, I did receive considerable assistance, always courteous and helpful, from the staff in the Manuscript Division of the Library of Congress.

A word of thanks goes out to my friend, Bill Kotwas, who dodged traffic on Connecticut Avenue and tour buses in Arlington Cemetary to obtain the photographs that appear in this work.

My heartfelt thanks are extended to Michael Nagy, whose initial reading of the early drafts of each chapter weeded out a tremendous amount of written debris before it ever reached anyone else's hands. Moreover, his continued support and encouragement helped save this project from an untimely demise.

George B. McClellan AND CIVIL WAR HISTORY

I

Of Statues and Shadows

IT STANDS IN METALLIC SILENCE, IMPASSIVE TO NINETY years of the commercial and residential growth that surrounds it. The statue, like the person it honors, remains difficult, almost hazardous to approach, its access constrained by two major District of Columbia arteries. Much like the man, the memorial rests on an island awash in a sea of confusion–aloof and distant from most other prominent Civil War statuary. Curiously, it adorns no rotary circle, graces no park or mall, commands no conspicuous city square as more and less heralded contemporaries do. Had not generations of urban sprawl engulfed it, the statue would go unnoticed. Tourists, providing they are alert, will stumble across it as they emerge from their hotel lairs for a day's sightseeing in the nation's capital. Its peculiar location reinforces the ambiguity besetting the one who created and first led the Army of the Potomac. And in a final touch of irony, the statue is flanked by such an irregular grid of street construction as to give rise to the amusing, if not judgmental, chestnut that the general was provided with three avenues of retreat but only one for advance. Fittingly, both the statue and the man, George Brinton McClellan, strike an enigmatic pose.[1]

1. The initial pages of this introductory chapter appeared earlier in somewhat altered form as Thomas J. Rowland, "In the Shadows of Grant and Sherman: George B. McClellan Revisited," *Civil War History* 40 (Sept. 1994): 202–25. The McClellan memorial is situated two miles north of the Mall and is framed by the convergence of Connecticut Avenue,

Looking resolutely southward. McClellan's memorial has been the subject of many jibes aimed at the general's timidity and extreme caution in fighting the enemy.

Photo courtesy of William E. Kotzwas.

In sharp contrast to the McClellan memorial are those to his brother officers, Ulysses S. Grant and William T. Sherman. In the District of Columbia alone, streets, avenues, and rotary circles pay homage to their memories. Their statues dwarf all other Civil War memorials, both in size and prominence of location. Grant's is an imposing statue, graced by splendidly animated horse-drawn artillery, and is located at the east end of the reflecting pool at the base of the capitol building itself. Located in East Executive Park, Sherman's statue is parked immediately behind the United States Treasury Building, fronting the Ellipse, and flanked by the White House. The respect paid to their memories is not confined to the District of Columbia. Perched above a stretch along the Hudson River in New York City, Grant's Tomb, a most impressive structure, houses the general's remains. Sherman, no doubt, would have had a similar edifice to his memory, except that he specifically ruled it out. While his understated burial rituals were respected, neither he nor Grant, had he wished, could constrain generations of urban and rural officialdom from dedicating scores of expansive parkland, town squares, libraries, and other fitting testimonials in their honor. If for no other reason, Grant is remembered in countless fiduciary transactions conducted on a daily basis. Although initially a seldom-used issue of currency, his stamped facsimile, printed on the fifty-dollar bill of legal tender, is increasingly being lifted out of American wallets and pocketbooks. Grant and Sherman stand head and shoulders above all of their Union commanders, casting a near-impenetrable shadow over them.[2]

On the other hand, one finds little to dispel the riddle posed by McClellan's memorial in the historiography of the Civil War era. Early McClellan biographies are generally so tainted with either panegyric or

---

Columbia Road, and California Street in the northwest quadrant of the District. For details on the McClellan statuary, see Mildred Baruch and Ellen Eckman, *Civil War Monuments* (Washington, D.C.: Daughters of Union Veterans of the Civil War, 1978), 24. Another old saw about the statue is how it looks defiantly in the direction of Richmond yet remains perfectly stationary. As an example of how entrenched disparaging views of McClellan are in the popular domain, the following is a tourist guide description: "Believed by many to be a Southern sympathizer, McClellan then ran unsuccessfully against Lincoln in 1864 on a platform for ending the war and letting the South go its own way. His statue is now condemned to look perpetually to the south over the city and directly toward the appropriately grand memorial to his nemesis and better, the martyred president." See Bob Bruton, *Exploring Washington on Foot* (Washington, D.C.: Rockrose Publications, 1995), 142.

2. Bruton, *Exploring Washington*, 126, 130.

vitriol that they have become useless in arriving at any sober and objective assessment of the man. In them, McClellan is alternately vilified as traitor and coward by some or hailed as patriot and genius by others. The polemical nature of these works detracts from even the useful biographical information that might otherwise be gleaned from them. At any rate, by the Second World War, these arguments had exhausted themselves and a new generation of historians were prepared to debate his place within the broad parameters of the Civil War itself.[3]

Scholarship in the second half of the twentieth century, focusing on McClellan and his contemporaries, Ulysses S. Grant, William T. Sherman, and even Abraham Lincoln, has tended to sweep McClellan into the background. In suppressing the controversy surrounding McClellan, Unionist historians of this period have forged a characteristic figure of the man. In finding McClellan's military career to be essentially an unsuccessful one, they have tended to agree with T. Harry Williams's verdict that McClellan was "not a good general, was even a bad one." Bruce Catton found him to have "all of the virtues necessary in war except one–he did not like to fight." Kenneth P. Williams blandly dismissed McClellan as the antithesis of a military leader by refusing to consider him a "real general." And while his judgment of McClellan as a "vain and unstable man who sat a horse well" contains some basis in reality, Williams distorts McClellan's active military ambitions in claiming he "wanted to be President."[4]

McClellan remains the "problem child" of the Civil War because his military performance still invites debate, although less now than at the beginning of this historiographical period. If not a winner, he was not exactly a loser. Nearly all historians admit he was the competent organizer and administrator of an army that had been shattered at First Manassas. Some point out that, unlike Grant, McClellan had taken on the Confederacy when it was young and strong. Others have seized upon Robert E. Lee's purported verdict that of all Federal commanders he faced, McClellan was his most difficult adversary. Warren W. Hassler and James G. Randall speculated that had McClellan's efforts in the Peninsula campaign not been undercut by an antagonistic administration, he might have taken

3. For an excellent and comprehensive view of the early McClellan historiography, see Harsh, "On the McClellan-Go-Round," 101–8.

4. T. Harry Williams, *McClellan, Sherman and Grant* (New Brunswick: Rutgers Univ. Press, 1962), 11; Bruce Catton, *Reflections on the Civil War* (New York: Doubleday, 1981), 82; Kenneth P. Williams, *Lincoln Finds a General*, 5 vols. (New York: Macmillan, 1949–59), 2:479.

Richmond and convinced the Confederacy of the futility of a protracted war. All of this might have been accomplished nearly three years before Grant finally cornered Lee in about the same location.[5]

There are formidable obstacles to surmount in approaching McClellan objectively. Joseph L. Harsh has astutely observed that the more negative appraisals of McClellan became increasingly solidified in the face of a growing acceptance of the Unionist interpretation of the Civil War. Evaluations of Federal military leaders, and the ever-popular ranking of them, became conditioned by the rigid conclusion that the rebellion was not crushed, slavery was not abolished, and the magisterial Lincoln was not vindicated until the final years of the war. To that effect, all before 1864 has been reduced to a herculean struggle marked by adversity and disappointment. Kenneth P. Williams's multivolume work underscores this frustration by implying that Lincoln despaired of finding a real general in the East until Grant was summoned in 1864. In this framework McClellan can only fail ignominiously. To McClellan's claims that he was victimized by political machinations, historians have responded by charging that he suffered acute psychological delusions. Students of American strategic thought have squarely placed McClellan as a shortsighted commander. The Civil War had outgrown the limited, professional war of the strategist Henri Jomini. It had taken on Clausewitzian dimensions; it was the total, unlimited, annihilative struggle between peoples that Grant and Sherman, however unwittingly, pursued. In strategic perception, McClellan tops the list of commanders who failed to comprehend that difference.[6]

5. T. Harry Williams, *Lincoln and His Generals* (New York: Knopf, 1952), 25; A. L. Long, ed., *Memoirs of Robert E. Lee* (Secaucus, N.J.: Blue and Grey Press, 1983), 267; Warren W. Hassler, Jr., *Commanders of the Army of the Potomac* (Baton Rouge: Louisiana State Univ. Press, 1962), 64; James G. Randall, *Lincoln the President*, 5 vols. (New York: Simon and Schuster, 1945–53), 2:65–86, 108–25.

6. Harsh, "McClellan-Go-Round," 101–9; Kenneth P. Willliams, *Lincoln Finds a General* 2:479; Allan Nevins, *The War for the Union*, 4 vols. (New York: Scribner's, 1959–71), 2:231–32; James Fry, "McClellan and His Mission," *Century Magazine* 48 (1894), 931–45; Russell F. Weigley, *Towards an American Army: Military Thought from Washington to Marshall* (New York: Columbia Univ. Press, 1962), 81–93; T. Harry Williams, *McClellan, Sherman and Grant*, 45–77; David Donald, ed., *Why the North Won the Civil War* (Baton Rouge: Louisiana State Univ. Press, 1960), 52–53; Charles Royster, *The Destructive War: William Tecumseh Sherman, Stonewall Jackson, and the Americans* (New York: Knopf, 1991), 79–143. More recently, the idea that Grant and Sherman pursued total, unrestricted warfare has been challenged. See Mark Grimsley, *The Hard Hand of War: Union Military Policy towards Southern Civilians*

An objective study of McClellan becomes particularly difficult when he is compared to Lincoln, Grant, and Sherman. Lincoln is perhaps one of the most revered presidents in America. His heroic perseverance and force of personality preserved the Union from dissolution. He was martyred for that cause at the very moment his struggles became vindicated. McClellan's own memoirs and his defenders' apologies appear insipid by contrast. Nor do McClellan's chances for an honest appraisal increase when he stands up to scrutiny with the likes of Grant and Sherman. Along with Phil Sheridan, Grant and Sherman are the heroic Union figures in the war. They emerge as both the architects and executors of victory. McClellan cannot and does not fare well by comparison.[7]

In the face of such commanding and summary verdicts, ongoing interest in the McClellan controversy largely languished in the immediate post-Civil War centennial period. All the same, a firm foundation had been constructed for future scholars to build upon. Acknowledging a debt to those early Unionist historians, James B. McPherson recently wrote: "A generation ago, fine studies by two historians named Williams–T. Harry and Kenneth P.–told us everything we might want to know about Lincoln's search for the right military strategy and for the right generals to carry it out." McPherson is dead-on in his appraisal. While elements of Unionist interpretation have been targeted for revision, the body of their work, particularly as it relates to the quality of Civil War commanders has remained largely intact and greatly respected. "Grant deserves the lion's share of credit for the Union triumph," Gabor S. Boritt plainly stated, and along with Sherman, "He provided the strategy and the victories that, in time, won the war." For Boritt, "These conclusions appear to be no longer

---

(Cambridge: Harvard Univ. Press, 1995); and Mark E. Neely, Jr., "Was the Civil War a Total War?" *Civil War History* 37 (Mar. 1991): 15–28. Even though McPherson warned that the unrestricted comparisons of Civil War generals was "a minefield through which historians had better maneuver carefully," it remains a very popular activity in the literature. See James M. McPherson, "American Victory, American Defeat," in Gabor S. Boritt, ed., *Why the Confederacy Lost* (New York: Oxford Univ. Press, 1992), 38.

7. Unlike Grant and Sherman, McClellan lost the only draft of his memoirs to a warehouse fire and was in the process of reconstructing them at the time of his death. However, his literary executor, Edward C. Prime, did publish selected letters, many of which McClellan meant to suppress, of the Civil War period in George B. McClellan, *McClellan's Own Story* (New York: Charles L. Webster and Co., 1887). His official papers are housed in the Manuscript Division of the Library of Congress. Historians are indebted to Stephen W. Sears for having produced an excellent guide to McClellan's correspondence during the war in his *Civil War Papers of George B. McClellan* (New York: Da Capo Press, 1992).

controversial." This sentiment is shared by Gary W. Gallagher, who acknowledges that only a handful of "critics continue to fight a rearguard action against Grant." For him, the "historical consensus clearly recognizes his [Grant's] indispensable role as the architect of northern military victory." Perry D. Jamieson, in reviewing Stephen W. Sears's biography of McClellan in the *Journal of Southern History,* has correctly analyzed that kinder works on the general by Warren W. Hassler, Jr., and Edward Hagerman simply have not been as influential as those by T. Harry Williams and others of his generation.[8]

Renewed interest in McClellan emerged with the arrival of Stephen W. Sears's version of the controversy. Appropriately hailed as the literary successor of Bruce Catton, Sears has, through meticulous research, including previously untapped sources, established himself as the authority on McClellan. Resurrecting McClellan as a figure worthy of controversy, he has reinterred him as a grievously flawed and ineffective commander, much in keeping with the views of Kenneth P. Williams, Bruce Catton, and T. Harry Williams. Noting that McClellan shared with Lincoln, Grant, and Sherman the honor of shaping the course of the Union during the Civil War, Sears concludes that of all commanders of the Army of the Potomac "he was inarguably the worst." This message, particularly its psychological profiling of the general, has found fertile soil. Joseph T. Glatthaar concluded that only "an exploration into what psychiatrists and psychologists term 'paranoid personality disorder'" would explain why a seemingly intelligent and charismatic person like McClellan could fail so miserably.[9]

8. James M. McPherson, "Lincoln and the Strategy of Unconditional Surrender," in Gabor S. Boritt, ed., *Lincoln the War President* (New York: Oxford Univ. Press, 1992), 35. While Bruce Catton has exerted the greater influence in the popular perception of Civil War commanders, T. Harry Williams has had a greater impact in the academic community. Frank B. Vandiver reflects the general sentiment that Williams's *Lincoln and His Generals* "stands at the top of a select group of books on the Civil War." See Frank E. Vandiver, "Williams and His Generals," in Roman J. Helniak and Lawrence L. Hewitt, eds., *The Confederate High Command and Related Topics: The 1988 Deep Delta Civil War Symposium: Themes in Honor of T. Harry Williams* (Shippensburg, Pa.: White Mane, 1990), 1. Gabor S. Boritt, *Why the Confederacy Lost,* 9; Gary W. Gallagher, "'Upon Their Success Hang Momentous Interests,'" in Boritt, *Why the Confederacy Lost,* 91–92. Jamieson's review is found in *Journal of Southern History* 56 (Feb. 1990): 127–29.

9. Stephen W. Sears, *George B. McClellan: The Young Napoleon* (New York: Ticknor and Fields, 1985), xii; Joseph T. Glatthaar, *Partners in Command: The Relationship Between Leaders in the Civil War* (New York: The Free Press, 1994), 237.

Because the Unionist interpretation has made its imprint on how the entire course of the war is viewed, those who have embarked on general military histories of the Civil War, or on topics that only vaguely deal with McClellan, have been similarly influenced. For many, he has become a benchmark or bellwether for their assessments of other Civil War commanders. Consequently, William Marvel is able to elevate Ambrose Burnside's reputation because, in the final analysis, Burnside was not so poor when compared to McClellan. Jeffry Wert, a historian who has produced excellent studies of Southern military commanders, and whose concern with McClellan is merely peripheral, relied exclusively on Sears's view of the McClellan that James Longstreet faced at the beginning of the war. Yet, no verdict can quite match the invidious comparison that was summoned by a reviewer of the most recent biography of Union general Franz Sigel. William Shea leavens his critique of the truly hopeless Sigel by proporting that "Sigel resembled George B. McClellan, though he operated on a smaller stage and consequently did less damage to the Union war effort." These examples do not even begin to scratch the surface of the immense catalog of indictments levied at McClellan.[10]

Bruce Catton and T. Harry Williams, as well as Kenneth P. Williams, a mathematician by profession, will be forever remembered by succeeding generations in the professional historian community; after all, they have provided a basis upon which careers and livelihoods have been built. Their greatest contribution, however, is in the degree to which they have molded enduring popular perceptions of Civil War military leadership. One of the consequences of their undisputed influence is the unquestioned and matter-of-fact presentation of Civil War platitudes, analogies, and invidious comparisons employed by those who write for popular or public consumption. The Unionist interpretation of the Civil War is accepted lock, stock, and barrel.

It was hardly surprising, then, when political pundit and conservative columnist for the *Washington Post,* George F. Will, took humorous aim at McClellan's statue on Connecticut Avenue as a way of questioning why the major international airport in the Washington metropolitan area

---

10. William Marvel, *Burnside* (Chapel Hill: Univ. of North Carolina Press, 1991), xi–xii; Jeffry D. Wert, *General James Longstreet* (New York: Simon and Schuster, 1993), 80–81, 438nn.10, 11; review by William L. Shea of Stephen D. Engle, *Yankee Dutchman: The Life of Franz Sigel* (Fayetteville: Univ. of Arkansas Press, 1993), in *Journal of Southern History* 63 (Feb. 1995): 83–84.

should be named after such an unpopular figure like John Foster Dulles. McClellan is hastily dismissed as Lincoln's "tormentor," and a "paranoiac with real enemies, whom he called 'traitors.'" The statue, in his opinion, was a monument to a man "whose vainglory, political ambition and military incompetence put the Republic at risk." Tongue in cheek, he suggested that the statue had "cluttered the city long enough," and in view of Lincoln's upcoming birthday, it should be removed from its location. Similarly, Harry Truman, a student of the Civil War, found in his nemesis, Douglas MacArthur, a suitable precedent in Lincoln's–George B. McClellan. Appearing in a best-selling biography by David McCullough is Truman's recollection of having sent a staff member to the Library of Congress for information on the Lincoln-McClellan crisis. He learned that Lincoln had to deal with a subordinate who refused to attack when commanded and who ventured into political matters outside the military arena. For Truman, the lesson gained was quite simple. Lincoln had exercised tremendous patience with his obstreperous general, "But at long last he was compelled to relieve the Union Army's principal commander." Now he was prepared to sack MacArthur. All could be reduced to simple truths.[11]

Periodically, McClellan's name is dredged up to provide insightful analysis in contemporary discussions of military and civil policy. At the height of the war with Iraq, when it was being suggested that allied armies should move on Baghdad to unseat Saddam Hussein, William Safire, in a *New York Times* op-editorial titled "McClellan's Way," hauled the general's reputation into his argument. Critical of attempts by the Soviet Union and France to fight a limited war, seeking settlement, Safire characterized them as a "McClellanesque mission." Safire claimed that, "McClellan lives; we hear his counsel of delay in Moscow, in Paris, in the seventh floor of our State Department." Calling upon President George Bush to seize the mission of protecting future freedom in the world, Safire cried, "Send for Grant." Bush was not the only president who should take heed of spurious military counsel. Upon the sudden retirement of Les Aspin as secretary of

11. George F. Will, "A Man Despised By the Chattering Class," *Washington Post,* Feb.11, 1990. A *New York Times* book review of Sears's biography of McClellan that echoes the standard interpretation is Tom Wicker's *New York Times Book Review,* Oct. 30, 1988, 30–31. David McCullough, *Truman* (New York: Simon and Schuster, 1992), 837–38. The Truman dilemma is also discussed in James V. Murfin, *The Gleam of Bayonets: The Battle of Antietam and the Maryland Campaign of 1862* (New York: Yoseloff, 1965).

defense in 1993, President William Clinton was forced to cast about for a replacement. One of his first choices was the retired admiral, Bobby Ray Inman, who quickly became somewhat of an embarrassment for Clinton, since he hedged accepting the assignment until certain uncomfortable military-political policies were clarified to his liking. Seizing upon this unusual posturing was syndicated political cartoonist Herblock. Lapooning Inman's demands, Herblock featured a nineteenth-century reporter standing in front of a strutting George McClellan, asking: "And you feel, Gen. McClellan, that the President is not providing you the proper comfort level?"[12]

Similarly, during the international crisis spurred by ethnic tensions in Bosnia, McClellan's name was trotted out once again. Again, a *New York Times* editorial writer was the instigator. Critical of the military's apparent reluctance to offer military options to intercede in the Bosnian slaughter, the writer suggested that Bush could tell General Powell what President Lincoln once told General McClellan: "If you don't want to use the Army, I should like to borrow it for a while." Unwilling to take a pasting without a fight, Colin Powell, chairman of the joint chiefs of staff, responded in an op-editorial days later. Powell took exception with the claim that the military was not responsibly responding to the crisis; he argued that there were no clear military goals in Bosnia. He concluded by setting the historical record "straight on President Lincoln's frustrations with General McClellan." The problem with McClellan was different from his own, Powell responded in a forthright manner. "McClellan would not use the overwhelming force available to him to achieve a decisive result. Lincoln had set out clear political objectives. McClellan acted in a limited, inconclusive way." With measured smugness, Powell concluded that the military establishment had "learned the proper lessons of history, even if some journalists have not."[13]

The last decade has seen a dramatic revival of public interest in the Civil War, spurred, no doubt, by the highly successful and well-received Public Broadcasting System's production of Ken Burns's documentary, "The Civil War." And it is in the arena of film, audiovisual presentations, and highly readable spin-off books that the Unionist interpretation of the

12. William Safire, "McClellan's Way," *New York Times*, Oct. 22, 1990; Herblock, *Washington Post*, Dec. 22, 1993.

13. *New York Times*, Oct. 4, 1992; Colin L. Powell, "Why Generals Get Nervous," *New York Times*, Oct. 8, 1992.

Civil War has found a solid footing. There is no denying the immeasurable impact upon memory, perception, and emotion–"The essential ingredients of history and the human experience,"–that film and television create. Yet the medium itself is not conducive to extended controversy or theoretical disagreement. Scope is almost always constrained by the limits of time and the need for conciseness and clarity in interpretation. Thus, historical consultants hired for many of these films and documentaries are compelled, most likely against their better instincts, to provide the incisive, uncomplicated sound bytes necessary to bypass the editors and splicers of the cutting room floor. The result, then, is not necessarily bad history; in fact, it is frequently very good history. The difficulty comes in judging the complex and arguable military records of Civil War commanders. The interpretation has to be consistent, straightforward, and unshackled by any divergence of opinion. In this regard, it is not surprising that McClellan's record is portrayed along the lines of consensus opinion.

Consequently, McClellan in the hands of Burns, who hailed Stephen Sears as the one who has "brought the complicated and contradictory life of George B. McClellan into such clear focus," does not come across as a shining example of military or personal competence. The popular "Civil War Journal," hosted and narrated by film star Danny Glover, likewise relies on historical consultants who provide an almost typecast rendition of the general in its volume titled "McClellan's Way." And the series, "Smithsonian's Great Battles of the Civil War," narrated by actor Richard Dreyfuss, provides a stark photographic contrast between the virtues of Ulysses Grant and the vices of George McClellan. Grant, who is pictured in a dusty, rumpled uniform, is praised for his "moral courage" in combatting his illness (drinking), a strength that allowed him to take unprecedented risks. This is immediately followed by a photo of the immaculately attired McClellan, surrounded by his aristocratic staff, and the comment that, unlike Grant, such "haughty generals" were never capable of taking serious gambles. Even in conceding that there is an element of truth to this characterization, it still does not justify the oversimplification that consumer-oriented history conveys.[14]

14. Ron Briley, "Nixon and Historical Memory in the Classroom," *Perspectives* (Washington, D.C.: American Historical Association, 1996), 6. Burns's comment is found on the dust jacket of Stephen W. Sears, *To the Gates of Richmond* (New York: Ticknor and Fields, 1992). The cinematic version of Gore Vidal's *Lincoln* features a pompous, self-absorbed,

Of all of America's wars, the Civil War has produced such an incredible variety of intriguing military personalities as to lend itself easily to the standard characterizations that the film industry adopts. In many respects, writers and producers of historical documentaries and dramas have merely tapped into a broader social and cultural dynamic in American society. One of our most treasured national assumptions is that of all peoples in the world, it is the Americans who most love the underdog. There is something attractively egalitarian and republican about seeing the aristocrat and the privileged fail miserably, while the underdog, who has had to struggle against all odds and adversity, triumphs at the end. Thus it is that we admire and cheer on the slow tortoises and industrious ants rather than the flashy hares and cavalier grasshoppers of this world. Nowhere in the Civil War do we see this dynamic in full flower like we do in the case of McClellan on one hand and Grant, Sherman, and Lincoln on the other.[15]

Certainly, in any historical discussion of the Lincoln-McClellan relationship, the contrasts are gallingly transparent, and many historians have capitalized upon them. Glatthaar sizes up the superficial differences between the two and recognizes that McClellan made a much better first impression. "Their differences transcended physical and social qualities," Glatthaar maintains. McClellan was a "gentleman" and an "aristocrat," a man of obvious discriminating tastes. And as difficult as it might be to imagine today, his hailing from a "refined Philadelphia family" signified a man with great credentials. On the other hand, there was Lincoln. "Unlike the new army commander, who was groomed for a career in leadership," Glatthaar notes, "Lincoln had no such background or birthright." Here was a roughhewn backwoodsman who had had to fight for anything he wanted in life. His informality and crude humor rankled the sensitivities of McClellan, who, assuming Lincoln to be an inferior, never took him seriously. Yet during the long course of the war, McClellan became for Lincoln what T. Harry Williams calls a "problem child." Lincoln, the architect of a righteous cause, was thwarted by the wayward, prodigal son.

---

even vindictive McClellan whose hauteur is cast unfavorably against Lincoln's genuine and generous behavior.

15. Jim Cullen has recently argued that the lines between popular culture and professional history are a great deal more blurred than many historians might admit. See Jim Cullen, *The Civil War in Popular Culture: A Reusable Past* (Washington, D.C.: Smithsonian Institution Press, 1995), 202.

Unable to redirect his difficult general, Lincoln was forced to turn him out. He eventually found someone else with whom he could work. That someone else, of course, was Grant. Needless to say, McClellan's flashy credentials proved no guarantee of success, and it was Lincoln who ultimately garnered all the kudos.[16]

Grant and Sherman could not have been scripted by Hollywood itself as better underdogs than they were in truth. Again, McClellan is unlikely to survive any comparisons with those two and serves as the perfect foil and antagonist to those immortals. The highly acclaimed Napoleon of the North, McClellan was expected by his peers, including Grant and Sherman, to be among the first to whom the nation would look to save it from dissolution. Alas, he did not fulfill that promise–he faltered. Perhaps, as Grant would say many years after the war, McClellan would have been better off having worked his way up to the responsibility that was conferred upon him from the outset. Grant and Sherman, by contrast, hailed from small towns in Ohio, far from the gaslights and cultured charms of the streets of McClellan's Philadelphia. Nothing came easy for them, even though Sherman, at least, enjoyed useful family connections. Their civilian careers prior to the Civil War were, in the main, unvarnished failures. Plagued by poor advice and bad fortune, and frequently manipulated by the deceitful counsel of business associates, they had little to show for all their hard work. They were even slow in getting out of the starting blocks during the first years of the war. In part, Grant was victimized by the jealousy of his commanding general, Henry Halleck, and Sherman stumbled badly in his first independent command in Kentucky. Yet they hung in tenaciously and eventually rose through the ranks. Although T. Harry Williams was referring to Grant, he might well have included Sherman when he claimed that Grant "was a success because he was a complete general and a complete character." By 1864 they had already established sterling reputations; they merely had to uphold them until the war's end. Others, particularly McClellan, had reputations to live down by that time.[17]

McClellan also suffered from his inconclusive record as a field commander. Contrary to the popularity attached to the underdog syndrome, a splashy personality can be enthusiastically embraced, providing its owner becomes a proven winner. Professional athletes have long served as

16. Glatthaar, *Partners in Command*, 57–58.
17. T. Harry Williams, *McClellan, Sherman and Grant*, 110.

fitting examples of this phenomenon. Most of Grant's predecessors, at least those in the East, were losers to one degree or another. Some losers, however, can be absolved. Grant's principal opponent, Robert E. Lee, achieved mythic standing in a losing cause. Union commanders like McDowell, Pope, Burnside, and Hooker can at least be pitied, for their tenure was brief, and they departed the scene rather quickly. McClellan's tenure was longer and his stature was higher than theirs. Besides, he should have been able to win. He had exceptional promise and all the right credentials, but his hubris proved his undoing. He became the Civil War's equivalent of Horatio Gates or, according to some, Benedict Arnold—men who were full of bluster and bravado but who came up short in delivering on their promise. For the story of the Civil War to be told in mythic proportions, McClellan must receive the condign censure he deserves.[18]

None of the preceding analysis is intended to suggest that Unionist historians and their adherents have conspired to consign McClellan to the lowest ranking among Civil War commanders. It does suggest, however, that a sturdy, almost impregnable, framework or construct has been established to interpret the war that does not admit McClellan to be viewed in anything but a dismal light. Civil War history lends itself to sweeping myths and generalizations. As a result, it becomes easy to see how the noble Lee could become "marbleized" over the years and how the Union's immortals, Grant and Sherman, could become "lionized." Similarly, McClellan becomes a conspicuous target for being "demonized." This is not to say that myths do not serve useful purposes. They provide a context for understanding a shared communal or national experience. For the generation sharing that experience, or immediately inheriting it, myths allow a way to validate the worthiness of one's involvement in a cause or movement. However, history has a way of catching up with myth. Since World War II, historians have largely recognized that the extreme characterizations of Civil War participants have been played out. The armor of the South's Lost Cause has been pierced, and Lee's inviolable position within this myth has been receiving a more balanced and enlightened review. The greatest casualty of the myth is James Longstreet, the South's

18. In his study of the "mythic Lee," Alan Nolan has written that "it is often difficult for Americans to think about the war with objectivity and detachment. Instead it is defined in our consciousness by the cliches with which historians and the purveyors of popular culture have surrounded it." See Alan T. Nolan, *Lee Considered: General Robert E. Lee and Civil War History* (Chapel Hill: Univ. of North Carolina Press, 1991), 3.

most controversial personality; as historians have come to see, he was as much a victim of a theoretical construct as he was a loser in the war of words and memories following the war.[19]

McClellan remains the North's most intriguing personality, if not its most controversial one. In many respects, Unionist historians still perpetuate a myth by insisting that McClellan's was such an extreme personality. In many ways, he is still being victimized by a mythical construct, and as long as he continues to be compared directly to Grant and Sherman without any contextualizing, he will continue to languish in their shadows. This is not to infer that many of the judgments historians have issued concerning McClellan's flaws are inaccurate or unfair. But what seems to be missing is any sense of balance, perspective, and proportion. What follows is an attempt to ease McClellan from the shadows cast by Grant and Sherman and review his career in a different light.

19. On Lee, see Nolan, *Lee Considered,* and Thomas L. Connelly, *The Marble Man: Robert E. Lee and His Image in American Society* (New York: Knopf, 1977). Longstreet's career has most recently been rehabilitated in Wert, *General James L. Longstreet.*

2

A Foray into the
Twilight Zone

CLEARLY, THE MOST DAMAGING FLAW ATTRIBUTED TO George McClellan is that he labored under innate psychological defects so severe as to preclude him from ever attaining excellence as a military leader. The psychological defects that historians have described in McClellan are his most crippling shortcomings, for all of his other weaknesses (i.e., political meddling, chronic overestimation of enemy strength, and the like) necessarily stem from them. The argument repeatedly presented is that McClellan not only lacked the temperament for waging war but operated under such significant psychological disabilities as to ensure his ineffective handling of the Army of the Potomac. In a reprise of early, and admittedly polemical, scholarship, one writer concluded that McClellan suffered from manic depressive illness that dated back to his childhood. Alternating between fits of "arrogant confidence and wretched self-abasement," the adult McClellan revealed an indulgent insolence displayed by those who are "congenitally incapable" of acknowledging authority because it would "make them feel inferior." Thus, any attempt to write a biography of McClellan inevitably "devolves into a psychograph."[1]

---

1. This chapter expands upon the ideas raised in my previously cited article. Irving Stone, *They Also Ran: The Story of Those Men Who Were Defeated for the Presidency* (New York: Doubleday, 1943), 160.

A host of scholars have also identified McClellan's psychological composition as the root cause of his failure. Kenneth P. Williams could find nothing attractive in McClellan's personality and went to great lengths to tie defects of character to the dilatory progress of his campaigns. To the charge that McClellan was vain and unstable, Williams added that the general was also inherently undisciplined and untruthful, another way of suggesting that McClellan was a pathological liar. Allan Nevins tarred McClellan's character with a messianic complex, which, he felt, sprang from the commander's unrestrained ego. T. Harry Williams viewed McClellan as a neurotic who entertained delusions of grandeur and who held the distorted apprehension that his enemies were everywhere, and at all times, plotting his undoing.[2]

One does not find any rehabilitation of McClellan's reputation in Stephen Sears's analysis. In fact, in his welcomed biography of McClellan (1988), Sears takes the analysis of the general's psychological health to even higher levels. He contends that McClellan's inability to prosecute war stemmed from the incontrovertible fact that he was a "man possessed by demons and delusions." While allowing that his analysis pertains to McClellan's performance as a military commander, Sears has, nonetheless, reached far back into McClellan's adolescence, West Point days, and pre-Civil War career to establish a consistent pattern of psychosis. Thus it is that Sears sees the development of a "morose view of the unfairness of life" when the young McClellan described the rigors of Academy life. When the cadet McClellan attempted to comfort his sister on the passing of her three-year-old daughter, Sears, while admitting it was an "awkward groping" for condolence, discerns an incipient dark fatalism in his writing, a sure harbinger of eventual adult immaturity. Similarly, the junior officer McClellan's occasional grumblings directed at volunteer officers in the Mexican War and his rows with the Academy superintendent, Captain Henry Brewerton, once described as "something of a martinet," are further grist for the psychological mill. The logical deduction here is that McClellan's later discord with the Lincoln administration and the Radical Republicans stemmed from an innately querulous nature that bristled at all forms of authority. By the time of the Civil War, when McClellan

---

2. Kenneth P. Williams, *Lincoln Finds a General* 2:479; Nevins, *War for the Union* 2:331–32; T. Harry Williams, *Lincoln and His Generals*, 26–27; T. Harry Williams, *McClellan, Sherman and Grant*, 40–42.

failed so ignominiously, the budding peevishness and disagreeable nature demonstrated early in his life had fully blossomed into a persecution complex. He became the deluded, out-of-control figure that could easily have been predicted.[3] Sears's message found fertile soil. In commending his editing of McClellan's Civil War correspondence (1989), Harold Holzer pronounced that Sears has accomplished "nothing short of convicting McClellan of raving paranoia," and with dramatic flair proclaimed that McClellan "emerges as the Captain Queeg of the Civil War."[4]

Just when it appeared that nothing more remained to be said about McClellan as a psychological marvel, Joseph T. Glatthaar's study of the general appeared. Leaning heavily upon Sears's analysis, Glatthaar parades McClellan as the one responsible for souring any hopes for a constructive and effective working relationship with his commander in chief. For Glatthaar, McClellan possessed qualities that were "all symptomatic of what modern psychology calls paranoid personality disorder with narcissistic tendencies"; these prevented him from "performing his duties as commanding general and general in chief satisfactorily." Glatthaar goes well beyond Sears's tour de force psychiatry when he anchors his conjecture with interpretations gleaned from professional psychiatric diagnostic manuals. To cement his case against McClellan, he devotes specific attention to plumbing the depths of the general's "tragic flaws" in an appendix to his overall study of command partnerships during the Civil War. Joining Sears, Glatthaar concludes that McClellan's poor relationship with Lincoln was but "another in a long line of failed relationships with superiors."[5]

A specious line of reasoning underlies these conclusions. Many historians have acted upon their own prejudices and have invoked a form of inductive reasoning to ferret out evidence for preordained conclusions.

---

3. Sears, *George B. McClellan: The Young Napoleon*, 1–29. Victorian society dealt with death in a very maudlin manner. Upon the death of his son, Willy, Sherman wrote: "We did all we could for poor Willy in life and in death, and it may be that he has escaped a long life of anxiety and pain mentally and bodily." Fellman also believes that the mourning ritual for Willy was "both obsessive and extremely protracted" and that it became the focus of correspondence between Sherman and his wife until their own deaths decades later. See Michael Fellman, *Citizen Sherman* (New York: Random House, 1995), 202.

4. See dust jacket comments by Harold Holzer (*Chicago Tribune*), found in Sears, *Civil War Papers of George B. McClellan*.

5. Glatthaar, *Partners in Command*, 92; see also the appendix, 237–42. Glatthaar also mentions in his preface that he obtained the services of a psychiatrist for a review and commentary on the McClellan chapter.

They have concluded that McClellan was a failure and that he was psychologically incapable of achieving success. Sears and Glatthaar, in particular, extrapolate from selected details in McClellan's past to conclude that the evidence they have uncovered conforms to a pattern—one that, all along, has supported their forgone conclusions. Additionally, the ad hominem nature of their attacks on McClellan's psychological character appears to serve them well in their final verdicts on the military dimensions of the general's performance. By establishing him as a psychological powder keg, they are able to reject any serious consideration of McClellan's strategy. Of all the reasons why McClellan may have been a gravely flawed commander, the exploitation of the psychological model is the most flawed itself, especially when employed by historians who see psychological reasons as the a priori condition for McClellan's failure. And it is so, for reasons beyond mere suspect reasoning.

Before looking at some of the specific psychological disorders attributed to McClellan, a general caveat is required. Critics of McClellan's leadership have a tendency to invoke specific clinical terms with disregard for precision. The terms hallucinatory behavior, delusional paranoid, and the like, are dropped very liberally, frequently overlapping and enmeshing with other characterizations. In our own "twelve-step" society, clinical terms are mouthed so readily and carelessly that they have become part and parcel of our vernacular usage. Common parlance is rife with descriptors borrowed from psychiatric literature (e.g., people are described as paranoid, hallucinating, delusional, and so forth). These terms are ascribed without regard to the clinical content meant to be captured by the words and thus represent empty, imprecise, pseudopsychiatric pronouncements.[6]

For example, a number of historians, looking at McClellan's penchant for overestimating enemy troop strength, have concluded that the general was delusional. According to the current classification of psychiatric illness from the *Diagnostic and Statistical Manual-IV (DSM-IV)*, a common

6. In response to an inquiry from the author, Dorothy M. Bernstein, M.D., editor of the history column of the *Psychiatric News,* published by the American Psychiatric Association, offered several warnings that should be heeded by psychohistorians, or those who practice psychiatric analysis from a distance. First, they must acknowledge the influence of the cultural, social, and political milieu upon the subject under review. Second, "Psychohistorians should recognize their [own] personal ideological approach and qualify their responses accordingly. If they are applying modern day concepts and diagnoses to another period, they should do so with qualification." Dorothy M. Bernstein, M.D., to author, March 12, 1996.

error is "to assume that a belief that is unusual (at least from the clinician's perspective) is necessarily a delusion." A look at the *DSM-IV* glossary definition of delusion elicits some pertinent inferences in McClellan's case, and it merits full citation:

> A false belief based on incorrect inference about external reality that is firmly sustained despite what almost everyone else believes and despite what constitutes incontrovertible and obvious proof or evidence to the contrary. The belief is not one ordinarily accepted by other members of that person's culture or subculture (e.g., it is an article of religious faith). When a false belief involves a value judgment, it is regarded as a delusion only when the judgment is so extreme as to defy credibility. Delusional conviction occurs on a continuum and can sometimes be inferred from an individual's behavior. It is often difficult to distinguish between a delusion and an overvalued idea (in which case the individual has an unreasonable belief or idea but does not hold it as firmly as is the case with a delusion).[7]

However inaccurate McClellan's assessments of enemy strength might have been, he was not delusional in the clinical sense of the word. Incontrovertible proof to the contrary did not exist. He was supplied reports on enemy strength by informed, or in this case misinformed, sources. While he may have been predisposed to accept those figures, as they were in keeping with his own perceptions, he did not manufacture the information. Moreover, Lincoln and Stanton, while they may have thought McClellan wrong, did not insist they were right. In fact, many of their decisions during the course of the Peninsula campaign, much to McClellan's chagrin, were based upon that erroneous information. The Northern press also reflected a great deal of confusion regarding enemy numbers based upon their own independent investigation; some news organs even reported figures that eclipsed McClellan's. In his military subculture many grossly overestimated enemy strength and appreciated the difficulties in obtaining accurate information. In hindsight, the information provided may appear incredible, but it was nowhere close to being uniformly rejected during the war itself. McClellan may very well have placed too

7. Michael B. First, M.D., Allen Frances, M.D., Harold Alan Pincus, M.D., *DSM-IV Handbook of Differential Diagnosis* (Washington, D.C.: American Psychiatric Association, 1995), 41.

much value in the estimates given him, and he may very well have manipulated those figures to his advantage, but he was not deluded in the clinical definition of the term.[8]

Historians, charged with rendering in language the events of history would do well to be more precise when they employ terminology so laden with value judgments. More than precision is at stake. In many respects, the issue of fairness is involved. It is one thing to maintain, as James M. McPherson has, that McClellan's personality "lay at the root of his military failure." It might also be appropriate for a historian to speculate or suggest the presence of psychological disorders as the basis of such failure. It is, however, quite another matter to assert with such clinical assurance that he was a victim of a catalog of psychological illnesses. Invoking psychological disorders as the underlying cause of McClellan's failures tempts us to dismiss his thoughts and actions, who he was and what he did, as unworthy of sober reflection. It is all the more important to be circumspect since personal deficiencies form the basis of the historical assessment of his overall performance during the war. This is not to say that historians act inappropriately in assessing and assigning interpretations to issues of behavior, personal character, and motivational dynamics in order to fully understand their impact upon decisions made and actions taken. To conclude on the basis of evidence that a person exercised unwarranted caution; made exaggerated claims of factual information; and appeared to be arrogant, argumentative, even egotistical would seem to reside well within the parameters of a historian's expertise. Indeed, history can easily be viewed as being a complement to, and having an advantage over, psychological analysis, for the latter is frequently limited by temporal and spatial provincialism of the kind that only historical inquiry can amend. As one custodian of the historical profession has put it, historians "possess many advantages in retrospection that ought not to be relinquished."[9]

The matter is complicated, however, when historians issue psychological verdicts that function as definitive evaluations of the status of a

8. George Meade, for example, overestimated Lee's strength at Gettysburg by a full 33 percent. See W. H. Taylor, "The Campaign in Pennsylvania," *The Annals of the Civil War* (New York: Da Capo Press, 1994), 317.

9. The McPherson quote is found on the dust jacket to Sears, *Civil War Papers of George B. McClellan*. David Hackett Fisher, *Historians' Fallacies* (New York: Harper Torchbooks, 1970), 213.

person's mental health and capacity. The injudicious characterization of McClellan as an individual who suffered from crippling neuroses, wild hallucinations, manic depression, paralyzing persecutory and grandiose delusions, and, most improbably, demonic possession violates basic tenets of medical diagnosis. Factors such as severity, duration, frequency, measurable impact on normal functioning, to name a few, must be considered before offering what is tantamount to a clinical diagnosis. Indeed, if any or all of these significant psychiatric disorders had afflicted McClellan at any time, it is doubtful that he would have been capable of anything resembling normal functioning, let alone any sustained measure of success. If, indeed, McClellan had been so adversely afflicted, the prognosis for full recovery from such illnesses would most likely have been rather grim. He would have been a man in dire need of professional therapeutic intervention and, possibly, psychotropic treatment. Of course, neither option was available in any sophisticated professional form to McClellan. Just as a responsible therapist or physician refrains from forming a clinical assessment without a full understanding of the personal and historical context of George McClellan's life, so too should historians resist issuing uninformed psychological pronouncements.[10]

The evidence historians draw upon for their psychological profiling of George McClellan is his correspondence. A review of their selections demonstrates that they relied almost exclusivly upon letters he wrote to his wife, Ellen. One may find the complaining, peevish, ambitious, or insulting McClellan in his correspondence to friends and associates, but the so-called truly damaging psychological exposé is generally found only in his letters to Ellen. Sears is joined by a number of other historians in believing that the candid expressions of feelings revealed in his letters to Ellen provide an insight into the true McClellan. They have seized upon one of his early communications wherein McClellan informed Ellen that whenever he wrote or talked to her, he felt like he was "communing with myself–you are my alter ego, darling. . . ." The obvious conclusion one

---

10. Although I hesitate to offer this information, see the following for a clinical discussion of the myriad disorders ascribed to McClellan's mental health status: Steven A. Schroeder, Marcus A. Krupp, Lawrence M. Tierney, Jr., and Stephen J. McPhee, eds. *Current Medical Diagnosis and Treatment* (East Norwalk, Conn: Langer, 1990), 693–710; and American Psychiatric Association, *Diagnostic and Statistical Manual of Mental Disorders* (Washington, D.C.: APA, 1987), 199–204, 213–34, 335–58.

should draw, then, is that everything he would subsequently write or say must necessarily be "mirrors of self-revelation."[11]

The few McClellan supporters in recent historical literature shrink from contesting, or at least engaging in, any discussions that involve the personal McClellan. Consequently, one does not see Ellen Marcy McClellan's name mentioned in any of their works. Joseph Harsh deplores the fixation Unionist historians have on McClellan's personality because it detracts from any serious consideration of his strategy. Edward Hagerman omits any reference to the general's personal background and his embroglios with the administration in favor of studying McClellan's appreciation for tactical and staff reorganization. And Rowena Reed, who praises McClellan's strategic brilliance at the expense of his principal antagonists, largely avoids the psychological dimensions of the literature. The only drawback to these omissions is that when the psychological profiling is ignored, it assumes a degree of general acceptance or, to borrow the cliche, silence breeds consent. The power of the psychological argument is strong and compelling. One of the reasons it becomes easy to scoff at McClellan's strategy and his skills and talents is that the psychological dimension to the argument always garners more attention. Why bother to deal with McClellan as a respected strategist or skilled administrator when he has been rejected as a person incapable of producing a positive result?

The only one ever to question seriously the content and possible meanings of McClellan's letters to his wife–that have become, if you will, the prima facie case against McClellan's mental health status–was James G. Randall. Nearly a half century ago, Randall suggested that McClellan's letters to his wife were a "kind of unstudied release, not to be taken seriously." Randall's is a valid point that has been brushed aside altogether too hastily.[12] McClellan's assertion that his wife was his alter ego was written during the year they were engaged to be married. What

11. Sears, *George B. McClellan: The Young Napoleon,* 62. Glatthaar identifies the general's wife, Nelly, as McClellan's "single true confidante." See Glatthaar, *Partners in Command,* 83. Perhaps the expression "alter ego" was used loosely during that time. Sherman used it to describe his relationship with his son Willy, shortly after the boy's death in 1863, though it is doubtful that he ever bared his soul to him. See Fellman, *Citizen Sherman,* 204.

12. Randall, *Lincoln the President* 2:73. Sears addresses Randall's judgment but claims that Randall based it upon only "slight familiarity with the larger body of the general's correspondence." Moreover, he asserts that there was nothing "unstudied" in McClellan's correspondence about Lincoln and the administration. See Sears's introduction to the *Civil*

people throughout the ages have intimated in love letters during the span of a courtship ritual can be left to one's own experience or imagination. Moreover, while that designation of "other self" suggests that McClellan felt free to bare his soul to his wife, it does not necessarily imply that he meant every jotted word to be explored in its literal sense. The "communing with myself" comment was as likely, if not more likely, a harmless flirtation, consistent with the amorous tones of his early letters to his wife. McClellan's letters to his wife are a weak foundation upon which to construct a definitive and indisputable case for his supposed psychiatric disarray.[13]

One such claim of psychiatric illness, the origin and basis of which are as puzzling as the claim is unwarranted, requires a closer look: it is Glatthaar's assertion that McClellan had difficulty making friendships. "Only a handful of people–his wife, Fitz John Porter, and a few others," Glatthaar observes, "maintained long-term bonds with McClellan, and in those cases he clearly retained the dominant role." The reason for that, according to Glatthaar, was that McClellan's ingrained distrust of people, rooted in a paranoid personality disorder, prevented him from forming true friendships. It is a particularly harsh accusation. Few things are more pathetic than a person without friends. With no friends during your life, or none remaining after your passing, there is no one available to validate that your life had worth or meaning. It is easy to characterize a friendless person as an object of scorn and derision. However, in McClellan's case, this judgment is entirely without merit. There is a great deal of evidence to suggest that McClellan formed and maintained a considerable, and let us assume acceptable, number of friends. Some of his friendships survived

---

War Papers of George B. McClellan, xii. I am contending that this general correspondence, while full of frank opinion and personal invective, even conniving and braggadocio, does not reflect in any substantive way the serious psychological disorders attributed to McClellan.

13. In taking her husband's side in his interpretation of events, Mrs. McClellan frequently encouraged him to unburden himself fully and freely. On July 22, 1862, she wrote him filled with indignance, and perhaps some humor: "To have a man [Halleck] put over you without even consulting you is rather more than I can endure–& if you do not resign I will!!!" See McClellan Papers, Manuscript Division, Library of Congress. It should also be observed, as Sears indicates in his discussion of the material selected for McClellan's memoirs, that the general did not intend to include his letters to his wife. He considered them private and only to be used to refresh his memory as to dates and other such information. His literary executor, William C. Prime, elected to include them. See Sears, *George B. McClellan: The Young Napoleon*, 405.

from the days he attended West Point. They included A. P. Hill, Dabney Maury, Cadmus Wilcox, John Gibbon, and William Gardner. Upon hearing that James Stuart, another West Point classmate, died during an attack in Indian country, McClellan recorded in his journal: "On the 18th of June 1851, at five in the afternoon died Jimmie Stuart, my best and oldest friend." McClellan also held conspicuous long-term friendships with others he became acquainted with through the army. Beauregard, Fitz John Porter, Franklin, Hancock, W. F. "Baldy" Smith, and Joseph Johnston, to name but a few, were steadfast friends. Johnston, one of McClellan's principal antagonists during the war, survived to become one of his pallbearers, and he genuinely mourned the loss of "a dear friend whom I have so long loved and admired." He also cherished friends made from his contacts in the business and political world. Sam Barlow, Augustus Belmont, Manton Marble, William Prime, and Abram Hewitt are names that immediately come to mind. While the McClellans were content to enjoy the comforts of home and family, they were hardly wallflowers. They frequently participated in the social calendar, whether it was in Chicago, Cincinnati, or New York, and they made a great number of casual friendships as a result. If during the war itself, men like Franklin and Fitz John Porter appeared to be dominated by their superior officer, there is nothing unusual about this phenomenon, unless, of course, they suffered from, shall we say, dependent personality disorders. It can be a very tangled web that is woven when one embarks upon psychological profiling. Some sense of perspective and comparison needs to be employed. Otherwise, in casting the nets to ensnare other Civil War illuminaries for inspection, such as Grant and Sherman, one would quickly discover they have opened a chaotic Pandora's Box of psychological speculation and conjecture.[14]

One particularly damaging indictment in the psychological portfolio collected on McClellan is that he suffered from a messianic complex. By today's standards, it is the most unnerving and alarming of all his purported disorders. A close look at his correspondence, especially with his wife, reveals a string of pronouncements and revelations that support the view that he earnestly believed he had been called by God to save the Union. The tone was set from the very beginning. Writing to Ellen on

14. Glatthaar, *Partners in Command,* 91–92, 237; George B. McClellan, *The Mexican War Diary of George B. McClellan,* ed. William Starr Meyers (Princeton: Princeton Univ. Press, 1917), 14n; Sears, *George B. McClellan: The Young Napoleon,* 64, 398–402.

August 10, 1861, he professed that he felt "God has placed a great work in my hand . . . how weak I am–but I know that I mean to do right & God will help me & give me the wisdom I do not possess." Two days before he superseded Scott, he wrote again, declaring that "with God's help & a single eye to the right I hope that I may succeed." After reviewing the obstacles placed in his way, both human and logistical, he remained confident that the ultimate "result remains in the hands of God." Noting that he was not a worthy instrument of God's calling, he consoled himself with the belief that he did not seek it–"It was thrust upon me," he declared. "I was called to it, my previous life seems to have been unwittingly directed to this great end," he reasoned, "& I know that God can accomplish the greatest ends with the weakest instruments–therein lies my hope." His conclusion to this letter reflected the prevailing religious interpretation of the underlying cause of the war. "I feel too that, much as we in the North have erred, the rebels have been far worse than we–they seem to have deserted from the great cardinal virtues."[15]

To the predominantly secular society of today, that stark expression of Calvinist theology and highly stylized piety reverberates discordantly. The first reaction is to recoil from the apparent conceit that underlies McClellan's intimations, as it hearkens of the wily charms of contemporary television evangelists. How is it possible, we ask ourselves, for someone to presume that his vocation in life has preordained him to be the savior of the Union and a martyr for the cause? The self-abasement and expressions of unworthiness come across as thinly veiled false humility. The inherent fatalism of his remarks is further cause for suspicion. In a strict context, those remarks might well be viewed as surpassing mere expressions of self-confidence or religious conviction and indicating a distorted sense of purpose. This has been the reaction of many historians, and their interpretations rest compatibly with our own cultural and social sensibilities.[16]

Nevins, for one, felt this way. One of the principal criticisms he reserved for McClellan was that he was always "religiously certain of divine guidance." That messianic conviction, in Sears's opinion, clouded all per-

---

15. Sears, *Civil War Papers of George B. McClellan*, 81–82, 112–13.

16. The notion of consigning oneself over to God's plan was a common principle in all Christian denominations of the time. Even the agnostic Sherman, in one of his darker moments, expressed regret over the inevitable and destined pain of life. Hoping that his nine-year-old daughter Lizzie could be spared life's tribulations, he expressed the wish that she could "quietly slumber in eternal rest and escape the sad events in store for us." See Fellman, *Citizen Sherman*, 108.

ceptions of reality. The foe took on dimensions in strength of legendary proportions, far exceeding any rational calculation. Likewise, McClellan could summarily dismiss the enemies from within, because in their ignorance or intrigue, they opposed not only his will but that of God. It became, as Sears viewed it, a dangerous "prop for his insecurity and the shield for his convictions." Moreover, that vision was tainted by a dark fatalism. When deeply held, it became the "ultimate escape from responsibility." If he failed, it was not his fault; others would have to account for it. Glatthaar also sees McClellan's vision of reality as greatly distorted. In his darker and more desperate moments, McClellan gave way to a very unbecoming purple fatalism. "Like Jesus Christ before him," Glatthaar insinuates, "McClellan refused to alter or avoid that fate. His sacrifice would cleanse the government of its rascals and cowards. . . . from his martyred career would emerge a united public that would cry out for fresh leadership to save the Union."[17]

In the movement away from the narrow to the broader perspective, McClellan's declarations do not appear demonstrably delusional within the general parameters of his own social and cultural milieu nor as inconsistent with his own deeply held religious convictions. Before his courtship with Ellen, McClellan, by his own admission, never professed or adhered to any specific Christian denominational creed. By 1859, however, it became clear that he had undergone an evangelical religious rebirth that fundamentally altered his outlook on life. He openly embraced the rigid Calvinistic dogma of mainstream Presbyterianism, particularly the doctrine of predestination, a belief characterized by a pervasive fatalism in which the hand of God rested upon those He had elected. McClellan shared those convictions with his wife, whose influence undoubtedly assisted the conversion process. During their betrothal, he would write his "little Presbyterian" that the "mere thought of uniting your pure religious soul to an unrefined irreligious immoral, or tainted man is to me sacrilege itself," thus integrating conjugal aspirations with a generous sprinkling of religious humility. Fate and election had brought them together, and it would carry them through this life into the glorious future of eternal life. When war broke out in 1861, which he also accepted as God's will, he would continue whenever possible to commune on a daily basis with his dear Nelly. Surely, a conflict of this magnitude had the

17. Nevins, *War for the Union* 2:332; Sears, *George B. McClellan: The Young Napoleon,* 106–7, 189; Glatthaar, *Partners in Command,* 91.

will of God written all over it, and McClellan would interpret it as such to his wife along the lines of their mutually shared religious outlook.[18]

McClellan should not be viewed as a quirky fundamentalist, standing apart from the religious mainstream of his day. He lived in an age of deeply held religious belief and sentimental expression; an age of Protestant reawakenings and camp revivals, which grew very popular during the war itself. The millennialist spirit peppered religious conversations in Protestant circles, and itinerant preachers suffused the atmosphere with calls for repentance and righteous behavior. Protestants of all denominations were called upon to proclaim their faith in public and let their actions lend testimony to the second coming of Christ. Mainstream Protestant morality was dominated by various forms and nuances of predestination doctrine, particularly as it related to man's need to submit to the will of God. It was also the age of fortress Catholicism. Nurtured by their immigrant Irish hierarchy, and extremely sensitive to the slights of Anglo-Saxon bigotry, Catholics strove to publicly demonstrate the exemplary quality of their piety and religious devotion in their adopted homeland. While the rigorous, almost fatalistic, influence of Jansenism over Irish Catholic theological praxis was losing its grip, the American Catholic world view was still dominated by the conviction that without God's grace and the Church's guidance, mankind was utterly depraved. Religion, then, was a dominant, pervasive force in American society. Indeed, that reality has led some to the arguable but plausible conclusion that one of the principal reasons for the rise and fall of the Confederacy was the way in which religion first sustained, then diminished, and finally undermined Southern society.[19]

Religion also remained a constant buttress to the moral framework in which the war was fought. Lincoln, a much more dispassionate believer, acknowledged as much in his second inaugural address. "Both [North and South] read the same Bible, and pray to the same God," he observed. "Each invokes His aid against the other . . . and neither has been fully answered." In retrospect, the war seemed to Lincoln to be the payment for the transgressions of both sides, and slavery was most likely but one of those offenses. While fervently praying that the scourge of war would be lifted from the nation, Lincoln, nonetheless, saw the divine aim in the war,

---

18. Sears, *George B. McClellan: The Young Napoleon,* 63.

19. Richard E. Beringer, Herman Hattaway, Archer Jones, and William N. Still, Jr., *Why the South Lost the Civil War* (Athens: Univ. of Georgia Press, 1986), 3.

and it required his submission to God's will. "Yet, if God wills that it continue," he intoned, "until all the wealth piled by the bond-man's two hundred and fifty years of unrequited toil shall sunk [*sic*], and until every drop of blood drawn by the lash, shall be paid by another drawn with the sword . . . so still it must be said the judgments of the Lord, are true and righteous altogether."[20]

God's will in the war frequently assumed apocalyptic dimensions, as victories and defeats were interpreted as the consequence of divine retribution or reward. One articulate Union veteran ascribed the defeat at Chancellorsville to General Joseph Hooker's profane challenge that even God Almighty could not dislodge his position, by riposting that there was "not much wonder that we were whipped." This was a war in which soldiers went to battle with Testaments, rosaries, or some conspicuous religious artifact in their pockets. Nor was it unusual that the faithful were led into battle by the church militant incarnate. While many marched along as chaplains, many ecclesiastics clutched the bible in one hand and the sword in the other. Most prominent among them was Leonidas Polk, the Episcopal bishop of Louisiana, who died as a result of shrapnel fragments from a well-aimed Union cannon outside Atlanta. But there were many others as well, including Nathan Bedford Forrest's chief subordinate, the Reverend Major D. C. Kelley; Robert E. Lee's artillery commander, the Episcopal priest William Nelson Pendleton; and Stonewall Jackson's aide-de-camp, the Presbyterian minister Robert L. Dabney. Both sides were also vigorously supported by their clergy on the home front. It was common to hear sermons from Northern and Southern ministers of the same denomination excoriating the principles of the other's cause while espousing the sanctity of their own.[21]

Like McClellan, many commanders brought their own religious convictions and eccentricities to the forefront during the Civil War. On the Union side there was the staunch Roman Catholic William Rosecrans, who, fearful of violating the Lord's second commandment, made an exquisite distinction between vulgarity and profanity. Any junior officer he caught voicing an example of the latter would be expelled from his

20. Roy P. Basler, *The Collected Works of Abraham Lincoln*, 8 vols. (New Brunswick: Rutgers Univ. Press, 1953), 8:332–33.

21. The Union veteran is quoted in Gerald F. Linderman, *Embattled Courage* (New York: The Free Press, 1987), 106; W. Harrison Daniel, "Protestantism and Patriotism in the Confederacy," *Mississippi Quarterly* 24 (Spring 1971): 119–23.

presence, but not before being upbraided by Rosecrans with a healthy dose of the former. Converted to Catholicism at West Point, Rosecrans tried to attend Mass at least twice a week, abhorred skirmishing on Sundays, and forced his subordinates to sit up well into the wee hours of the morning, listening to him expound on theological matters. General Oliver O. Howard was a paragon of virtue and religious devotion, and everyone in the army knew it well. In his retirement, Joseph Hooker, Howard's superior officer in 1863, sarcastically remarked that the pious general "would command a prayer meeting with a good deal more ability than an army." William T. Sherman, who spent a lifetime resisting his wife's entreaties to become a Catholic and who lived with regret to see the day his son Thomas became a priest, was a believer. Sherman acknowledged a deity, but saw it in fatalistic terms. God was the dispenser of fate. His own experience told him that he had been dealt a dismal hand, and he could only do his best to escape the inevitable doom. Had he been a more conventional believer, as were his peers, the vanity that reeks in the letters to his wife suggests that he may well have ascribed messianic overtones to his military career. But religious meaning for Sherman was often obscured by the penetrating depression, mood swings, shame, and self-loathing he experienced, and at times the difference between the religious fatalist and the afflicted individual became indistinguishable.[22]

The South quite possibly outdid the North in producing commanders with evangelical fervor. Robert E. Lee, whose religious beliefs and piety reflected the moderation of the Episcopal church, was, nevertheless, a primary sponsor of camp revivals in the Southern army of 1863. In a general order to the army on August 13, he linked the waning fortunes of the Confederacy to national hubris and beckoned his troops to amend their depraved ways. "Soldiers! we have sinned against Almighty God," he announced, "[and] we have forgotten His signal mercies, and have cultivated a revengeful, Haughty, and boastful spirit . . . and we have relied too much on our own arms for the achievement of our independence." Lee was also willing to believe that God manipulated the forces of nature. He was staggered to find the normally drought-stricken Potomac at flood stage during the retreat from Gettysburg, fearful as he was that Meade might trap him on the northern side. "Had not the river not unexpectedly

22. Hooker is quoted in Walter H. Hebert, *Fighting Joe Hooker* (Indianapolis: Bobbs-Merrill, 1944), 294; Nevins, *War for the Union* 3:185–87; Fellman, *Citizen Soldier,* 44–45, 63–68, 373–92.

risen," Lee wrote his wife, "all would have been well with us. But God, in His all-wise providence, willed otherwise." His principal biographer, Douglas Southall Freeman, has determined that Lee struggled on against all odds to the bitter end, despite the inevitability of defeat, because he sensed that it was God's will he should do so. Lee's own divisional commander, George Pickett, was renowned for marching his men into battle to the strains of a popular religious anthem, "Guide Me, O Thou Great Jehovah." And, then there was Thomas Jackson whose militant religious principles virtually unnerved his command. On one occasion he informed his subordinate, Richard Ewell, that through the aid of Providence he had captured an entire Union wagon train, to which the exasperated Ewell could only ask, "What has Providence to do with Milroy's wagon train?" The pious soldier, Jackson maintained, would always prevail in combat because God favored his every move. Jackson was an ardent supporter of camp revivalism, and his interest in evangelizing was not just because he wanted to bring sinners to Christ. A reborn army would ensure the survival of the Confederacy. Destiny would not be denied. If a nation of believers could be molded, Jackson opined, then God, who surely guided all events, would favor His own in the heat of battle. For Jackson, war was a purifying process which cleansed the soul of iniquity and transformed the baseness of human nature. For Jackson, the hand of Providence was omnipresent. Still, for all of his talk about God directing the course of human events and the manifestation of divine order during the course of combat, Jackson has more frequently been hailed as an eccentric genius than a self-styled messiah.[23]

McClellan's admissions to his wife about his role in saving the Union reveal more about his being caught up in a momentous historical event than they do about any truly messianic call. His summons to the capital in July 1861 and his recall to command the army in September 1862 came swiftly on the heels of significant Union reverses in the field, after which the safety of the capital was in the balance. In a manner of speaking, he was being called to save the Union. Much of the controversy associated

---

23. Capt. Robert E. Lee, *Recollections and Letters of General Robert E. Lee* (New York: Konecky and Konecky, n.d.), 105–6; Robert E. Lee to Mrs. Mary Custis Lee, July 12, 1863, in Clifford Dowdey and Louis H. Manarin, eds., *The Wartime Papers of Robert E. Lee* (Boston: Little Brown, 1961), 547; Douglas Southall Freeman, *R. E. Lee: A Biography*, 4 vols. (New York: Scribner's 1935), 4:504; Wert, *Longstreet*, 292; Royster, *The Destructive War*, 63, 77, 267–69. Ewell is quoted in Glatthaar, *Partners in Command*, 30.

with McClellan's references to saving the Union finds its parallel in the lively discussions circulating throughout the North of the need for a dictator to assume control of the government. It was certainly not uncommon in military circles for officers, who were frustrated with civilian interference in military affairs, to bandy about such opinions. Both Hooker and Sherman reflected upon the potential benefits that might be accrued by a government that waged war in a less democratic environment.[24] In Hooker's case, Lincoln's reprimand concerning his involvement with those conspiring to install a dictator did not carry the twentieth-century connotations of the totalitarian despot. Rumors of dictatorship in the mid-nineteenth century, that all sectors of the Northern population indulged in during the Civil War, were more akin to classical notions of the selfless patriot taking momentary control of the government during a period of acute crisis. The venerable Cincinnatus of Rome's republican history, who left his plow in the field to save Rome from her enemies, came to mind. In McClellan's case, his keen grasp of classical military history, coupled with his religious predilections, may have supplied him with prosaic analogies about saving the Union that suggested more than he actually intended. And it should be noted that most speculation about McClellan's taking over the government amounted to idle chatter by his subordinates. For his part, McClellan vigorously rejected any serious consideration of that topic.

In the early days of the war there was a great deal of wildly exaggerated talk, not the least of which was the claim that the Federal army was going to dismantle the Confederacy before its own ninety-day volunteer enlistments expired. On July 21, McClellan received a telegram of ominous brevity from Washington: "Circumstances make your presence here necessary. Charge Rosecrans or some other general with your present department and come hither without delay." A week later, after his arrival in Washington, the thirty-four-year-old McClellan wrote his wife of being caught up in a "new and strange position. . . . Presdt, Cabinet, Genl Scott

24. Despite hearing Hooker's name mentioned among those who thought the time was ripe for a dictator, Lincoln thought it harmless enough to appoint him as commander of the Army of the Potomac. See *The War of the Rebellion: A Compilation of the Official Records of the Union and Confederate Armies,* 128 vols. (Washington, D.C.: GPO, 1880–1901), ser, 1, vol. 25, 2:5 (hereafter cited as *OR).* Sherman's obsession with curtailing the freedom of the press, and his clearly authoritarian views, has lead Fellman to conclude that there was a "clear connection between Sherman the arbitrary censor and Sherman the principled antidemocrat." See Fellman, *Citizen Sherman,* 131.

all deferring to me." In jest, he suggested that even a small victory was likely to enable him to "become Dictator." On July 30, he wrote giddily that his visit to the Senate had "overwhelmed" him. He was repeatedly told how young he looked, and amidst the backslapping and handclasping, he recalled that everyone told him he was being "held responsible for the fate of the Nation. . . . Who would have thought when we were married," he mused, "That I should so soon be called upon to save my country."[25]

McClellan drank too deeply from the cups of praise and adulation offered him in those first weeks of his arrival in Washington. Others may have shrunk from the responsibilities being fashioned in those early days, but McClellan eagerly embraced them. Nevertheless, the crisis was real. His religious convictions endorsed a sense, however inflated, of destiny and calling. His references to saving the Union engendered little or no derision among his contemporaries. If he was so transparently out of touch with reality, no one, either friend or foe, made slight of it—not then, nor later in their memories of those headstrong days. Of all people, McClellan would recall how he and Stanton stayed up late into the evening during the fall of 1861, talking about how together the two of them would "save the Union." The salvific quality of his fervor struck a resonant chord with the religious expression of his time. No wonder he fell into the pitfalls of hubris, as Bruce Catton suggested.

"McClellan's boast was justified," Catton reasoned. "The people were calling upon him to save the country." Unless he succeeded in whipping the army into shape, many thought, the Confederates might well march into Washington. After all, fear that the Confederates might capture the capital was a constant companion of the president and his secretary of war, the latter of whom always kept a vigilant eye on the Potomac for the naval vessel that would cart him to safety. McClellan, a young and deeply religious man, was more likely swept up in the highly emotionalized mood of the time. Caught in a position unparalleled in American history since the days of George Washington, he allowed the compliments of important people to go to his head. Indeed, his apparent messianic language might well have been no more than an extension of his considerable vanity, which was fueled by the accolades he received in Washington. Couching his vanity within a framework of religious terminology would have been no more than a self-deceiving attempt

25. Sears, *Civil War Papers of George B. McClellan*, 70–71.

at self-effacement. While his statements most certainly showed he was susceptible to flattery, they are not indicative of a psychotic state of mind. He believed that God called men to fulfil their preordained destinies. There was nothing messianic, in the modern clinical sense of the term, in his perception of mission.[26]

By introducing psychological factors as the basis to judge McClellan's incapacity for waging war, historians have declined to look at McClellan as an integrated identity. Yet, in viewing the sum total of McClellan's life experiences, it is difficult to discern the presence or eruption of any of the disorders ascribed to him during his command of the Army of the Potomac. Notwithstanding earlier critiques of his moodiness as a cadet, his academic career at West Point was exemplary. He displayed intelligence, wit, initiative, and perseverance and was graduated second in his class of fifty-eight. Claiming that he was overly competitive and that he became sour when he failed to overtake Charles Stewart, ranked first in the class, is like pumping a well that is known to be dry. McClellan was the youngest in his class; in fact, he was below the legal age for entering the academy. Bright boys at that age are prone to competiton, and they tend to pout when they are frustrated. If his competitiveness was so overweening and transparent, it most likely would have alienated him from his classmates. Such was not the case. McClellan was well liked, and he was generous in helping other cadets who found their studies difficult. His evident self-confidence did not turn off his classmates. One of them fondly recalled that McClellan "bore every evidence of gentle nature and high culture, and his countenance was as charming as his demeanor was modest and winning." Erasmus Keyes, who later served under McClellan as a divisional commander, was one of his instructors at West Point; Keyes recalled that a "pleasanter pupil was never called to the blackboard." In the main, McClellan's adolescent years at West Point do not suggest themselves as a breeding ground for future psychological chaos.[27]

---

26. Ibid., 347; Bruce Catton, *Mr. Lincoln's Army* (Garden City, N.Y.: Doubleday, 1951), 61. Toward the end of the Peninsula campaign, McClellan may well have realized that his pride had got the better of him. He wrote Ellen: "I hope and trust that God will watch over, guide & protect me—I accept most resignedly all the adversity he has brought upon me— perhaps I have really brought it upon myself, for while striving conscientiously to do my best, it may well be that I have made great mistakes, that my vanity does not permit me to perceive." See Sears, *Civil War Papers of George B. McClellan*, 363.

27. John G. Waugh, *The Class of 1846* (New York: Warner Books, 1994), 8, 25, 41; Dabney H. Maury, *Recollections of a Virginian in the Mexican, Indian and Civil Wars*, 3d. ed.

McClellan's military career prior to 1861 was distinguished, if not spectacular. He was breveted twice during the Mexican War, had a respectable number of horses shot out from under him, and narrowly missed being seriously wounded by a canister fragment that glanced off the hilt of his sword. In the stupendously dull peacetime army, McClellan received respectable and challenging assignments. He made many friends, enjoyed army camaraderie, and was judged as pleasurable company. He continued to maintain a professional's attitude, attending postgraduate training and reading and writing military history. Before resigning his commission in 1857, he had participated in a number of topographical surveys that took him to the Red River country of Texas and Oklahoma, the Pacific Northwest, the Texas Gulf Coast, and the Caribbean. He was promoted to captain in 1855 and was selected as a commission member to observe military developments in Europe, arriving in time to see the allied siege of Sevastopol during the Crimean War. He concluded that portion of his military career by writing a field manual for American cavalry, leading to the adoption of the McClellan saddle as standard issue until the cavalry became mechanized. Only his survey to the Pacific Northwest was marred by significant disagreement, and that was with the leader of the expedition, Isaac I. Stevens. Any other difficulties he experienced during that period appear rather trifling. None of them derailed, or even sidetracked, a career deemed promising and successful. He was, in fact, well regarded in the old army.[28]

His civilian career before the outbreak of war in 1861 was marked by great achievement and personal success. Within a year of joining the Illinois Central Railroad as chief engineer, he was promoted to the vice

---

(New York: Scribner's, 1894), 59; Erasmus D. Keyes, *Fifty Years' Observation of Men and Events Civil and Military* (New York: Scribner's, 1884), 59. Of McClellan's formative years little is known. In Sears's biography, which is the most recent and best written, only a page and a half are given to his boyhood days before he entered West Point. Unfortunately, Sears sees an ominous portent of things to come when the youngster McClellan threw a tantrum over his teacher's accusing him of something he did not do. See Sears, *George B. McClellan: The Young Napoleon*, 4. Glatthaar suggests that McClellan suffered from paranoid personality disorder, and he notes that psychiatrists point to parental antagonisms and harassment experienced during early childhood as the underlying cause. After acknowledging that very little is known about McClellan's childhood, he states that it is "by no means inconsistent with the formation of paranoid personality disorder!" See Glatthaar, *Partners in Command*, 238–39.

28. McClellan's initial military service is explored in Sears, *George B. McClellan: The Young Napoleon*, 17–49, and Waugh, *The Class of 1846*, 73–130.

presidency. While it appears that his heart was not really in railroading, he acquitted himself well and demonstrated considerable determination in successfully weathering the financial crises attendant to the Panic of 1857. During that time, he remained attentive to fellow army officers in need. When Burnside's business ventures failed, McClellan secured a position for his friend with the railroad and allowed him to live with him at his own house in Chicago. Although his military expertise was repeatedly sought by those interested in the filibustering schemes of the time, McClellan prudently declined any offers of involvement. He remained a railroad executive of some distinction, nearly doubling the track mileage on the Illinois Central in 1858, and he was eventually courted for a more lucrative post with the Ohio and Mississippi Railroad. Following a long courtship with Ellen Marcy, the daughter of West Pointer Randolph B. Marcy, he was wed in May 1860. It would ultimately prove to be a fulfilling and loving relationship, marked by near-daily correspondence in times of separation, even though his letters resulted in rueful consequences for the McClellan legacy. McClellan was living in Cincinnati when the war began; he accepted one of several offers and became major general of the Ohio Volunteers.[29]

The point in this recapitulation of McClellan's career prior to 1861 is to suggest that in the balance he did not appear to be plagued by crippling mental instability. There was nothing in his past to intimate a lurking, brooding, out-of-control panic waiting to uncork on the Peninsula. McClellan advanced steadily and impressively in his military career, and the same confidence and verve marked his civilian ventures. Those who search McClellan's past to cull isolated, nonpatterned events to construct and substantiate their conclusions are patently unfair in their methodology. The broader examination of McClellan's life evinces no glimmer of instability or fragmentation. He was admired and respected by colleagues within the army and the railroad. Socially, he enjoyed a wide and intimate circle of friends. He related well with his family in Philadelphia and entered a marriage that was rich and rewarding. To the extent that it can be said that any family escapes being dysfunctional, McClellan's appears to have done so. His children did not grow up to hate him. His daughter, May, doted upon him, and his son, Max, who served a term as mayor of New York, would write a moving and loving tribute to his father in his own autobiography, *Gentleman and the Tiger*. McClellan's postmilitary

29. Sears, *George B. McClellan: The Young Napoleon*, 50–67.

career saw an unsuccessful, though respectable, bid for the presidency; a term as New Jersey's governor that was widely regarded as successful; and numerous commercial and literary enterprises. His later years, then, were characterized by the same vitality, organization, and sense of purpose that had animated earlier years. He may have mellowed somewhat toward the end of his life, but it was the vain and contentious McClellan who softened, and not the dysfunctional one envisioned by his critics and perpetuated by many historians.[30]

The psychological model suggested by historians is a red herring. Rather than encouraging a fair appraisal of McClellan's beliefs, attitudes, and abilities, it circumvents that endeavor from the outset. For the purpose of comparison only, one can see that when the standard of psychological profiling is employed in evaluations of Grant and Sherman, the construct is rendered suspect. In all likelihood, Sherman's and Grant's early disappointments, failures, and personality flaws and quirks were no barometer and had little to do with their reputations as Civil War commanders. And on the surface, it would seem as though both Sherman and Grant trailed a significant baggage of personality deficiencies into the Civil War. Yet the presence of those shortcomings did not prevent them from exercising military competence. Sherman's mental stability, in particular, was the subject of much speculation both during the war and in subsequent years. Every Sherman biographer has been compelled to address this issue.

Sherman, who had served under Irvin McDowell at First Manassas, was besieging Washington with desperate appeals for massive reinforcements in Kentucky at about the same time McClellan was being criticized for not taking the offensive in Virginia. If anyone came close to experiencing a psychotic episode during the Civil War it was Sherman in Kentucky. Situated near Elizabethtown, Sherman was convinced that he was confronted with vastly superior Confederate forces, although the enemy was as heavily concentrated in the Virginia theater and as thoroughly unprepared elsewhere as the federals were. In an estimate that far exceeded any McClellan would suggest, Sherman flatly declared that his opponent,

30. An overview of McClellan's career following his dismissal from command in November 1862 to his death on October 29, 1885, is ably covered in Sears, *George B. McClellan: The Young Napoleon*, 344–402. George B. McClellan, Jr. (Max), *Gentleman and the Tiger: The Autobiography of George B. McClellan, Jr.*, ed. Harold C. Syrett (Philadelphia: Lippincott, 1956), 1.

Simon Bolivar Buckner, outnumbered his force by a five to one ratio. Louisville, in Sherman's opinion, was in imminent danger; it was ripe for the enemy's taking. He was also convinced that Kentucky played host to a nest of spies and that its population was deceitful and treacherous. Northern reporters, moreover, were conspiring against him, and at one point, he threatened to hang a New York reporter who tried to remain near the army when all others had been barred. Using his family connections, he wrote to Lincoln directly concerning his desperate condition, and he ended one of his letters with the curt demand: "Answer." Sherman also sent foreboding and frantic messages to Grant and to the secretary of the treasury, Salmon Chase, warning them of the hopeless situation he had inherited in Kentucky.[31]

Not unlike McClellan on the Peninsula, whose exertions and frazzled nerves brought on a bout of a recurrent illness, Sherman succumbed to asthma attacks. Overwrought, Sherman took to sleeping too little and smoking and drinking too much. His utterings about impending disaster only intensified his craven fears. When the Northern press began to proclaim his manifest insanity, he only became more despondent. He remained intransigent in his belief that he needed two hundred thousand troops if the government wished him to take the offensive. That claim flabbergasted Secretary of War Simon Cameron and concerned McClellan and the War Department enough to send a delegation under Cameron to check on Sherman. When reports of the meeting made their way into the newspapers Sherman's claims and mood became public knowledge and led the assistant secretary of war, Thomas W. Scott, to declare, "Sherman's gone in the head, he's luny." Disturbing reports from many other quarters eventually convinced Halleck to ask McClellan to relieve Sherman of his duties. Buell replaced Sherman on November 13, 1861.[32]

Sherman admitted to his wife later that he had contemplated suicide in Kentucky, and he was accosted by his brother, John, with the analysis that he was not only wrong in his apprehensions but "laboring under some strange illusions." Still, Sherman remonstrated and forecast that hopes for preserving the Union were doomed unless major changes were inaugurated. Halleck, sensing that Sherman was unfit to command, or-

---

31. John F. Marszalek, *Sherman: A Soldier's Passion for Order* (New York: The Free Press, 1993), 161; Fellman, *Citizen Sherman,* 92–93.

32. Marszalek, *Sherman: A Soldier's Passion for Order,* 161–63; Fellman, *Citizen Sherman,* 96–99.

dered him to St. Louis where he thought Sherman could regain his equipoise. He was wrong. Sherman worried that the enemy force in Missouri was ready to pounce on the scattered and disorganized Union forces assigned to that region. After seeing a physician, who diagnosed him as too nervous to remain in command, Sherman returned to his family's hometown of Lancaster, Ohio, for a three-week sabbatical. Sherman's early Civil War career, then, was a signal failure, capping a life that had been marred by personal, financial, and commercial collapses. It was also a time marked by long periods of despondency and an unusual marriage in which his wife preferred living with her own parents more than she did with him. Although his subsequent war record was not without blemish, he regained his composure and redeemed himself, as well as his ultimate reputation, when he accepted a command under the watchful eye of his mentor, Grant.[33]

Of Sherman's early war career, historians have seen what they wanted to see. Some have viewed his mental afflictions as a sign of a simple collapse; others have called it a nervous breakdown; still others are convinced he was manic depressive. Marszalek has concluded that Sherman, like other men under the extraordinary strain of military leadership, experienced a searing episode of anxiety and depression that nearly incapacitated him. His desire to achieve success and avoid failure led him to exaggerate enemy strength and underestimate Union resolve. Like others in the Union command structure who had digested the poorly prepared and ill-advised effort at Bull Run, Sherman was afraid the same disaster might occur under his command. Eventually restored to command by McClellan, Sherman's shaky confidence grew stronger with Grant's patient guidance and example. Prompted in large part by an increase in irregular partisan warfare, Sherman would embrace harder measures of warfare for which he is mostly remembered. Sherman's active imagination, nimble intellect, volatile emotions, and palpable anxieties sparked the cathartic personal disarray in his early command positions. When more advantageous conditions for waging war emerged in 1864, those

---

33. Marszalek, *Sherman: A Soldier's Passion for Order,* 163–65. Sherman grudgingly admitted that he overreacted in Kentucky, but shortly after his dismissal he wrote his father-in-law, Thomas Ewing, that in "these times tis hard to say who are sane and who insane." See Ibid., 165. Fellman insists that the death of his son Willy cast Sherman into an exaggerated period of grief. It became, in Fellman's opinion, a subject of obsession with him, lasting throughout the Civil War. See Fellman, *Citizen Sherman,* 200.

characteristics proved to be the catalyst for a successful career. Underlying psychosis was not the basis for either his failure or his success.[34]

While in many ways McClellan and Sherman were temperamentally alike, Grant was atypical of other commanding generals in the Federal army. He was remarkably devoid of ostentation and practiced self-promotion with great care. While hardly a breezy, carefree personality, he was a most refreshingly forthright one. Laconic in speech, Grant put his trust in actions rather than promises. He exerted tenacity, determination, and aggressiveness, traits that eventually surmounted criticisms of his character and led a hopeful Lincoln to summon him east for command. If imaginable, Sherman's pre-Civil War failures were exceeded by Grant's, as a peacetime army officer, a farmer, a businessman, and a clerk in his father's general store in Galena, Illinois. One winter Grant sold firewood on the streets of St. Louis and pawned his watch in order to make ends meet. Some of his failures were attributable to bad luck and unfortuitous circumstances; others were a product of his chronic misjudgments in selecting business partners and colleagues. He was approaching his fortieth birthday when the outbreak of the rebellion presented yet another opportunity for renewal.[35]

Other than a fairly stimulating tour of duty in the Mexican War, Grant's early military career had been scarred by significant periods of boredom, loneliness, and depression. He enthusiastically greeted his assignment to the Pacific coast in 1852, even though it meant leaving his pregnant wife in St. Louis. However, once he was stationed at Camp Humboldt on the coast of California, Grant became deeply despondent and lonely. Like McClellan, Grant chafed under the despotic rule of the post commander, Lt. Col. Robert Christie Buchanan. Despising each other, Grant and Buchanan quarrelled frequently, leading, in part, to Grant's resignation from the army in 1854. Before he did so, however, Grant's despair had reached a point where he apparently sought and found solace in the dubious comforts of alcohol, initiating a life-long reputation for heavy and constant drinking that is more apocryphal than true. His drinking habits became the source of great interest and speculation throughout the Civil War, enabling Halleck to stall his career at one point and goading

34. Charles E. Vetter, *Sherman: Merchant of Terror, Advocate of Peace* (Gretna, La.: Pelican Press, 1992), 96; Fellman, *Citizen Sherman,* 100–109; Marszalek, *Sherman: A Soldier's Passion for Order,* 169.

35. William S. McFeely, *Grant: A Biography* (New York: Norton, 1981), 29–66.

the unctuous Stanton to send Charles Dana to snoop around Grant's camp. Loneliness, idleness, and depression have been described as the trigger mechanisms, although experts in the field of alcohol abuse view the process in reverse. His celebrated drinking sprees have been termed benders, occasions of abuse, overindulgence, and outright alcoholism. Irrespective of the most appropriate term, he did appear dependent upon alcohol on certain occasions. Grant was aware that his drinking was a liability that could interfere with his chances of landing a respectable command at the beginning of the war. His efforts at lobbying were rebuffed, and it was not until his own congressman interceded that he received his colonel's commission. Grant eventually won admirers with his successes in the western theater, and it has been humorously suggested that once he became commanding general of all the armies, half the state of Illinois claimed credit for getting him his commission.[36]

Grant's drinking customs and the moodiness that surrounded their initiation bespeak a discernable clinical disorder more easily identifiable than those possibly attached to McClellan or Sherman. Although there is a tendency to slough off hard drinking as harmless when it comes to military heroes,[37] it can hardly be laughed off in Grant's case. It was a problem for Grant throughout the remainder of his life. In one sense, he was lucky to have John Rawlins constantly at his side during the war, for that adjutant served in many ways to head off potential problems when warning signals flared. However, in a way, Rawlins was the classic enabler to Grant, for his efforts helped Grant avoid having to confront his compulsion during long periods of idleness. His was a very strange relationship with Grant. He is reputed to be the only one, other than Julia,

36. McFeely, *Grant*, 52–55, 74–76. See also John Y. Simon, *Grant and Halleck: Contrasts in Command*, The Frank L. Klement Lecture, September 16, 1996 (Milwaukee: Marquette Univ. Press, 1996), 12.

37. When it was reported that at Chancellorsville Hooker had abstained from the hard drinking that was his trademark, George Armstrong Custer wrote McClellan: "If anything except his lack of ability interfered or prevented him from succeeding, it was a wound he received from a projectile which requires a cork to be drawn before it is serviceable." See Custer to McClellan, May 6, 1863, McClellan Papers, Manuscript Division, Library of Congress. Hooker's corps commander, Darius Couch, sneered that the absence of alcohol was to blame and that Hooker would have been better off had he maintained his customary habit. See Darius Couch, "The Chancellorsville Campaign," in Robert Underwood Johnson and Clarence Clough Buel, eds., *Battles and Leaders of the Civil War*, 4 vols. (New York: Century, 1888), 3:170 (hereafter cited as *Battles and Leaders*).

whom Grant would allow to issue orders about his personal life. His bearing toward Grant smacks of a strong maternal instinct, occasionally mixed with a potent potion of Calvinistic probity that served as the general's "alter superego." At one point, Rawlins was so incensed with Grant's drinking that he wrote him a sharp rebuke over the matter. After chiding Grant for indulging his vice in the company of bad men, he reminded Grant of an earlier promise: "Had you not pledged me the sincerity of your honor early last March that you would drink no more during the war, and kept that pledge during your recent campaign, you would not to-day have stood first in the world's history as a successful military commander." Whether Rawlins did an ultimate disservice to his chief is arguable, but he helped Grant pass Stanton's litmus test in the spring and summer of 1863. After the great victory at Vicksburg, Dana suppressed some of his findings and wrote Stanton that whenever Grant "commits the folly of tasting liquor, Rawlins can be counted on to stop him."[38]

When the standards of evaluation are uniformly applied, it is clear that Grant, Sherman, and McClellan each came to their command positions with a less than extraordinary mix of successes, strengths, weaknesses, and failures. To the untrained eye, none of those men were incapacitated by neuroses or psychoses that singularly exempted them from command ability. Under different circumstances and environments, each of them felt the strain of war and coped with varying degrees of success. If McClellan's correspondence, especially in the preponderant portion addressed to his wife, is used as the measure to assess his state of mind, an examination of Sherman's correspondence yields similar results. If McClellan's fits of pique with superior officers were truly prescient indicators of a troubled future, then Phillip Sheridan should never have been placed in command. After all, he had chafed under the yoke of several superior officers, had engaged in several celebrated rows with Stanton, and had been suspended for a year at West Point for assaulting his cadet sergeant after refusing to obey a command. And if the pompous and overrated McClellan never should have aspired to be the commanding general of all Northern armies, then Grant's reputation as a pathetic drunkard entitled him to no more than a corporal's stripe.

38. The Grant-Rawlins relationship is astutely explored in McFeely, *Grant*, 85–88, 133–35.

The same standard when applied to Lincoln, who served as commander in chief to Grant, Sherman, and McClellan, makes one wonder why he was ever elected president and how he succeeded so well in his job. His bouts of depression, which on one occasion in Illinois convinced friends to remove razors, knives, and pistols from his room, were well known. His own awareness of depression, generated by family tragedies, deaths of friends, thwarted romance, and even political defeats profoundly affected him, serving to inspire the impression that he was wholly and entirely a melancholic person. William McFeely may have been correct in observing that "Sherman, Grant and, Lincoln might well have been in therapy . . . than in command of the nation's fortune" had the Civil War been fought in our own time. His melancholy notwithstanding, Lincoln remained a steadfast and capable executive.[39]

The assessments of professional historians have trickled down and sunk fast roots in the perception of the Civil War. In the process, we have inherited simplistic, golden-rule impressions of that war's military leaders. Matters complicated are reduced to avowed truths. Thus it is that Robert E. Lee becomes the solemn and wise patriarch, the venerable dean of the Southern cause. His was a valiant uphill struggle. For many, the South did not lose. Its greatest commander was merely outmatched by Northern manpower and industrial might. William T. Sherman emerges as the excitable genius of the war, who conceived and implemented a total war strategy that brought the South to its knees. Stonewall Jackson is viewed as the eccentric warrior-evangelist whose lightening-quick tactics amazed friend and foe alike and whose untimely death deprived Lee of his best commander and the South of ultimate victory. Grant is enshrined as the dogged, unpretentious, bulldog of the war. He validated Lincoln's long and futile search for a general who would fight the hard and grimy war necessary to win. His drinking habits are viewed as a badge of honor, or at worst, they are winked at. And then there is McClellan. He emerges as the privileged, fair-haired boy-general of whom great things were expected. He failed to deliver on his promise because his colossal ego, erratic personality, and psychological composition rendered him incapable of doing so. He became the Civil War's biggest dud.

39. Charles B. Strozier, *Lincoln's Quest for Union* (New York: Basic Books, 1982), 44–45, 204–9; William S. McFeely, ed., *Memoirs of General William T. Sherman* (New York: Da Capo Press, 1984), x.

When the overall, more complex, picture is viewed instead, one might appreciate that the injudicious claims many historians have levied against McClellan's mental health not only are unwarranted, they are unnecessary. It is not required that McClellan be diminished for Sherman and Grant to appear praiseworthy. Nor is it necessary to dismiss McClellan as a pretender in order to vindicate Lincoln's military acumen. To borrow Joseph Harsh's suggestion, the time has come to get McClellan "off of his merry-go-round of make-believe controversy" and to consider his place in Civil War history with less passion and greater balance.[40]

40. Harsh, "On the McClellan-Go-Round," 118.

3

Little Mac's Peccadilloes

I F G E O R G E M C C L E L L A N ' S P S Y C H O L O G I C A L H A N D I C A P S
constitute the basis for his inability to succeed as a military commander, then his lesser faults, or peccadilloes, serve to undermine his credibility even further. In equivalent theological terms, McClellan's psychological flaws comprise his mortal sins in the eyes of his critics, and for
these he receives the condign censure of the historical literature. His peccadilloes, on the other hand, represent his venial sins. These have assumed
a tremendous importance in any review of McClellan's personality, for
if his psychological disabilities render him a figure of pity or derision,
his personality limitations make him an object of scorn and contempt.
For many historians, his smaller flaws, whether they be his purported arrogance, rudeness, vanity, secretiveness, or insubordination are magnified
out of proportion to their substance. No other commander's venial shortcomings have been subject to such intense scrutiny as McClellan's. Any
browsing of Civil War history is quite likely to lead the reader into believing that those peccadilloes were the exclusive property of George Mc-
Clellan. Until a more discerning and expanded view is conducted of the
full panoply of characters who played out that great moment of history,
there is no reason to expect any change in this perception.

McClellan's relationship with Lincoln is central to any understanding
of why historians judge him as a flawed personality. For Unionist historians like T. Harry Williams, Bruce Catton, Kenneth P. Williams, and their
successors, Lincoln has attained a stature that sets him apart from other

mortals. Their interpretations are firmly set in a profound respect for Lincoln's personal and executive qualities. He is clever but remains endearingly folksy. His homespun anecdotal wit belies a keen insight into the nature and motivation of humankind. He is able to rise above the base criticism of petty politicians, generals, and bureaucrats in keeping his eye on the prize. He transcends temporal and spatial parameters to stand as an ideal for all generations, or as his secretary of war declared upon the close of the Lincoln death watch on Tenth Street, "He belongs to the ages." He is the one who truly preserved the Union.

While Lincoln deserves all of the credit lavished upon him, it has often come at the expense of others, and none more than George McClellan.[1] The tone for dealing with the historical McClellan might well have come from the first custodians of the Lincoln legacy–John Nicolay and John Hay. During the course of revising their monumental history of the Lincoln presidency, Hay advised Nicolay that handling McClellan would be an important and delicate matter. After toiling through ten chapters that involved McClellan, Hay was satisfied that he had proven the general's "mutinous imbecility," and he proudly remarked that only on one occasion had he resorted to the use of an "injurious adjective." It was of paramount concern for Hay that "we should seem fair to him, while we are destroying him." Despite that professed intention, Hay enjoined his partner to be impartial and unsparing with all other historical figures, excepting the departed president, for both of them were "Lincoln men all the way through."[2] While it would be inaccurate to suggest that Unionist historians have appropriated Hay's partiality, it might not be unfair to suggest that some of the stark judgments they have formed about McClellan still reflect a dynamic of that bias. To be sure, McClellan unwisely chose to consider Lincoln as thoroughly inimical to him personally and to his outlook on the war. Nevertheless, many aspects and dynamics of the Lincoln-McClellan relationship suggest the relationship suffered from mutual mishandling.

One of the most striking criticisms leveled at McClellan is his outright rudeness to Lincoln, the man, and his patent disrespect for the office

1. T. Harry Williams, *Lincoln and His Generals*, 7–14; Bruce Catton, *Reflections on the Civil War* (New York: Doubleday, 1981), 28–33; McPherson, "Lincoln and the Strategy of Unconditional Surrender," 31–35, 61–62; Glatthaar, *Partners in Command*, 229–30; David H. Donald, *Lincoln* (New York: Simon and Schuster, 1995), 599.

2. Hay is quoted in William Roscoe Thayer, *The Life and Letters of John Hay*, 2 vols. (Boston: Little Brown, 1915), 2:31–33.

Lincoln held. Given the president's preeminent position in the history of the war years, McClellan's purported discourtesy towards Lincoln is tantamount to insulting an icon. As usual, a great deal of supporting evidence is drawn from McClellan's correspondence with his wife. Therein is found the reference, actually borrowed from Stanton, to the president as the "original gorrilla." On another occasion, as he railed against the entire administration, he referred to Lincoln as "nothing more than a well meaning baboon." We also see an annoyed and irritated McClellan escaping the company of a "browsing" president at Stanton's house of all places. McClellan resented the near-daily visits, at any hour of the day and night, from the president and increasingly considered them fruitless intrusions. From other sources come tales of McClellan's arrogance and mean-spiritedness. Heintzelman recorded that after the president entered a conference room to offer unsolicited and uninformed military advice, McClellan saw him out the door and remarked to Heintzelman, "Isn't he a rare bird?"[3]

But the supreme insult, and what John Hay called the "unparalleled insolence of epaulettes," was the reported snub McClellan delivered the president on November 13, 1861. It is the one story that finds its way into virtually every biography of Lincoln or McClellan. According to Hay, he, along with Lincoln and Seward, went to visit the general's home on Jackson Square to confer with McClellan. When they arrived, the porter informed them that McClellan was out attending the wedding of an officer. Electing to wait, they sat until they heard McClellan arrive home. Then, according to Hay, the general brushed past the parlor, paying no attention to the porter's announcement of visitors, and went straight upstairs. After a half hour passed, Lincoln reminded the porter they were still waiting to see the general; he received the response that McClellan had already gone to bed.[4] Even the most neutral observer would be forced to think very poorly of McClellan.

Although it may be recorded as but another item in the record of McClellan's insolence, Hay's recollection deserves a closer look. The fact that it appears as an incident worth citing in any review of the Lincoln-

3. Sears, *Civil War Papers of George B. McClellan*, 106, 113, 135; entry for November 11, 1861, *Journal of Samuel P. Heintzelman, 1861–1865*, Manuscript Division, Library of Congress.

4. Tyler Dennett, ed., *Lincoln and the Civil War in the Diaries and Letters of John Hay* (New York: Dodd, Mead, 1939), 34–35.

McClellan relationship points to its significance in the literature. A number of McClellan supporters have tried to mitigate the callous aspects of the event by impugning Hay's truthfulness or by making excuses for the general's behavior.[5] In part, these objections are valid, but they have usually been ignored or dismissed.[6] Still, there are many unsettling matters with respect to the use of this story. Most importantly, historians have accepted at face value the integrity of the story, both in its explicit content and in the value Hay placed upon the incident. No one prefaces any narration of the story by relating that this is the "way Hay saw it," or "according to Hay," or even "Hay reported." The story is repeated as is, presumably for its full impact.

The strange thing about that incident is that not one of the principals involved corroborated it in any way. Beyond Hay's assertion that Lincoln made light of the matter, there is no mention of it in anything Lincoln wrote or said, and the same may be said for Seward. McClellan, who is on record for sharing most of his contempt for the president with his wife, made no mention of it, even though he wrote her the very next day. Such a snub would surely have been worthy of sharing with Ellen. Lincoln did not use the incident, as some have maintained, to stop visiting McClellan's home and begin summoning the general to the White House. He visited the general on the very next evening, and at least one more time, on the evening of November 18. Shortly after that, McClellan's wife, with her infant daughter in tow, came to live with the general, and that may have been a factor in the switch in meeting places. Consequently, it seems plausible that the incident, assuming it did occur, came off very differently than described and that it carried none of the general's insolence or the president's humiliation that Hay perceived.[7]

5. Randall impugns Hay's integrity in light of the comments he made to Nicolay about how they should handle the historical McClellan. See Randall, *Lincoln the President* 2:68, 72. Hassler suggests that perhaps McClellan had drunk too much at the wedding and did not want to see the president in that condition. See Warren W. Hassler, Jr., *General George B. McClellan: Shield of the Union* (Baton Rouge: Louisiana State Univ. Press, 1957), 41.

6. Sears, *George B. McClellan: The Young Napoleon,* 426n.10. Sears's own diligent research points to Lincoln having met with McClellan on at least fifty-seven occasions during the intervening months between his arrival in Washington and his departure for the Peninsula. See Stephen W. Sears, "Lincoln and McClellan," in Gabor S. Boritt, ed., *Lincoln's Generals* (New York: Oxford Univ. Press, 1994), 11.

7. Sears, "Lincoln and McClellan," 133. See also Sears, *Civil War Papers of George B. McClellan,* 121, 132.

McClellan was undoubtedly responsible for playing a prominent role in undermining the working partnership with his commander in chief. This is all the more unfortunate because the president, despite his exasperation with the general's excessive caution, actually liked elements of McClellan's personality. The indelible impression in the historical literature is that Lincoln played no role in the failure of his partnership with McClellan. As Glatthaar maintains, throughout the entire course of this relationship, Lincoln "supported his general wholeheartedly." In addition to his unreserved support, Lincoln also "articulated military goals for his commander and provided the necessary manpower and equipment to accomplish them." Unfortunately, that is not exactly true. At various times throughout McClellan's tenure as commander, Lincoln upbraided him in disrespectful tones and with biting sarcasm. If anything, Lincoln showed he could give as well as he could take. Lincoln also demonstrated that he could be as insensitive as his commander on occasion. He waited until McClellan had embarked for Fortress Monroe before issuing the order that relieved McClellan as general in chief. As it was, McClellan learned through the grapevine that the order had already been published in the press. If anyone was graceful, it was McClellan, for he accepted the demotion without grumbling, even though it was a clear setback to his public image. Nor is it exactly true that Lincoln was entirely candid in articulating military goals and sustaining his commander's every need. Although he shelved his own preferences for the spring offensive of 1862 in favor of his commander's, he nursed his reservations throughout the entire Peninsula campaign and acted upon them in a number of decisions that were decidedly to McClellan's disadvantage. At critical moments during the campaign he reneged in committing the manpower originally promised McClellan, an act that actually imperiled the general's troop dispositions. And the president was not frank about how military goals were to be shaped by the political dimensions of the rebellion. In part, that was because those aspects were in a state of flux, and McClellan was a general who clearly opposed the direction they were heading. Whatever might be said by way of propriety and timeliness of the Harrison's Landing Letter, at least McClellan was clear as to where he stood and was straightforward with the president. Lincoln did not reciprocate in kind. As Phillip S. Paludan has observed, Lincoln might have taken the occasion of this letter to discuss military strategy with his commander. Instead, he thanked McClellan, tucked the letter in his pocket, and did not read it until he returned to Washington. McClellan was left to ponder where the president stood on the matter.[8]

Just as any military commander bears the responsibility for the statements and actions of his subordinates, so, too, does the president for the members of his cabinet. Unfortunately, the member most responsible as the liaison in the Lincoln-McClellan relationship was Edwin M. Stanton. Despite his impressive administrative talents, Stanton did nothing to facilitate a harmonious relationship between the commanding general and the commander in chief. He was, in the opinion of many, a most disagreeable man. And when speaking of difficult personalities, if anyone during the Civil War approached being a genuine misanthrope, it surely was Edwin Stanton. It was truly a monument to Lincoln's greatness as president that he was able to work effectively with the man and enlist his best talents in the service of the government. Virtually every commander who had to report to the secretary of war disliked him intensely. Despite his relative distance from Washington, and the comfort of having Grant as a buffer, Sherman came under the lash of Stanton's poisoned pen. When Sherman ill-advisedly initiated peace negotiations with Johnston's surrendering army, Stanton rebuked him publicly. Nursing a grudge, Sherman did not stew in his anger; he got even. When the victorious western armies marched past the reviewing stand in May 1865, Sherman alighted from the stand and shook everyone's extended hands. When Stanton pushed his way forward, Sherman abruptly withdrew his own hand. Sherman's was a calculated snub, played out for effect, and he was pleased that everyone took notice of it. Grant, on the other hand, made a career of avoiding Stanton whenever he could, although after the war, his dislike of the secretary played a significant part in Stanton's removal from office. It is said that Grant was generally magnanimous in his judgments of people in his memoirs. However, when it came to his reflection on Stanton, none of that spirit of cordiality was evident. Stanton, in Grant's reckoning, "Cared nothing about the feelings of others." Indeed, Grant decided that "it seemed to be pleasanter to him to disappoint than to gratify." Even Phil Sheridan, who did not have to report directly to the secretary until very late in the war, felt Stanton's wrath and was put in his place by secretarial edict.[9]

---

8. Glatthaar, *Partners in Command,* 93; Sears, *Civil War Papers of George B. McClellan,* 515; Basler, *Collected Works of Lincoln* 5:474; Phillip Shaw Paludan, *The Presidency of Abraham Lincoln* (Lawrence: Univ. Press of Kansas, 1994), 137–41.

9. William T. Sherman, *The Memoirs of William T. Sherman,* 2 vols. (New York: D. Appleton, 1875), 2:377; Ulysses S. Grant, *Personal Memoirs,* 2 vols. (New York: Charles L.

Stanton held a special dislike for McClellan. Theirs had been an unusual relationship. At the outset of the war, Stanton, a Democrat, found a kindred spirit in McClellan, egging him on in his denunciation of Scott and others who stood in the general's way. Stanton's own residence served as McClellan's refuge from the prying eyes of Washington in the fall of 1861. However, shortly after Stanton replaced Cameron as secretary of war on January 13, 1862, the relationship soured. It was perhaps one of the fastest transformations in political alliances during the war. The same Stanton who, according to McClellan, actually sought the general's approval before accepting his cabinet position, was by month's end haranguing McClellan's inactivity and trumpeting that the "champagne and oysters on the Potomac" had to come to an immediate end. Stanton made his animus toward McClellan manifestly clear by February. First, he actively courted the support of his erstwhile enemies among the radical elements of the Republican party, and then he collaborated with Horace Greeley of the *New York Tribune* in what amounted to an unmistakable public slap at McClellan. Seizing upon Grant's victories at Forts Henry and Donelson, Stanton derided McClellan's strategic thinking in a cloaked indictment that not only betrayed his skewed understanding of military history but underscored his strategic naivete and religious euphoria. The article read:

> Much has recently been said of military combinations and organizing victory. I hear such phrases with apprehension. They commenced in infidel France with the Italian campaign, and resulted in Waterloo. Who can organize victory? Who can combine the elements of success on the battlefield? We owe our recent victories to the Spirit of the Lord, that moved our enemies with dismay. The inspiration that conquered in battle was in the hearts of the soldiers from on high; and wherever there is the same inspiration there will be the same results.

Coming from McClellan's immediate superior, such a message was not calculated to inspire confidence and goodwill. With his wife residing in Washington with him, we have been spared whatever McClellan's

---

Webster, 1885–86), 2:537; Roy Morris, Jr., *Sheridan: The Life and Times of General Phil Sheridan* (New York: Crown, 1992), 235–36. John Hay is reported to have begged his friend Nicolay to never send him to Stanton to ask a favor, by saying, "I would rather make a tour of a smallpox hospital." See Nevin, *War for the Union* 2:35.

immediate reaction to this statement might have been. Another unmistakable gesture of Stanton's complete lack of confidence in the commanding general was his invitation to Maj. Gen. Ethan Allen Hitchcock
to assume command of the Army of the Potomac before it embarked for
the Peninsula.[10]

Stanton's dislike of McClellan, in and of itself, should not have played
a conspicuous role in the failure of the Peninsula campaign. It was not required that the two of them like each other to achieve success, although
it undoubtedly would have helped. Furthermore, Stanton was not necessarily at fault or wrong in his conviction that McClellan did not possess
the stuff of which great commanders are made. And, to a certain degree,
McClellan's political connections and outspoken views on the civil policy
of the war made him a somewhat legitimate target for attack. What is
important about Stanton is that he held a position of immeasurable importance in the cabinet and that his obvious distrust of his primary subordinate led him to make decisions during the course of the campaign
that affected its outcome.

Like all others during that time, the secretary was new to his responsibilities and made his fair share of mistakes in the process. Certainly, his
decision to suspend recruitment in the North in April was a blunder. In
part, McClellan's seemingly unrealistic expectations and pleas for reinforcement late in the campaign were adversely magnified by that decision.
Stanton also played the principal role in Lincoln's decision to deny Mc-
Dowell's timely participation in the Peninsula campaign. He seized upon
Brig. Gen. James S. Wadsworth's analysis of the troops allocated for the
defense of Washington and brought the full power of his office and personality to persuade the president to suspend McDowell's movement
toward McClellan. Perhaps Grant, who managed to forge a viable working relationship with both Lincoln and Stanton, had the best insight into
the secretary's unwelcome intrusion into military affairs. In his analysis,
Stanton could not help himself from "interfering with the armies covering
the capital when it was sought to defend it by an offensive movement

---

10. Charles A. Dana, *Recollections of the Civil War: With the Leaders at Washington and in
the Field in the Sixties* (New York: D. Appleton, 1898), 5; U.S. Congress, *Report of the Joint
Committee on the Conduct of the War*, 3 vols. (Washington, D.C.: GPO, 1863), 1:62–63 (hereafter cited as *CCW*); *New York Tribune*, Feb. 20, 1862. Stanton's offer to Hitchcock, a sixty-
four-year-old man in ailing health who knew more of religious mysticism than commanding armies, was fitting testimony to the secretary's total lack of confidence in McClellan. See
Hassler, *General George B. McClellan*, 72.

against the army guarding the Confederate capital." By Grant's accounting, Stanton, unlike Lincoln, was too "timid," even hinting that the secretary was altogether too motivated by fear for his own personal safety. "He could see our weakness," Grant declared, "but he could not see that the enemy was in danger." Any analysis, then, of the presumably flawed relationship between Lincoln and McClellan is incomplete if the role played by Stanton is not included. And while Lincoln most likely emerged the least tarnished in that debacle of cooperative leadership, Stanton certainly gave McClellan a run for his money in the race for most sullied.[11]

A vital component of the McClellan personality forged over the last half century is that his rude and arrogant stance towards the president was an intrinsic character flaw. His rudeness towards Lincoln was not an exception to the rule; it was only an example of the rule in action. The president was but one in a long series of persons to find themselves at the receiving end of McClellan's unattractive personality traits. He has been seen as a particularly petty, vindictive, vain individual, overly sensitive to what he perceived were his special prerogatives and secretive and furtive in his dealings with others. Many historians have not only noted those flaws, they have frequently identified them as if they were peculiar to McClellan. Again, as in so many other particulars concerning his actions during the Civil War, McClellan is singled out as the chief sinner. Consequently, we have received a very distorted picture.

There can be little doubt that McClellan could be petty, vain, and vindictive on occasion. Those unlikable traits were not, however, characteristic of the man, nor were they his special province of behavior. During his tenure in command and in the responsibilities incumbent to that position, he undoubtedly upbraided subordinates in an undeserving manner for what he perceived as dereliction of duty. It appears that he treated McDowell shabbily and subjected him to the public humiliation of reenacting the Federal defeat on the plains of Manassas. Most likely, he was uncharitable towards Burnside in his retrospective analysis of the Antietam campaign, although that officer was culpable for many mistakes during the battle, and his subsequent performance during the remainder of the war only served to confirm his manifest incompetence. At other times, McClellan could be incredibly vain. He inflated the significance of minor victories, boasted about his importance to the war effort, and

11. Sears, *To the Gates of Richmond*, 34; Grant, *Memoirs* 2:537.

became self-absorbed in attempting to secure the adulation and approval of others. In many ways and at many times, McClellan was those things; he could be petty, vain, and vindictive. In truth, his display of those vices helped contribute to his estrangement from those whose support he needed most. But that is not the entire story.[12]

McClellan's public persona was of a man charming and engaging, possessing an outstanding faculty for remembering the names of even junior officers. As is readily acknowledged, he was held in high esteem by the rank and file of the army, and he worked hard to sustain their morale, pride, and self-respect. He attended to their physical needs and was affected by the loss of human life on the battlefield. Throughout his tenure, he retained the loyalty and respect of the majority of the officer corps. His dispatches to Washington were not entirely self-absorbed. He took special notice of any exemplary actions undertaken by his subordinates. Despite his estrangement from his superiors, he was able to transcend petty considerations when circumstances called for it. When the Lincolns suffered the death of their son Willie, McClellan wrote a sincere and heartfelt letter of condolence. Similarly, he overlooked his extreme dislike for Stanton by offering his sympathies over news that the secretary's child had become seriously ill.[13]

Many who played significant roles in the Civil War possessed personalities that appear in the balance to be less attractive than McClellan's. The North had more than its fair share. For sheer malevolence, Joseph Hooker had no equal. No one escaped his sarcasm, and no one had anything kind to say about him after the war. Had it not been for Gen. Daniel Butterfield, his principal adjutant, and the Southern general, John B. Gordon, it is altogether possible that he had no friends. McDowell and Buell possessed McClellan's hauteur but none of his grace and charm to offset it. Both of them were disliked by their subordinates, and in McDowell's case, it is widely acknowledged that his soldiers would not accept his leadership after his performance at Second Manassas.

---

12. Sears, *George B. McClellan: The Young Napoleon,* 86–88; Glatthaar, *Partners in Command,* 56; Nevins, *War for the Union* 2:47; Marvel, *Burnside,* 126. McClellan has frequently been criticized for his less than respectful attitude toward his mentor, Winfield Scott, and for the fact that he was responsible for their falling out. McClellan's predecessor, Irvin McDowell, a longtime favorite of Scott's, fell out of the commanding general's favor by opposing the Anaconda policy. See *CCW* 2:37.

13. Sears, *Civil War Papers of George B. McClellan,* 187; McClellan, *McClellan's Own Story,* 477.

Halleck commanded respect in some quarters for his administrative abilities but garnered no awards for a winning personality. Meade, while well respected in the army, had a way of distancing himself from others by explosions of his uncontrollable temper. Stanton was obsequious enough to ingratiate himself with those he relied upon for advancement, but once he attained the object of his desire, he usually assumed the role of antagonist. In the South, the universal criticism levied at its leader, Jefferson Davis, was his inability to get along with people. The greatly revered Stonewall Jackson inspired respect and admiration, but he was altogether too austere, unyielding, and eccentric to make his an approachable personality. And Johnston and Beauregard were as adept at preening and massaging their own egos and ambitions as McClellan ever was.[14]

Sherman and Grant, too, demonstrated some of the same venial flaws as McClellan. When success, which had eluded him for so long, finally came his way, Sherman could be as vain as McClellan. The fulsome praise he accorded himself in his letters to his wife vie with McClellan's for sheer braggadocio. After Shiloh he basked in the glow of his own disingenuous self-appraisal. "I have worked hard to keep down," he swallowed, "but somehow I am forced into prominence and might as well submit." That bombast was rapidly followed by the next: "I noticed that when we were enveloped and death stared us all in the face my seniors in rank leaned on me." In the wake of his success, he advised his wife Ellen that she would eventually convince herself that he was "a soldier as famous as General [Nathaniel] Greene," although he demurred from taking any personal satisfaction from such praise except to win it for his family. That parade of self-inflicted backslapping continued to the end of the war and beyond. With his march to the sea concluded, Sherman confided to Ellen that he had been told if he were to travel up North, he "would be feted and petted." As he began his ascent through the Carolinas, he noted that he had suddenly emerged as a "leader to whom not only my soldiers look to but the President and the People. Not only our own but foreigners and

14. Hebert, *Fighting Joe Hooker*, 295; John J. Hennessy, *Return to Bull Run: The Campaign and Battle of Second Manassas* (New York: Simon and Schuster, 1993), 466; T. Harry Williams, *Lincoln and His Generals*, 48, 260; Waugh, *Class of 1846*, 283–88; Royster, *Destructive War*, 45–47, 77–78; Steven E. Woodworth, *Davis and Lee at War* (Lawrence: Univ. of Kansas Press, 1995), 16–20, 26–28, 74–75, 91. Following his dismissal from command, John Pope, Lincoln's erstwhile friend, characterized the president as "feeble, cowardly, and shameful." See Wallace J. Schutz and Walter N. Trenerry, *Abandoned by Lincoln: A Military Biography of General John Pope* (Urbana: Univ. of Illinois Press, 1990), 176.

the South now accord me one of the Great Leaders of armies, endowed with extraordinary powers." As Fellman concluded, after Grant, the person Sherman admired most was himself, "A hero to whom he quite often referred in the third person." Throughout his retirement, the "icon" Sherman thought of himself "as the eternally plucky warrior." It was Fellman's discernment that Sherman's "urgent vanity was quite apparent," while his "attempts at dissembling his egotism were transparent."[15]

Sherman the vindictive warrior was also a force to be reckoned with. Like so many other junior officers during the peacetime army, when hinterland assignments proved monumentally dull and opportunities for advancement were extremely limited, Sherman's intensity got him entangled in peevish disputes with other officers. One notable instance was a row he had with a fellow lieutenant with whom he would collide later during the Civil War—Henry W. Halleck. At one point in California, Sherman became so incensed with Halleck that he wrote his senior officer, Col. R. B. Mason, asking him to indicate which of the two quarreling subordinates had first mentioned that they were not on speaking terms. When Mason unwisely endorsed Sherman's version of the tiff, Sherman chided Halleck for squealing to a senior officer. "I shall expect you to acknowledge this simple fact," he gloated in a letter sent to Halleck. Without a martial outlet for pent-up ambitions, many junior officers, like Sherman and McClellan, bristled when they thought their prerogatives were being trampled upon. Had Sherman been an officer of a generation earlier, such a petty argument would have been sufficient provocation for him to have invited Halleck to a duel.[16]

Sherman's well-timed reproach, delivered to Stanton on the reviewing stand in Washington, D.C., was viewed with wide approval within army circles and might have been overlooked as a well-deserved comeuppance for a haughty politician. It did, however, reveal that Sherman savored the sweet taste of revenge. It also showed that he would not accept insults passively; he rarely allowed his resentment to go unavenged. To Halleck's misfortune, he had thrown his hat into the ring with Stanton over Sherman's unauthorized peace feelers extended to Johnston. When Halleck ordered other officers to ignore Sherman's peace initiatives, he earned that general's wrath. Sherman's estrangement from Halleck was quite different

    15. Fellman, *Citizen Sherman*, 117–18, 190, 301, 337.
    16. Ibid., 28; Edward M. Coffman, *The Old Army: A Portrait of the American Army in Peacetime, 1784–1898* (New York: Oxford Univ. Press, 1986), 66–70.

from his rift with Stanton. For all his aloofness, Halleck had always taken a personal interest in safeguarding Sherman's career. When the hue and cry was raised against Sherman in Kentucky, it was Halleck who intervened to save him from self-destruction. Halleck nurtured Sherman's reintegration back into the army and was instrumental in coaxing McClellan to assign him to Grant's command. As late as the fall of Atlanta, Sherman acknowledged Halleck as a true friend. "I confess I owe you all I now enjoy of fame," he confided to Halleck, "for I had allowed myself in 1861 to fall into a perfect 'slough of despond,' [and] you alone seemed to be confident, and you gradually put me in the way of recovering from what might have proved an ignoble end." That candid admission, however, did not make Sherman hesitate for an instant to seek revenge the following April when Halleck transgressed. Sherman rebuffed Halleck's attempts at making apologies and amends, and when "Old Brains" invited the hero of Atlanta to stay with him in Richmond as his army was passing through in May 1865, Sherman replied: "I cannot have any friendly intercourse with you." Believing that his hunger for revenge was not fully satiated, Sherman, through public advertisement, informed Halleck he was not welcome to review the march of his army through Richmond. "I beg you to keep slightly *perdu*," he advised, "for if noticed by some of my old command I cannot undertake to maintain a model behavior, for their feelings have become aroused by what the world judges an insult." Forewarned, the humbled and humiliated Halleck hunkered down in his Richmond headquarters with the curtains drawn over the windows. For Sherman, the bigger prize—Stanton—was waiting in Washington. By anyone's standards, Sherman's treatment of a fellow officer was outrageous.[17]

McClellan's intention to keep his wartime correspondence with his wife out of his official memoirs at least suggested that his desire for vindication had limits, and he was aware of the malignant tone in them. Sherman remained relentless in his pursuit of self-adulation and revenge in his retirement. With the possible exception of Longstreet and his detractors, no one exceeded Sherman in that mission. In a battery of letters, articles, and essays during the two decades following the war, Sherman engaged in a protracted war of words, and he launched a series of bitter feuds with the partisans of Generals Don Carlos Buell and George H. Thomas. His contentiousness never mellowed during that time, and aside from James Schofield and John Logan, he made amends with no one.

17. Fellman, *Citizen Sherman*, 249–53; Sherman, *Memoirs* 2:372–74.

When Halleck's widow asked his assistance in organizing that general's memoirs, he quickly abandoned an initial attempt at conciliation by dredging up his still-simmering resentment. His memoirs became the crucible for defining his place in the annals of the Civil War, and many fellow officers were maligned in the process. John S. Logan, John A. McClernand, and Joseph Hooker received predictably scathing reviews. His attempts to balance the ledger with the now-deceased George Thomas only fanned the flames of partisanship. Perhaps Thomas's greatest error was that he accomplished what the "plucky warrior" Sherman had never done. Thomas, the "Rock of Chickamauga," had stolen the glory on Missionary Ridge and, despite criticism from Grant and Sherman, had actually destroyed an enemy army at Nashville. In his memoirs, Sherman should have erred on the side of magnanimity rather than ambivalence and let it go at that. But Sherman was not going to allow the feelings of others to stand in the way of his perception of the truth.[18]

Ordinarily, Grant's phlegmatic personality did not lend itself to high-strung rhetoric such as that used by Sherman. This does not mean, however, that he did not give in to the darker side of his nature. In some respects, Grant might have been better off had he released some of his resentments more openly, for his responses to the pressures of life and career led him down murkier pathways. Grant's resignation from the peacetime army in 1854 was occasioned by a deep depression. His last assignment at Camp Humboldt in northern California featured yet another of those martinet colonels for which the army was infamous. In California, he allowed his intense dislike for Lt. Col. Robert Christie Buchanan to cloud his outlook on life. With little or no hope for advancement or transfer, he engaged in idle distractions to assuage his restlessness, and it was in California that he cemented his reputation for hard drinking. At any rate, the outbreak of the war resuscitated his military career, and he was delighted with his commission as colonel.[19]

During that time, the McClellan and Grant legacies lend themselves to some incidental comparison. Junior officers, like McClellan and Grant, sometimes chafed under the constraints of dealing with older officers who merited their superior positions by seniority alone. Part of the cumulative case made against McClellan's argumentative nature is based upon his discourtesy toward Maj. Richard Delafield and Maj. Alfred Mordecai, the

18. Fellman, *Citizen Sherman,* 318–36; Sherman, *Memoirs* 2:214–16.
19. McFeely, *Grant,* 52–56.

two other commissioners designated to study European military developments in 1855. Both Delafield and Mordecai were roughly twenty-five years older than McClellan. At one point during the tour, McClellan wrote his brother John, characterizing his fellow officers as "d—d old fogies!! I hope that I may never be tied to two corpses again–it is a hell upon earth." Although the intention of the comment seemed more like an expression of boredom and humor, it ends up as part of the indictment of McClellan's personality. McClellan was hardly the only one peeved with the company of older officers. When he received his first assignment, Grant wrote Julia of the burden of having to deal with the two senior officers with whom he was assigned. "One is a preacher and the other a member of the Church," he groaned, adding that he doubted he would ever "have a game of Eucre with them."[20]

Again, in the early days of the war, the Grant and McClellan legacies collided again, although that time it was by way of their failure to meet. A seemingly small matter, it has become part of the mythology in which Grant's stock is elevated and McClellan's lowered, for a decided element in the redeemed pathos of Grant's military career was the desperation with which he sought a commission or an assignment to another West Pointer's staff. Learning of McClellan's assignment as major general of the Ohio volunteers, Grant raced to Cincinnati, hoping to meet with McClellan to ask for a position on his staff. Grant's biographer, McFeely, noted that the irony of Grant, the supplicant, and McClellan, Grant's junior and the potential bestower of favor, was palpable. "I called on two successive days at his office," Grant remembered, "but failed to see him on either occasion and returned to Springfield." In his celebrated postpresidential world tour, Grant recalled that "McClellan never acknowledged my call, and, of course, after he knew I had been at his headquarters, I was bound to await his acknowledgment." The juxtaposition of the quintessential outsider, rejected and cast off by his peers, to the ultimate insider, acclaimed and respected by those same peers, could not have been better scripted.[21]

20. Sears, *George B. McClellan: The Young Napoleon,* 44–45; Glatthaar, *Partners in Command,* 241; "U.S. Grant to Julia D. Grant, June 26, 1861," in John Y. Simon, ed., *The Papers of Ulysses S. Grant,* 19 vols. (Carbondale: Southern Illinois Univ. Press, 1967), 2:49.

21. Grant, *Memoirs* 1:241; McFeely, *Grant,* 75; John Russell Young, *Tour Around the World with General Grant: A Narrative of the Visit of General U.S. Grant, Ex-President of the United States, to Various Countries in Europe, Asia, and Africa, 1877–1878,* 2 vols. (New York: D. Appleton, 1879), 1:214–15. Others include that incident in their narratives. Herman Hattaway and Archer Jones state that "McClellan was too busy to talk to him." See Herman

While the story is worth reciting in the apotheosis of Grant's legacy and literature, it has unfortunate connotations for McClellan's. The clear suggestion is that McClellan went to extraordinary efforts to avoid an interview with Grant. There is, however, a great deal of ambiguity regarding the dates of Grant's visit and whether McClellan was even in Cincinnati at the time. In light of Grant's subsequent success, McClellan appeared anxious in his memoirs to cover his tracks to avoid being tagged as the one who declined Grant's services. He claimed that he was away in Indianapolis at the time, and once he returned, he was informed by his staff that Grant had been there to see him, but he had already accepted a position elsewhere. Grant had written Julia on June 10 that he had arrived in Covington, Kentucky, and that he intended to visit army headquarters in Cincinnati within a couple of days. He next wrote Julia from Springfield, Illinois, on June 17 that he had just returned from his visit and that he had earned a colonel's commission. That implies he was in the Cincinnati area between June 9 and June 16. McClellan, on the other hand, left Cincinnati on the evening of June 12 and returned on June 17. One of two things happened. Either Grant did visit McClellan's headquarters on June 11 and 12, and McClellan did, in fact, give him the cold shoulder, or Grant did not visit until the thirteenth or fourteenth, in which case, McClellan was out of town.

Without a clearer understanding of the exact days on which Grant called upon McClellan, it becomes difficult to substantiate that McClellan treated him with deliberate disrespect. In any event, it would not been out of character for McClellan to have denied Grant's request. He certainly would not have been the first to have done so. While hardly a teetotaler himself, it is not difficult to conceive of his frowning on anyone with a reputation for hard drinking. McClellan had seen Grant's prowess with the bottle in 1853 when he came across Grant at Fort Vancouver. Moreover, assignments to personal staff were the prerogative of each commanding general. Grant would not have measured up to McClellan's standards. In that regard, McClellan most certainly was disingenuous in his

---

Hattaway and Archer Jones, *How the North Won* (Urbana: Univ. of Illinois Press, 1983), 54. Sears asserts that Grant was "one officer he [McClellan] did not seek for his staff." Moreover, Sears conjectures that the reason McClellan might have avoided an interview with Grant was his knowledge of Grant's drinking spree when the two of them had met at Fort Vancouver in 1853. See Sears, *George B. McClellan: The Young Napoleon,* 73.

claim that he would have given Grant a position had he seen him. Nevertheless, there is no conclusive evidence that he purposely snubbed Grant by avoiding him in Cincinnati, and he was under no obligation whatsoever to offer him a position on his staff.[22]

Grant's judgments of peers and subordinates during the war itself were relatively free of rancor. If he was somewhat harsh with Hooker, Burnside, Butler, McClernand, and Sigel, his complaints seemed warranted. His criticisms of William Rosecrans and George Thomas seemed less justified. Grant tried to placate the sensitivities of George Meade, but his outright assumption of control of the Army of the Potomac and his clear preference for favorites like Sherman and Sheridan made Meade feel ignored and useless in the end. At times, Grant could be as disingenuous as any Federal commander. During the summer campaign of 1864 he became disenchanted with Halleck's influence in Washington, and he wrote Stanton that Halleck should be sent to the Pacific Coast to replace Irvin McDowell, whom he characterized as "inefficient" in his administration. Stanton, however, would not take the bait and replied that there were no complaints with McDowell's performance.[23]

Grant also played the political game with considerably more aplomb than McClellan and Sherman. He kept whatever dislike and contempt he had for Stanton in check and did not become embroiled in disputes that would reflect poorly on him. Although Grant chose the higher ground in most of his characterizations of the generals of his time, when it came time to write his memoirs, he was not altogether generous. His wartime prejudices against McClernand and Butler were repeated and explained. Burnside was described as affable but not one "fitted to command an army." Hooker was "a dangerous man," insubordinate to his superiors and so inordinately ambitious as to care "nothing for the rights of others." To those whom he realized some degree of respect needed to be paid, like Meade, Thomas, and Edward Canby, Grant was at his ambivalent best. After painstakingly pointing out their strengths and

22. McClellan got carried away with his excuse for not having seen Grant when he claimed that Grant was lucky not to have received a position from him, since "he would have probably remained with me and shared my fate." See McClellan, *McClellan's Own Story*, 47; Sears, *George B. McClellan: The Young Napoleon*, 38, 73, 419n.10; Simon, *Papers of Ulysses S. Grant* 2:41–48.

23. Grant to Stanton, Aug. 15, 20, 1864, and Stanton to Grant, Aug. 18, 1864, *OR*, vol. 50, 2:945–51.

accomplishments, he qualified them with so much attention to their deficiencies as to render his praise quite faint.[24]

McClellan's was but one of many colossal egos colliding with others during the Civil War. Criticisms that single him out as especially guilty of weaknesses in character appear unfair. They are much ado about nothing. His unattractive qualities were not spectacular, and any comparison with his peers suggests he was no different from them. To be sure, at times his inappropriate behavior offended people. On the other hand, he endeared himself to a great number of people. More often than not, his personality attracted rather than repelled. Much the same can be said of his contemporaries—Lincoln, Grant and Sherman.

Of all of McClellan's peccadilloes, his rudeness, arrogance, vanity, and vindictiveness are the most obvious corollaries to or derivatives of the psychological disorders discussed earlier. For many historians, however, a host of other minor drawbacks to McClellan's personality comprise the composite picture. Chief among them are an inability to delegate responsibility and a penchant for secretive and furtive behavior, both of which are perceived as logical by-products of his profound distrust of others. Also hovering above any consideration of his career is the presentation of McClellan as a bungler, the recipient of comical embarrassments and the creator of unbelievable gaffes and mishaps. Some accounts of his campaigns carry the whiff of physical and moral cowardice. Finally, McClellan is held responsible by some for imbuing the Army of the Potomac with a collective inferiority complex. According to this theory, the army was influenced by McClellan into believing they always faced a stronger and more determined foe, and they could take justifiable pride in merely holding their own against the enemy. Again, any narrowly focused review of McClellan's Civil War career is likely to produce suggestive examples or half-truths of such behavior. However, a wider perspective on the war and an examination of the record of other Civil War commanders diffuses the strength and pertinence of these judgments.

As deemed by some historians, McClellan's unwillingness and inability to appropriately delegate responsibility was a reflection of an in-

---

24. McFeely, *Grant,* 158; Grant, *Memoirs* 2:538–41. Reid has suggested that Grant's air of modesty in his recollections was transparent, even, at times, "overdone." See Brian Holden Reid, "Another Look at Grant's Crossing the James, 1864," *Civil War History* 39 (Dec. 1993): 315.

flated opinion of his own abilities and a mark of his deep-seated distrust for fellow officers. Sears sees the seeds of McClellan's distrust from the very beginning. In the western Virginia campaign, Sears noted McClellan's displeasure with three of the four brigadier generals assigned to his command. That sentiment only increased when he arrived in Washington, where he discovered he had to conduct detailed inspections of the army camps. He lamented that because he had "no one on my staff to whom I can entrust the safety of affairs–it is necessary for me to see as much as I can every day." Even as the organization of the army was taking shape in the fall of 1861, McClellan never shed his distrust, and at critical moments in the field, he would frequently be found bogged down in administrative minutiae. His absorption with the details of organizing the army was physically exhausting and served to distract the general from more important strategic concerns.[25]

For some, the same McClellan, who was not capable of trusting the delegation of logistical minutiae, was equally distrustful of revealing his operational plans. It became a trademark of McClellan to say as little as possible in the presence of politicians. Keeping his own counsel, McClellan rationalized the secrecy by using the excuse that few civilians were competent to critique military operations, or worse, any discussion on the subject would invariably land in the newspapers. He most likely, in the opinion of some historians, used as an excuse his quip that the president revealed operational plans to his son Tad as a cover for the fact that he had no real plans for assuming the offensive. McClellen's secrecy has become a symbol of his willful stubbornness and peevish obstinacy that were ultimately marks of disrespect to the president.[26]

Of the plethora of negative assessments of McClellan, his failure to delegate authority and his obstinate secrecy are the most deserving. And both were in part the result of his distrustful nature. There was, however, nothing pathologically delusional about that distrust. To a great degree his suspicion was reality based. The shortage of capable officers bothered most professional West Pointers at the beginning of the war. Sherman

25. Sears, *George B. McClellan: The Young Napoleon*, 86, 112–13, 162, 183; Glatthaar, *Partners in Command*, 62. McClellan's fear that Edwin Sumner, the senior corps commander, would succeed him in the event of his being disabled or killed led McClellan to keep out of harm's way and to remain ambiguous in his delegation of field command. See Sears, *To the Gates of Richmond*, 71, 87, 107, 160, 265, 281.

26. Kenneth P. Williams, *Lincoln Finds a General* 1:137–38; Sears, *George B. McClellan: The Young Napoleon*, 132, 140–41; Glatthaar, *Partners in Command*, 62, 237–38.

deplored the lack of trained officers both in his first action at Manassas and later in Kentucky. When he returned from his sabbatical in a subordinate position, he was relieved of that anxiety because he no longer was in a primary command position. Later, during his Atlanta campaign, Sherman served as virtual quartermaster to his army, supervising the minutest of details concerning supply and transportation.[27]

To his credit, Grant quickly came to terms with the fact that volunteers would play a key role in a civil war, although he remained wary of political generals like McClernand, Sigel, Logan, Banks, and Butler. As seen earlier, Grant gave Sherman the green light to make a precipitous move on Vicksburg, resulting in the disastrous attack at Chickasaw Bluffs, because he wanted Sherman off and moving before McClernand arrived to assume command of his force. Even in the final months of the war, Grant remained acutely sensitive of seniority, as Butler happened to be the next in line for command of the Army of the Potomac should something happen to him. Grant's chief adversary in the East, Robert E. Lee, had been appalled by the generals he inherited from Johnston during the Peninsula campaign. He distrusted their abilities to play any key role during the Seven Days' Battle, and as soon as he was able, he had generals like Holmes, Huger, and Magruder transferred or relegated out of harm's way.[28]

To lay the charge of excessive secrecy on McClellan alone is a travesty. And any attempt to tie it directly and solely to the general's distrustful nature is equally unfair. Waging war in an open and democratic society, with all the trappings of a free press, was a most difficult and, at times, vexing matter. It had become well known that Beauregard had received complete warning of McDowell's advance by way of ciphered messages sent to him by Rose Greenhow, a socialite and Confederate spy extraordinaire, of Washington, D.C. Her access to vital information by way of contacts and probable assignations with high-standing military

27. Marszalek, *Sherman: A Soldier's Passion for Order,* 160, 260–61.

28. Grant, *Memoirs* 1:145, 152; Nevins, *War for the Union* 1:321; Emory M. Thomas, *Robert E. Lee: A Biography* (New York: Norton, 1995), 246. The Confederate army, a place in which honor really meant something, was plagued by tremendous haggling and hypersensitivity to seniority ranking. Davis was constantly at odds with Johnston and Beauregard over the matter, and the normally unpretentious Stonewall Jackson actually tendered his resignation at one point over a dispute concerning seniority with Secretary of War Judah Benjamin. See *OR,* vol. 5, 1:1053; and Craig L. Symonds, *Joseph E. Johnston* (New York: Norton, 1992), 336–39.

and political leaders was astounding. McClellan eventually had her shadowed by Allan Pinkerton, which led to her arrest and imprisonment. Sherman's celebrated rage against the activities of the press, though a partial attempt to stem their criticism, was a function of his desire to keep the army's plans secret from the enemy. Grant, too, was not exactly a great communicator. He ascribed his image problems in the Northern press to the fact that he "would not divulge my ultimate plans to visitors." He would suffer the criticisms that he was "idle, incompetent and unfit to command men in an emergency" if it meant keeping his plans from reaching the ears of the enemy. Similar to Sherman, Grant "admired the South . . . for the boldness with which they silenced all opposition and all croaking by the press or by individuals within their control." Grant could also be uncommunicative with his staff, as he was in holding back on his plans for the Vicksburg campaign, presumably for fear of leakage. "I did not therefore communicate this plan, even to an officer on my staff," he recalled, "until it was necessary to make preparations." If McClellan was inappropriate in withholding operational plans from the president for fear of exposing his hand to the enemy, then Grant merely followed suit in 1864. Following Halleck's advice to withhold from Lincoln his campaign plans for the spring offensive for fear of exposure, Grant extended his web of secrecy, noting that his designs were kept from Stanton and Halleck as well. What remains to be determined is whether Grant, like McClellan, was dishonest and obstinate or whether he was merely prudent.[29]

If pride truly precedes a fall, then the arrogant, haughty McClellan logically became the victim of numerous embarrassments. Virtually every narrative of McClellan's campaigns and every discussion of his personal characteristics highlight those episodes. Thus, when his engineers misgauged the width of the lock passages on the Chesapeake and Ohio Canal near Harper's Ferry, thus preventing the passage of boats, it reflected poorly on McClellan's leadership. Consequently, McClellan was forced to endure the circulating wisecrack that his expedition had died of lockjaw. When his army stormed the enemy's defenses at Manassas, only to find Quaker guns pointed in its direction, McClellan's stock fell. The scene was more or less repeated weeks later at Yorktown. For a general

---

29. William C. Davis, *Battle at Bull Run* (Baton Rouge: Louisiana State Univ. Press, 1981), 52–53. Sherman's tirades about the Northern press can be found in John F. Marszalek, *Sherman's Other War: The General and the Civil War Press* (Memphis: Memphis State Univ. Press, 1981); Grant, *Memoirs* 1:271–72, 363.

who was boldly predicting grand campaigns that would demolish the enemy, those incidents gave the appearance of ludicrous ineptitude. Farce gave way to tragedy when Colonel Edward Baker, a close friend of Lincoln's, made an injudicious crossing of the Potomac to attack a Confederate force near Leesburg, Virginia. The result was the debacle known as the Battle of Ball's Bluff, wherein the Federal force was shoved back into the river where many in Baker's regiment drowned. Included in the number killed was Baker himself. Although Baker was entirely at fault, his immediate superior, Gen. Charles P. Stone, shouldered most of the blame; however, congressional inquiries into the sad affair aimed for bigger game, George McClellan. McClellan also suffered the ignominy attached to Jeb Stuart's end-around runs of the Army of the Potomac, both on the Peninsula and in the wake of the Maryland campaign. Although Stuart's highly celebrated rides accomplished little of military importance, the image of an annoying, pesky fly getting the better of an immense, plodding behemoth filled newspapers throughout the North. Although errors of that nature were experienced in many other campaigns of the same size, those occurring under McClellan's watch are invariably portrayed in the worst possible light. They are tendered as incontrovertible proof that the general did not have the capacity for high command.[30]

The unfortunate affair at Ball's Bluff has given rise to another misrepresentation aimed in McClellan's direction. Some have disparaged McClellan's attempts to distance himself from the inquiries of the Committee on the Conduct of the War, which investigated the Ball's Bluff affair, by claiming he sacrificed Charles Stone to the congressional wolves. Rather than accept ultimate responsibility for the incident, he let Stone be the scapegoat. Veiled suggestions of his cowardice fill campaign narratives where McClellan is caught absent from the front lines of the Seven Day's battle. Because of his conference with naval commander John Rodgers aboard the gunboat *Galena,* ostensibly about the new base for the retreating army, McClellan was viewed as a general whose moral courage had evaporated. When he did return to Malvern Hill, it was only "as far as pos-

30. Sears, *George B. McClellan: The Young Napoleon,* 120–23, 144–45, 156–58, and *To the Gates of Richmond,* 17, 22; Catton, *Reflections on the Civil War,* 182–85; James M. McPherson, *Battle Cry of Freedom* (New York: Oxford Univ. Press, 1988), 362–63. Stuart's exploits on the Peninsula are detailed in Edwin C. Bearss, "Jeb Stuart's Ride Around McClellan," in William J. Miller, ed., *The Peninsula Campaign of 1862: Yorktown to Seven Days,* vol. 1 (Campbell, Calif.: Savas Woodbury, 1993), 71–142; Kenneth P. Williams, *Lincoln Finds a General* 1:123–24; Nevins, *War for the Union* 2:326.

sible from the scene of combat." The gunboat *Galena,* then, became synonymous with a breakdown in the general's stamina, and it would emerge
as the subject of considerable lampooning during McClellan's presidential
bid in 1864. Similarly, his perch at the Pry House, overlooking the battlefield of Antietam, was seen as a remote refuge from the hard fighting going
on below. Another legacy of Antietam is that McClellan's lack of moral
courage induced him to select Burnside as the scapegoat for failing to
destroy Lee's army there. Burnside's recent biographer, William Marvel,
waxes eloquently and floridly over McClellan's perfidy. "But the thought
of having his thunder stolen at the brink of the great battle was more than
Little Mac could stand," Marvel explains, "and Burnside fell, like Ger-
manicus, his reputation slowly poisoned by the one closest to him."[31]

The notion that McClellan was somehow the butt of more embarrassing incidents than anyone else is greatly diminished by any extended review of the war's comical and tragic mistakes. In fact, a more
complete comparison with Grant and Sherman uncovers another interesting facet of the literature. In assigning overall responsibility for failures and successes, the literature is frequently slanted in favor of Grant
and Sherman. Sherman, for example, is usually not held responsible for
James B. McPherson's failure to press his advantage at Resaca. Having isolated a part of Johnston's army at Resaca, while the bulk of it was still at
Dalton, McPherson inexplicably pulled back, allowing the Confederates
to reunite their army. Historians generally weigh in on Grant's side when
it comes to evaluating his shortcomings. Thus it is that subordinates like
Burnside, Warren, Smith, Rosecrans, Butler, and McClernand take their
pratfalls across the stage of Civil War literature, while Grant's reputation
remains untarnished. McClellan, on the other hand, is generally assigned
blame for campaign mistakes while his subordinates are accorded credit
for his successes. In the western Virginia campaign, Rosecrans, the subordinate, is given most of the praise resulting from the success there.
Likewise, any skill McClellan might have exercised in extricating the
army from impending disaster during its retreat from the Chickahominy is

31. Nevins, *War for the Union* 1:298–99; Sears, *George B. McClellan: The Young Napoleon,*
120–23, 144-46, and *To the Gates of Richmond,* 280–81, 330; T. Harry Williams, *Lincoln
and the Radicals* (Madison: Univ. of Wisconsin Press, 1941), 101–4; A. Wilson Greene, "'I
Fought the Battle Splendidly,': George B. McClellan and the Maryland Campaign at Antietam," in *Essays on the 1862 Maryland Campaign,* ed. Gary Gallagher (Kent, Ohio: Kent State
Univ. Press, 1989), 67, 72, 80; Marvel, *Burnside,* 126.

denied him and given to his corps commanders. On the other hand, responsibility for all reverses are laid to rest directly at McClellan's feet. For example, the literature acknowledges the contributions of Sumner and Burnside to the failure at Antietam, but it is nearly unanimous in holding McClellan accountable for it.[32]

During the course of the war, Grant found himself both the agent and victim of a number of cruel embarrassments, yet his ultimate success has absolved him of much of the responsibility. Perhaps the greatest embarrassment of the entire Civil War occurred during his command at the siege of Petersburg. It was an incident that involved Burnside yet again. In an attempt to break Lee's entrenched works outside Petersburg, or as Grant claimed, "As a means of keeping the men occupied," he approved Burnside's plan to dig a tunnel under the enemy. The mined tunnel was filled with explosives and would be detonated at a designated time. Troops would be assembled to rush in through the breach and exploit the opportunity, despite the fact that Grant had observed that the lay of the land was not particularly favorable to the success of the operation. When the explosives were finally charged and the air cleared of the human and material debris caused by the earth's upheaval, the battle of the Crater ensued. It was, in Grant's own words, "A stupendous failure." Grant's own analysis of where the fault lay was both candid and accurate. The selection of James H. Ledlie as the divisional commander to lead the charge was a mistake in itself, compounded by the fact that it came about by way of drawing names out of a hat. When the attack commenced, Ledlie was nowhere to be found; he was off hiding and drinking. The carnage that ensued in the crater itself was stultifying in its grotesqueness. The blame

32. On the western Virginia campaign, see Sears, *George B. McClellan: The Young Napoleon*, 88–92; Glatthaar, *Partners in Command*, 56; Nevins, *War for the Union* 1:225; Kenneth P. Williams, *Lincoln Finds a General* 1:105–12. On the retreat to Harrison's Landing, see Sears, *To the Gates of Richmond*, 280–81, 309; Glatthaar, *Partners in Command*, 78; Kenneth P. Williams, *Lincoln Finds a General* 1:239. On the Antietam campaign, see Stephen W. Sears, *Landscape Turned Red: The Battle of Antietam* (New York: Ticknor Fields, 1983), 37; Greene, "'I Fought the Battle Splendidly,'" 69–80; McPherson, *Battle Cry of Freedom*, 539–44; Nevins, *War for the Union* 2:224. Marszalek claims that Sherman was justified in being upset with McPherson's performance at Resaca, noting that the latter was wrong in insisting that it was too dangerous to press the enemy. See Marszalek, *Sherman: A Soldier's Passion for Order*, 265. Albert Castel, who is decidedly critical of Sherman's military skills during the campaign to Atlanta, demurs only in that Sherman did not explicitly order McPherson to take Resaca and did not give him sufficient means. See Albert Castel, *Decision in the West: The Atlanta Campaign of 1864* (Lawrence: Univ. of Kansas Press, 1992), 182.

for the failure at the Crater was correctly assigned by Grant to "inefficiency on the part of the corps commander [Burnside] and the incompetency of the division commander [Ledlie]." And that is pretty much the way historians see it. Grant, who held ultimate responsibility for the actions of his subordinates, comes out relatively unscathed. As McFeely has suggested, "Grant was lucky," for Lincoln, who was scheduled to meet with him the day following the explosion of the crater, "could have seen the episode as evidence of incompetence lunatic enough to put McClellan and all of Grant's predecessors in Virginia to shame." While this was but one incident in the harvest of death that was the Civil War, and while it does not detract from Grant's success one bit, it is illustrative of how Grant's setbacks and errors in judgment are minimized or trivialized in the literature.[33]

The Crater was hardly Grant's lone mistake and embarrassment during the war. His approval of McClernand's assault on the Vicksburg fortifications was, by his own admission, an inadvisable decision. At both Fort Donelson and Shiloh he was absent from the front when the fighting began. He also joined Halleck and Sherman in falling victim to Beauregard's ruses at Corinth. If McClellan looked foolish at Manassas and Yorktown, staring down the harmless barrel of a Quaker gun, then so did the troika at Corinth. There, they mistook the loud cheering and the constant running of empty trains as a sign of enemy reinforcement instead of the massive evacuation that was underway. When they entered Corinth, they, too, were greeted by Quaker guns. And while it must be admitted that McClellan was forced to abandon a base of supply on one occasion, he did not lose one to Confederate raiders like Grant did at Holly Springs. Again, Grant's advanced intelligence that an incompetent commander had been left at Holly Springs did not induce him to name a replacement, and it almost led to his wife being captured by the enemy. Finally, there was Cold Harbor. Even Grant knew that that was his biggest mistake in the war. In a battle that started at dawn on June 3, 1864, in which Meade reported that Grant honored "the field with his presence

---

33. Grant discusses the Battle of the Crater in Grant, *Memoirs* 2:314–16. McFeely notes how Grant escaped censure for his role at the Crater in McFeely, *Grant*, 177–79. Those narrating the incident who assign blame to Grant are: McPherson, *Battle Cry of Freedom*, 758–60; Hattaway and Jones, *How the North Won*, 614–16. Scant attention is paid by Nevin, *War for the Union* 4:51, 104, 132; and no mention is made by T. Harry Williams, *Lincoln and His Generals*, or Glatthaar, *Partners in Command*. Even Marvel, in his sympathetic treatment of Burnside, does not hold Grant responsible. See Marvel, *Burnside*, 390–412.

only about one hour in the middle of the day," thousands of men were misdirected at first, then directed straight into the deadly fire of the entrenched enemy. A more useless slaughter than this could only be remembered at Fredericksburg in 1862.[34]

If Grant is said to possess the moral courage necessary in great commanders, an attribute McClellan did not possess, nothing about his actions in the hours and days following Cold Harbor are testimony to it. For a man who was personally sickened at the sight of blood, he took no pains to alleviate the suffering of his own soldiers who were pinned down, wounded in the killing zone between the opposing armies. Instead he engaged in a protracted war of words with Lee over the protocol for requesting a truce with both armies remaining on the field. In fact, the whole affair reflected poorly on both of them. Technically, Lee was correct, for by any estimation, he had prevailed at Cold Harbor, and both tradition and the popular understanding of the rules of warfare compelled the losing general to request a truce. Grant remained truculent over the matter, and by the time the two of them got around to settling the dispute, three whole days had elapsed with the wounded remaining on the field. It was hardly a surprise, then, when Grant noted that "all but two of the wounded had died."[35]

Thinly disguised attempts to suggest that personal cowardice was an intrinsic element of McClellan's personality fall way off the mark. Certainly, his failure to supervise the final actions of the Seven Days' Battle is not commendable. He should have remained near the field and taken his chances with a staff member in choosing the site for the army's encampment. As for his being at the front itself, this is a ridiculous expectation for a commanding general. His rightful place was behind the lines so that he could command all of the units engaged at the front. To a lesser

---

34. George Gordon Meade to M. S. Meade, June 4, 1864, in George Meade, *Life and Letters of George Gordon Meade,* 2 vols. (New York: Scribner's, 1913), 2:200. It remains amazing that Grant does not take a beating in the literature for his conduct at Cold Harbor. Other than describing the battle itself and Grant's admission of the assault as a mistake, little else is said. See McPherson, *Battle Cry of Freedom,* 733–35; and Nevins, *War for the Union* 4:39–42. T. Harry Williams skips right over it in *Lincoln and His Generals,* as does Glatthaar, *Partners in Command.* A more balanced perspective can be found in Hattaway and Jones, *How the North Won,* 578–81, and McFeely, *Grant,* 171.

35. Horace Porter, *Campaigning with Grant* (New York: Century, 1897), 62–63; Grant, *Memoirs* 2:273–76. Grant is criticized for his handling of the wounded at Cold Harbor. See Nevins, *War for the Union* 4:42–43; and McFeely, *Grant,* 171–72.

degree, the same standard applies to corps commanders. McClellan's selection of the Prys' farmhouse was as good as any place at Antietam. In a battle featuring a wide front, it afforded him the best possible view of the action unfolding below. Virtually all of the war's successful commanders relied upon their subordinates to execute the course of fighting in their own sectors. Grant, for example, never commanded the actual combat in any of his battles once he was the commanding general. In fact, one of the war's enduring images is that of Grant, sitting on a bench or stump in the Wilderness or at City Point, receiving reports of the battle's progress while he aimlessly whittled away at a stick and puffed on his cigar. Indeed, Grant relied on his ears rather than his eyes to monitor the progress of his attacks.[36]

The last of McClellan's personal failings, or at least the final one under consideration, is whether McClellan made the best use of the Army of the Potomac, whose creation was the one generally accepted contribution McClellan made to the Union war effort. That McClellan created and organized the Army of the Potomac and infused into it a resilient pride has long been held by both his defenders and detractors as his greatest single achievement. If, in the eyes of his critics, he failed to capably use that creation, at least it remained the cornerstone upon which Grant led the North to final victory. It should continue to be his one unassailable accomplishment. However, in one of the most provocative theses in the literature in this past half-century, Michael C. C. Adams has persuasively argued that McClellan was an overly cautious general because he instinctively believed that "he faced a militarily more efficient people and that his attitude was communicated to those who surrounded and adored him." Adams has effectively argued that McClellan stained the Army of the Potomac with such a thoroughly defeatist attitude that he succeeded in putting it on a continuously defensive footing. For Adams, McClellan's persistent inflation of enemy troop strength was less delusional in the psychological sense of the term than a product of his conviction of Southern military prowess. This thesis dovetails nicely with those of Unionist historians in that Adams believes it was not until Grant, a western man,

36. Porter, *Campaigning with Grant,* 50, 52, 60, 80. Thomas affirms that Lee's style of leadership was consistent with the expanded parameters of Civil War battlefields. He relied exclusively upon his subordinates to dictate the tactical flow of the battle once it began, preferring to supervise "at some distance from the hurly burly." See Thomas, *Robert E. Lee,* 246.

arrived in the East that the sway of McClellan's influence on the Army of the Potomac was finally dispelled.[37]

Adams's thesis, or as he terms it, speculation, has its merits. McClellan, indeed, was convinced that the South was not only better prepared at the outset of the war but furnished a social order that was more conducive to discipline and order. Consistent with his views on the influence of the slaveholding aristocracy in perpetrating secession, he believed that the deference shown them by the poor whites in the South made discipline an easy task. Along with Sherman and many other Northern generals, McClellan believed that during the secession crisis the North had allowed the South to seize federal property and arsenals and to begin drilling and training recruits for the army. The South, they believed, was fully prepared for war; the North was not.[38]

Adams enters the more speculative phase of his thesis when he argues that McClellan stamped an indelible print of inferiority upon the Army of the Potomac that was not erased until Grant came east in 1864. It is true that Grant was puzzled by many of his new subordinates in the East who counseled caution in dealing with the wily Robert E. Lee. Grant's apparent disregard for Lee's vaunted prowess was captured by a remark he made in the Wilderness to a general officer that was overheard by Horace Porter of Grant's staff. When the excited officer warned that Lee was capable of throwing his army between Grant's army and the Rapidan, thus severing their communications, the ordinarily unflappable Grant nearly exploded. "Oh, I am heartily tired of hearing about what Lee is going to do," he responded. "Some of you always seem to think he is suddenly going to turn a double somersault, and land in our rear and on both of our flanks at the same time." Although Grant remained unintimidated, he soon discovered that Lee was nearly capable of accomplishing just that feat. Grant's confidence was more likely a function of his conviction that he was facing a worn-out opponent and that he would be receiving all, if not more, of the reinforcements he requested in the next few months. After three years of ruinous fighting, Lee had finally reached the point

37. Michael C. C. Adams, *Our Masters the Rebels: A Speculation on Union Military Failure in the East, 1861–1865* (Cambridge: Harvard Univ. Press, 1978), 88, 92–96.

38. McClellan, *McClellan's Own Story,* 39–40. Sherman was considerably more expansive and supportive of this thesis. See Sherman, *Memoirs* 1:163–68, 175. Following the first Battle at Bull Run, Scott informed one lieutenant that the South had the best officers from the old army, remarking that he doubted that "we shall make head against them." See Michael C. C. Adams, *Our Masters the Rebels,* 80.

where his chances of using his army to thwart another overland Federal advance were exceedingly thin.[39]

At the beginning of the war, Grant was actually one with McClellan and Sherman in his respect for Southern strength, and for many of the same reasons. He acknowledged as much in his memoirs when he described the state of affairs in the waning days of the Buchanan administration. At another point he cited his admiration for the South "for the boldness with which they silenced all opposition and all croaking, by press or by individuals within their control," noting it as a sign of strength that a country did not have to "tolerate an enemy within their [own] ranks." In his discussion of the spring offensive of 1864, he seemed sensitive to the manner in which troop strengths were measured. At the time he was drafting his memoirs, Grant was, no doubt, annoyed by the popular argument, already enjoying wide circulation in the South, claiming he had faced an army much inferior in number to his own. "In the Confederate army often only bayonets are taken into account," he argued. "Never, I believe, do they estimate more than are handling the guns of the artillery and armed with muskets or carbines." He believed that throughout the course of the war the number of Lee's "forces was always lowered and that of the National forces exaggerated." Either Grant was engaging in puffing up the strength of his enemy to counter arguments that he had simply overawed Lee with great numbers, or he earnestly believed that the enemy was nearly equal in strength to the Northern force.[40]

Grant was exceedingly fortunate to have established his good reputation during the early years of the war in the Western theater. In

39. Porter, *Campaigning with Grant*, 69–70. For all of his efforts to destroy Lee's army, Grant failed to do so. The day after the embarrassing defeat at the Crater, Grant met with Lincoln at Fort Monroe. John Y. Simon suggests that at that point Lincoln was dissatisfied with Grant because he was recommending Meade and William B. Franklin for the unified command of the capital region's defense. Lincoln rejected the suggestion with a stroke of the pen, writing "McClellan" next to that agenda item. In July, after Early had staged his raid on the capital and Grant was settling in for a long siege, Lincoln may have viewed Grant as having become "McClellanized." See John Y. Simon, "Grant, Lincoln, and Unconditional Surrender," in Gabor S. Boritt, ed., *Lincoln's Generals* (New York: Oxford Univ. Press, 1994), 18–81.

40. Grant, *Memoirs* 1:135, 263, 2:513–14. Reid takes Grant to task, again, over his manipulation of Lee's strength during the campaign in Virginia. Observing that, during the war, Grant underestimated Lee's abilities, Reid claims that Grant "exaggerated Lee's strength after the war by almost one third, thus magnifying his achievement." See Reid, "Grant's Crossing of the James," 314.

many ways, experience in the West proved a useful training ground for success in the East. In the West he was able to exploit the many navigable rivers to his advantage and maneuver in wide-open spaces. He was not constrained, as were Eastern commanders, in dealing with the Washington-to-Richmond corridor. To a certain degree, Grant also enjoyed the advantage of waging war against the wooden-headed leadership of the Confederacy's western command. Not only were generals like Floyd, Pillow, Pemberton, Bragg, Johnston, and Hood less skilled than their Eastern counterparts, they also made made egregious tactical decisions that enabled Grant and Sherman to overpower them. Federal commanders in the West were also unhindered in their campaigns by any concern for protecting their nation's capital. Defending the banks of the Ohio River, the closest Western equivalent to the District of Columbia, was never a serious issue. Both the distance and the logistical realities entailed made that an unrealistic target for Southern ambition. By the time Grant arrived in the East, the time was ripe for success. No doubt, his success in the West had made him a confident commander, but it helped enormously that the foe he faced was but a mere shadow of its former self. Grant only needed to exploit his advantages and press the issue with Lee. It may well have been harder and taken longer than he thought it would, but he ultimately succeeded in the task.

Historians who attribute McClellan's disappointing performance to his psychological composition or his personality quirks have built a foundation on shifting sand. McClellan's personality deficits were neither symptomatic of psychological disarray nor the product of it. These same historians also have erred in viewing selected evidence of those flaws as intrinsic to his person or personality. In most cases, McClellan's exhibitions of unattractive behavior were in response to the provocations and stress that were produced by a war in which he held a responsible position.

Unionist historians are undoubtedly correct in assessing some of the real shortcomings in McClellan's leadership. He was excessively cautious. He did mismanage critical moments during his campaigns. His faculty for overestimating enemy strength, while hardly delusional in 1861–1862, nourished his sense of caution. And like many other Eastern commanders, and the Lincoln administration for that matter, his attempts to juggle offensive aggression with the need to protect the capital undermined any capacity to take risks. McPherson may be right when he argues that in order to be a great general, one has to be willing to take great risks. It is the nature of the game. McClellan was not willing to take those risks. In that respect, he was flawed and cannot be considered a great commander. It does not necessarily mean, however, that he was an irretrievably dismal one.

The excessive hunts for drawbacks to attach to McClellan's personality and attempts to establish him as a person incapable of military command become trivial pursuits. Not only are his faults viewed out of context, they also do not stand up to any measure of an objective standard. In any comparison with other Civil War commanders, particularly those to whom he is unfavorably compared, McClellan's personal shortcomings were not that remarkable. On any given day, Sherman, or any other Civil War commander, could be as ill-humored, vain, and vindictive as McClellan. McClellan held no monopoly in that respect. It is time the witch-hunt was called off. Factors other than McClellan's personality have a great deal more to do with why success in the eastern theater proved so elusive in the early years of the war.

4

The Struggle Becomes Remorseless

ALTHOUGH IT IS MᴄCLELLAN THE FIELD COMMANDER who is generally faulted, many of his critics take him to task for being a proponent of an unrealistic and flawed military strategy. Unionist historians have appropriated John Pope's derisive commentary on McClellan and his army to themselves. They concur with Pope that McClellan fought the war with kid gloves. McClellan is vilified for thinking that the war could be won by wielding a velvet hammer in dealing with the Confederacy.[1] Many feel he refused to countenance the hard reality that soldiers would die in battle and that he, as their general, would have to order them to their deaths.[2] His inordinate desire to avoid de-

1. T. Harry Williams surmised that McClellan wanted "to capture Richmond without a battle," and he noted that the "trouble with McClellan was that he liked to think of war as a bloodless strategy, as moves on a gigantic chessboard." See T. Harry Williams, *Lincoln and His Generals,* 51, 107. Grant, on the other hand, fully understood the political nature of the war, and his ability to rise above the staid "dogmas of traditional warfare" marked him as a "modern general." See T. Harry Williams, "The Military Leadership of the North and South," in Donald, ed., *Why the North Won the Civil War,* 40–42.

2. A statement of McClellan's frequently appears in critiques of his inability to sanction hard fighting. In a letter to his wife following the Battle of Fair Oaks, he wrote, "I am tired of the sickening sight of the battlefield with its mangled corpses & poor suffering wounded! Victory has no charms for me when purchased at such a cost." On another occasion he crooned, "Every poor fellow that is killed or wounded almost haunts me." Quoted in Sears, *George B. McClellan: The Young Napoleon,* 196. See also T. Harry Williams, *Lincoln and His Generals,* 107; and Waugh, *Class of 1846,* 359–60.

structive war unnecessarily prolonged the war, for the hard-nosed fighting initiated by Grant and Sherman would be the only way it would be
won.[3] Moreover, his strategic principles suffered from a case of acute
myopia as well. Unlike Grant, he failed to coordinate all Union armies in a
simultaneous concert of action, allowing the enemy to shuttle troops back
and forth across the Confederacy to counter sporadic and isolated Federal
military initiatives. Under Grant's aegis and Lincoln's benediction, Federal strategy called for all Union armies to begin campaigning at the same
time and with equal tenacity and vigor. The essence of Grant's idea was
captured in one of Lincoln's many homespun aphorisms. After listening
to Grant expound on his plan for the 1864 campaign season, Lincoln
quipped: "Those not skinning can hold a leg."[4] Finally, McClellan is often
taken to task for swimming against the tide of public opinion on the political and social nature of the rebellion and the consequent need to develop new military strategies and tactics to save the Union.[5]

What is generally overlooked in the indictments listed above is any
serious consideration of McClellan's strategic thinking vis à vis Northern perceptions of the nature and causes of the secessionist rebellion and
the political and national strategies designed to subdue it in its first year.[6]

3. Sears, "Lincoln and McClellan," in Boritt, ed., *Lincoln's Generals*, 50. In summariz-
ing a speech Lincoln gave to a convention of women in November 1862, T. Harry Williams wrote: "He [Lincoln] said that the people and the officers of the army had not made
up their minds that the country was in a terrible war. The officers, he said, thought the war
could be won by strategy. Hard, tough fighting would win it, he continued, not strategy.
The army must be officered by fighting men." See T. Harry Williams, *Lincoln and His Generals*, 178.

4. John Hay, *Lincoln and the Civil War in the Diaries and Letters of John Hay*, ed., Tyler
Dennett (New York: Dodd, Mead, 1939), 178–79.

5. McPherson contends that by July 1862, when McClellan presented his views in the
Harrison's Landing Letter, Lincoln had already "concluded that McClellan's conservative
counsel on national strategy was of a piece with the general's cautious and unsuccessful military strategy, fighting with 'elder-stalk squirts, charged with rose water,' as Lincoln put
it." See McPherson, "Lincoln and the Strategy of Unconditional Surrender," 49. See also
Glatthaar, *Partners in Command*, 81.

6. See Joseph L. Harsh, "George B. McClellan and the Forgotten Alternative: An Introduction to the Conservative Strategy in the Civil War: April–August 1861" (Ph.D. diss.,
Rice University, 1970). It is a study that looks at McClellan as a serious strategist, and I am
indebted to this scholarship during the course of preparing this chapter. His ideas are crys-
talized in two essays: "Battlesword and Rapier: Clausewitz, Jomini and the Civil War,"
Military Affairs 38 (Dec. 1974); and "Lincoln's Tarnished Brass: Conservative Strategies
and the Attempt to Fight the Early War as a Limited War," in Roman J. Helniak and Law-

With hindsight, McClellan came to see that "slavery was the real knot of the question and the underlying cause of the war." His Civil War career had been anchored in the belief that that was precisely the question that had to be avoided, since it obscured and complicated the importance of saving the Union. He had written his friend and mentor Samuel Barlow in November 1861 to ask his assistance in dealing with the political aspects of the slavery issue. "Help me to dodge the nigger—we want nothing to do with him," he pleaded. He believed that the issue of emancipation was entirely "incidental and subsidiary" to the matter of restoring the Union, and he was comforted by his perception that the "Presdt is perfectly honest & is really sound on the nigger question." He remained steadfast, however, in his conviction that the conflict was started by the "violent course of a comparatively small number of men, on both sides of the line, during the thirty years preceding the war." Despite his suspicion that northern abolitionists were most culpable for the rupture of the Union, he had unswervingly thrown aside all questions of responsibility once Fort Sumter was fired upon. "The Govt. is in danger, our flag is insulted," he declared, "[and] we must stand by it."[7]

Irrespective of the potentially questionable logic entailed, the bulk of informed opinion in the North subscribed to the belief that the slave-holding class of Southern planters was responsible for removing formerly loyal states from the Union. Nowhere was this theory more ascribed to than within the ranks of the Republican party itself; they had repeatedly witnessed the disproportionate power of the planter elite in the slave extension debates of the antebellum period. According to theory, the South had been virtually "hoodwinked" by a small number of the wealthiest planters to foment rebellion. In what was characterized as the great "Slave Power Conspiracy," planter aristocrats, relying on a tradition of subservience and deference to their position, had goaded their social inferiors into supporting secession. As Lincoln's Republican friend and advisor Carl Schurz put it, "One class of citizens is accustomed to rule, and the other to obey."[8]

---

rence L. Hewitt, eds., *The Confederate High Command and Related Topics: Themes in Honor of T. Harry Williams* (Shippensburg, Pa.: White Mane, 1988) 124–41.

7. Sears, *Civil War Papers of George B. McClellan*, 5, 127–28; McClellan, *McClellan's Own Story*, 29–30.

8. Quoted in Grimsley, *The Hard Hand of War*, 9. Grimsley's is an enlightened study of the evolution of military policy as it was directed at Southern civilians. It argues that there was a gradual evolution in this policy, marked by three stages: conciliatory, pragmatic, and

That perception was buttressed by another deeply held belief in the North that most Southerners were not dedicated secessionists. Their support was predicated on unquestioned obeisance to the whims of their social betters, and it was shallow at best. Moreover, many Northerners believed with good reason that many large pockets of loyalism were sprinkled throughout the South, and these had been suppressed during the voting on secession legislation. Lincoln endorsed that view in his address to a special session of the Congress on July 4, 1861. He articulated the prevailing sentiment that it "may well be doubted whether there is, today, a majority of the legally qualified voters of any State, except perhaps South Carolina, in favor of disunion . . . [and] there is much reason to believe that the Union men are the majority in many, if not in every other one, of the so-called seceded States."[9]

Even the two men who would take such an active part in dismantling the Confederacy in 1865 subscribed to the thesis that the Southern elite had led their section into open rebellion. In recalling the stormy years leading up to the war, Grant discerned that there were those in the South who wished a separate government in order to protect the "Divine institution of slavery." He entertained no doubts that the "prevailing sentiment of the South would have been opposed to secession in 1860 and 1861," except for the actions of "demagogues" in its midst who rallied on behalf of slavery while railing "vehemently and unceasingly against the North." He was never able to understand why the "great bulk of the legal voters of the South," who owned no slaves and needed "emancipation" themselves, would vote for secession, except for the control exerted upon them by the "old regime" of their social betters. Countenancing the possible objection that the "ballot was as untrammelled in the South as in any section," he reasserted his conviction that poor Southerners voted under the direction of the planter elite. There may not have been "masked men . . . intimidating the voters . . . [with] shot-guns," Grant conceded, "but there was a firm feeling that a class existed in every State with a sort of divine right to control public affairs."[10]

Sherman was not as expansive as Grant in his recollections about the causes of the rebellion. That may well have to do with the fact that he

---

hard. For my purposes, it is useful in the way it highlights the link between national and military policy during McClellan's tenure in command.

9. Basler, *Collected Works of Abraham Lincoln* 4:437.

10. Grant, *Memoirs* 1:222–26.

was the superintendant of a military school in Louisiana at the outbreak
of the secession crisis and regretted that his pursuit of financial stability
and career success was about to spin out of control again. The cadets en-
rolled in his school were the sons of the well-to-do planter aristocrats
with whom he enjoyed a cordial and beholden relationship. Nonetheless,
his memories revealed a great deal about the interests of slaveholders, as
illustrated in the conversation at a dinner party he attended at the home
of Louisiana's governor, Thomas O. Moore. Gathered there were "several members of the Louisiana Legislature, [Senator Richard] Taylor, [and
Braxton] Bragg," who were discussing the purported abolitionist lean-
ings of his brother John Sherman. Even in his recollection, Sherman,
after being invited to partake in the discussion, made but a tepid defense
of his brother's views. As for the issue of slavery itself, Sherman made
no disparaging remarks concerning its legality as an institution and
only suggested that the lot of "field hands" should be brought up to the
level of the domestic slaves. He was infinitely "relieved" when the discussion ended because he was well aware that "at the time all men in
Louisiana were dreadfully excited on questions affecting their slaves,
who constituted the bulk of their wealth." To his brother John, Sherman
wrote in April 1861 that the "question of the national integrity and slavery
should be kept distinct, for otherwise it will gradually become a war of
extermination–a war without end."[11]

Months later, on the eve of First Manassas, Sherman seemed almost
reluctant to embark upon a crusade against the South. He took time to
write a letter to his little daughter Minnie in which he spoke of his desire
to keep the intensity of the war on a limited and conciliatory basis. "We
must fight and subdue men in arms against us," he counseled her, "but we
mean them no harm. . . . We have not disturbed a single slave." He even
admonished Minnie to avoid getting caught up in the spiraling circle of
war hatred, for he was fighting "thousands . . . whom I used to know as
kind, good friends." Those same people, Sherman reasoned, must have felt
like they were fighting in self-defense of "their country, their houses and
famililies against foreign invaders." He concluded his fatherly advice by

11. Sherman, Memoirs 1:148–50; Rachel Sherman Thorndike, ed., The Sherman Letters:
Correspondence between General and Senator Sherman from 1837–1891 (New York: Scribner's
1894), 113. According to Marszalek, Sherman was clear in his support of slavery and his opposition to emancipation, and he even intended to purchase house slaves when Helen
joined him in Louisiana. See Marszalek, Sherman: A Soldier's Passion for Order, 126.

cautioning his "dear child" not "to get into the habit of calling [them] hard names of rebels, traitors." They were a people, who had been "deceived" by malignant forces in the South, and that, he proposed, was "easy enough for a people to do." At that stage of the conflict, despite his protestation that the nation was facing a long war with the South, he hoped that neither side would have to drink to the dregs from the cup of suffering.[12]

If, in Northern opinion, the great majority of Southerners had little at stake in the elitist rebellion, then the way to bring them back to their senses was to kindly, but sternly, demonstrate the error of their ways and the sheer folly of secession. Central to the enlightenment process was a show of irresistable force to convince Southerners of Northern might and determination. Yet that powerful demonstration had to be employed in such a way as not to alienate potential fence-sitters into the secessionist fold. Invoking an inchoate form of paternalism, Northerners would rescue their loyal brethren from the clutches of the slaveholding conspirators. In a nation founded upon the act of revolution, Northerners could still feel justified in coercing their compatriots back into the Union because they had been duped into seceding by a cabal of jackanapes.[13]

A very practical dimension of Northern thinking in the emerging struggle with the South was how to retain the loyalty of the border states of Missouri, Maryland, and Kentucky. Should any overt aggression push them into Confederate arms, the task of restoring the Union would become virtually impossible. At his first inaugural address in March 1861, at a time when Virginia and several other states had not yet left the Union, Lincoln was careful to stifle any expression of aggressive intent. "In your hands, my dissatisfied fellow countrymen, and not in mine, is the momentous issue of civil war," he declared. He would forsake using force to reunite the severed states unless they forced it upon him. "The government will not assail you, unless you first assail it. You can have no conflict, without being yourselves the aggressors."[14]

The bombardment of Fort Sumter and Lincoln's subsequent call for seventy-five thousand volunteers muted the abstract theorizing and stimulated discussions of the best means to end the rebellion. Many

12. Fellman, *Citizen Sherman*, 89.
13. Grimsley, *Hard Hand of War*, 9–11.
14. Basler, *Collected Works of Abraham Lincoln* 4:261, 271.

Northerners were deeply concerned that any active military operations directed at the South would only intensify the existing disaffection that existed. Lincoln was bombarded by respected opinions in that regard. His own attorney general, Edward Bates, after disparaging the strength of Southern resistance and perseverance, suggested a naval blockade of the South as the best alternative. Citing England's lamentable experience in Ireland as an example, Senator John Crittenden of Kentucky spoke out against an early attempt to pass a confiscation bill on the grounds that it would "stimulate your adversaries to still more desperate measures." Brigadier General George Meade concurred with that line of thinking when he wrote his wife that "the ultras on both sides should be repudiated, and the masses of conservative men may compromise and settle the difficulty." Seizure of rebel property, especially slaves, Meade reasoned, would "forbid any hope of the Southerners yielding so long as there is any power of resistance left in them." The secretary of state, William Seward, agreed that military action of any kind should be avoided, as it might undermine the efforts of Union supporters in the South who were working to effect reunion. No one was a more ardent supporter and champion of a conciliatory policy than Seward.[15]

In the waning days of the Buchanan administration, when the states that would form the Confederacy were seceding from the Union, Winfield Scott labored over the possible military responses the North might be called upon to make. Scott was not sanguine about the success of any plan to invade the South and force those seceded states into rejoining the Union. Of four options laid out by him, he was most pessimistic about the invasion plan. Arguing that it would require an army of three hundred thousand commanded by a brilliant general and take "two or three years" to subdue the South, he did not believe an invasion would justify the enormous waste in human life and treasure. It would only restore the Union in appearances, for in truth, the South would never be reconciled to its conquerors and would have to be garrisoned for generations.[16]

---

15. Grimsley, *Hard Hand of War,* 10; Glyndon G. Van Deusen, *William H. Seward* (New York: Oxford Univ. Press, 1967), 238–54.

16. Winfield Scott, *Memoirs of Lieut.-General Scott, L.L.D. Written by Himself,* 2 vols. (New York: Sheldon, 1864), 2:625–28. Scott's dour estimate was actually exceeded in the course of the war. It would take four years, more than twice as many men-in-arms, and an enormous toll in blood and expenditure.

A second option, in his opinion, was for the government to adopt the Crittenden compromise or some other policy aimed at assuaging Southern concerns. He favored that plan above all the others and predicted it would stem further secession and prompt the return of most, if not all, of those states that had already departed. Another military option, short of invading the South, was to establish a blockade of Southern ports to compel the seceded states to sue for reconciliation based on economic terms. His last option, and the one that earned him the suspicion of many in the Republican party, was to let the South go its own way undisturbed, or in his own words, "Wayward Sisters, depart in peace!"[17]

The events at Fort Sumter dampened and precluded any realistic implementation of Scott's nonmilitary options. Still, the old general would not endorse any military invasion of the South on the grounds that it remained impractical and would drive potential loyalists into the enemy camp. In May 1861, he fleshed out in greater detail his option of blockading Southern ports. In what would later be dubbed the Anaconda Plan by a critical press, Scott advised an immediate blockade against all Southern coastal ports, followed by the dispatch of a strong force to gain control of the Mississippi River. Following that, the government should wait to determine if economic asphyxiation would compel the South to submit.[18]

While Scott's proposal held sway for several weeks, the presence of rebel armies at Manassas and in the Shenandoah Valley ultimately made a casualty of it. On June 29, Scott's scheme of operation was shelved in favor of McDowell's plan to strike at Manassas. The groundwork for an invasion of the South was laid. Northern opinion had undergone a subtle shifting in the days since Fort Sumter. The belief that a demonstrated show of force would be a greater inducement for the resurrection of Southern loyalism had gained increasing popularity, particularly in the press. Within Lincoln's cabinet, Montgomery Blair, postmaster general, assailed the waiting game and convinced Lincoln that further hesitation would only serve to entrench secessionist support in the South. Both plans, however, shared the underlying resolution that any military operation would be conducted in such a way as not to alienate Southerners. Any action would have to be directed solely against men in arms.

17. Scott, *Memoirs* 2:625–28.
18. *OR*, vol. 51, 1:369–70.

Noncombatants were to see both the might and the right of Union resolve. Such a display would make reconciliation possible.[19]

The ill-prepared attack on Confederate forces at Manassas, which Scott deplored and McDowell resisted, led to the rout of the Union army. The retreating Federals carried with them any hope of seeing the immediate collapse of the Confederacy. Emboldened by that first flush of success, nationalist sentiment in the South blossomed. Summoned to command the forces in Washington in the wake of McDowell's defeat, McClellan was gravely perturbed by the consequences of the poorly planned offensive. While the "contest began with a class," he ventured, "now it is with a people." Before the defeat at First Manassas, McClellan's views on military strategy had contained elements of both Scott's and Lincoln's ideas. In response to Lincoln's request, McClellan detailed his views in a memorandum dated August 2, 1861. In it, he forged the salient benefits of both plans. Although he rejected Scott's long-term solution as no longer practical, he endorsed the idea that the Union offensives should be conducted in such a convincing and conciliatory manner as to encourage Unionist sentiment in the South, thus paving the way to ultimate reconciliation. One of the cardinal points in his strategy was to organize such an "overwhelming strength, as will convince all our antagonists, especially those of the governing aristocratic class, of the utter impossibility of resistance." Noting that the recent reverse at Manassas had forfeited any hopes to spare the "expense and labor of a great effort," McClellan vowed that only military success would crush the rebellion. With specific emphasis, he implored Lincoln to understand that "the authority of the government must be supported by overwhelming physical force." After making provisions for the Union's western armies and for an adequate defense of Washington, McClellan ventured an estimate of 273,000 for active operations in Virginia. This was consistent with Scott's forecast of April 1861. Hand in hand with this "overwhelming" force, McClellan added the qualification that it should be employed in a manner that pursued a "rigidly protective policy as to private property and unarmed persons, and a lenient course as to common soldiers." At the heart of McClellan's military policy was a "carrot and stick" approach. The stick would be the intimidating and pulverizing application of Union might. The carrot would be a conciliatory policy that would permanently restore a "peaceful Union." As he recalled in later years, he believed that it was a

19. Grimsley, *Hard Hand of War,* 29–31.

"matter of sound policy to do nothing likely to render ultimate reconciliation and harmony impossible, unless such a course were imperative to secure military success."[20]

In light of the spectacular failure at Manassas, McClellan believed that a lengthy period of time, preparation, and training would be required before that "overwhelming" strength could be marshaled and fine-tuned. Once those matters were resolved, McClellan intended to translate his military policy into strategic terms. Although Grant is usually the first to be credited with dictating that simultaneous pressure be applied in all theaters of the war, McClellan's memorandum of August 2 called for just such a concert of action. While he understood that the Virginia campaign would be the most significant, McClellan called for movements elsewhere, both on land and water. Specifically, he recommended the immediate pacification of Missouri and a movement down the Mississippi. He also suggested that once Kentucky was secured, a force should be sent into East Tennessee both to assist the "Union men of that region," and to seize the vital railroad link between Memphis and the East. A similar campaign in Texas would also profit by tapping into veins of Union loyalism there. With foresight, he envisioned the usefulness of railroad lines, remarking that they could assist in troop concentrations and in opening up new lines of operation. Amphibious operations likewise played a considerable role in his reckoning, and several were outlined in broad strokes. He realized that his troop requests would be as expensive as they appeared extensive. That was, however, the price of Bull Run's folly. If Lincoln wanted to "reestablish the power of the Government . . . in the shortest possible time," McClellan argued, then the North had to "crush the rebellion at one blow [and] terminate the war in one campaign." Nor did he think his recommendations were quixotic or unworkable when both the personnel and raw material required for assembling that overwhelming strength were the North's two distinct advantages going into the war.[21]

---

20. Sears, *Civil War Papers of George B. McClellan,* 71–73; McClellan, *McClellan's Own Story,* 35. Stanton was not a member of Lincoln's cabinet in August 1861. The following February McClellan sent him a memorandum outlining the military strategy in which he revisited many of the same themes of the August 1861 memorandum to the president. In Stanton's letter McClellan reviewed the reasons why operations could not commence in December 1861. See Sears, *Civil War Papers of George B. McClellan,* 162–64.

21. Sears, *Civil War Papers of George B. McClellan,* 72–75.

As Joseph Harsh astutely argues, most historians have refused to take the strategic thinking in that memorandum seriously, preferring instead to impugn the character of its author. Sears interprets McClellan's strategy not as a revision of Scott's concentric troop deployment, exerting pressure on all points of the Confederacy, but as a rejection of it. For Sears, McClellan merely desired the vast majority of the five hundred thousand men Congress had recently authorized for his own invasion of Virginia. T. Harry Williams declared the project "a defective one in almost every aspect." The plan was "unrealistic . . . a fantasia," Williams ascertained, speculating that Lincoln might have thought "the Young Napoleon was merely a little flighty and would settle down with experience." Despite noting that Lincoln had specifically requested strategic advice, Glatthaar seems to suggest that McClellan, who was "ever certain of his own judgment," was making an attempt "to dictate policy." Kenneth P. Williams, the inveterate McClellan critic, viewed the occasion of McClellan's submitting his recommendations over Scott's head, for which he faulted Lincoln, as the launching pad for the escalating hostility between those two generals. Noting that even in his infirmity, Scott was the picture of Mars himself, Williams perceived that it was McClellan's fate that "the name Little Mac became inevitable."[22]

Although T. Harry Williams was correct on one score–it did ramble a bit–McClellan's was, nonetheless, a well reasoned strategic proposal. His conservative views consistently reflected those holding widespread appeal throughout the North at the time. The war aims were truly conservative; the conflict was undertaken to restore the Union as it had been before the war. Other than a mere handful of abolitionists, no one was interested in destroying the South or in interfering with its social and economic institutions. Buell, McClellan's trusty subordinate in Kentucky, agreed that it was important to protect the constitutional rights of Southerners so as to not further divide the breach that divided the nation. From South Carolina, Brig. Gen. Thomas W. Sherman hailed McClellan's grand strategy as triumphant. "My opinion is that you have crushed this rebellion already," Sherman offered. "The Savannah and Charleston papers show a deeply saddened spirit among the people." McClellan's own experience in West Virginia, however limited, showed that a determined but

22. Harsh, "Lincoln's Tarnished Brass," 124; Sears, *George B. McClellan: The Young Napoleon,* 98–99; T. Harry Williams, *Lincoln and His Generals,* 30–31; Glatthaar, *Partners in Command,* 59; Kenneth P. Williams, *Lincoln Finds a General* 1:125.

conservative course of action had been well received by the local population. The conciliatory aspects of the limited war strategy were not as much a rejection of hard fighting per se, as they were grounded in the belief that wreaking devastation in the South would have an adverse impact upon the national goal of reconciling the country.[23]

McClellan, however, was not the master of his own destiny. He lacked the authority to implement that strategy in any systematic way until Scott retired on November 1. Moreover, as seen earlier, other Federal forces were nowhere close to being ready to take to the field. Sherman was in the midst of spinning out of control in Kentucky. His successor, Buell, assumed major challenges in reorganizing the army there once Sherman departed, and he would be hampered by genuine logistical problems for months to come. The outbreak of guerilla-style fighting after the Federal defeat at Wilson's Creek and the mismanagement of General John C. Frémont rendered the situation in Missouri chaotic. Halleck, who was appointed to sort out the mess in Missouri and to organize future operations efforts in western Kentucky, would not be ready until early 1862 to make any headway. Consequently, McClellan spent his time as productively as possible, organizing and training his newly assembled army. Had others been as prepared as the Army of the Potomac, McClellan claimed he would have commenced his campaign by December 1, 1861. While that deadline seems a trifle optimistic, it does not alter the fact that other sectors were totally unprepared for active collaboration any time in 1861. It was not until March 1862 that western armies were prepared to participate in the grand invasion of the Confederacy.[24]

The inability of all Federal armies to cooperate in a concert of action at that early stage of the war contrasts sharply with the military situation Grant inherited when he arrived in Washington in 1864. While Grant should be applauded for ordering the simultaneous advance of all Federal armies in the spring campaign of 1864, it was feasible only because the

23. On Buell's political views, see Stephen D. Engle, "Don Carlos Buell: Military Philosophy and Command Problems in the West," *Civil War History* 41 (June 1995): 94. Sherman's letter is in *OR*, vol. 6, 1:236–37. In the early stages of his western Virginia campaign, McClellan issued a proclamation to the inhabitants of the area, emphasizing that his army was an enemy "to none but armed rebels, and those voluntarily giving them aid." In his address to his own soldiers, he warned them that they were "in the country of friends, not enemies . . . that you are here to protect, not to destroy." See Sears, *Civil War Papers of George B. McClellan,* 34–35.

24. Harsh, "Lincoln's Tarnished Brass," 129–30.

Federal war effort had reached the apex of its development at the same time the Confederate war machine was at the nadir of its own rapid decline. Moreover, the idea was not exactly novel. Although the geopolitical realities had changed by the spring of 1864, McClellan had already submitted in 1861 a proposal strikingly similar to Grant's. If, as T. Harry Williams submits, it was actually Lincoln's idea to have all Federal armies act in concert, perhaps it was because he still possessed a dim memory of McClellan's memorandum of August 1861. Neither Sherman, nor any other commander for that matter, would have been prepared to swoop down into Georgia in May 1864 unless and until Confederate armies had been pushed out of the difficult terrain of Kentucky and Tennessee. And that task was not accomplished until two full years of hard fighting, punctuated by several reversals, had taken place. The claim that Grant's ingenious proposal to occupy the attention of all enemy armies in order to prevent them from shifting reinforcements to any one critical area is overblown. By 1864, neither the Army of Northern Virginia nor the Army of Tennessee were realistically capable of mutual support. Lacking the strength for any sustained offensives, both armies were back on their heels. Lee, remembering the positive effects of setting Jackson loose in the Valley in 1862, might have been willing to spare Jubal Early for a diversionary attack on the Federal capital in 1864, but he could hardly contemplate releasing any sizeable force for duty in the West.[25]

Between the date McClellan assumed Scott's mantle as general in chief and his departure to the Peninsula, very little transpired to persuade him that his conciliatory strategy had been scrapped. If anything, all indications pointed to its full and complete endorsement. True, Congress failed in December 1861 to muster a vote of confidence for the Crittenden-Johnson resolutions, passed earlier in July, that disavowed the abolition of slavery as one of the war aims. Yet, most of the votes that had switched since July had been Republican ones, and no actual reversal of policy had been authorized. In early September, Lincoln censured Gen. John C. Frémont for his surprising proclamation that freed the slaves

25. Davis, in April 1864, fearing that the great push of the enemy would come in Virginia, refused to grant Johnston substantial reinforcements in the West, leading Johnston to observe that "the U.S. have the means of collecting two great armies—here & in Virginia. Our government thinks they can raise but one, that of course in Virginia." Quoted in Gilbert E. Govan and James W. Livingood, *A Different Valor: The Story of General Joseph E. Johnston, C.S.A.* (Indianapolis: Bobbs-Merrill, 1956), 257.

in war-torn Missouri. Not only was Lincoln fearful of the potentially explosive consequences of that action in the border states, especially Kentucky, he was not prepared to make the abolition of slavery an issue in the contest with the South. When Frémont interpreted Lincoln's reprimand merely as a request to rescind his proclamation, the president clarified it for him by publicly ordering him to do so.[26]

In early December, Lincoln found it necessary to rebuke one of his own cabinet members over the slavery issue. Secretary of War Simon Cameron, in his annual report, advised that the government arm slaves to be used against the rebels. Lincoln was incensed when he read that section of the report; he ordered Cameron to recall it and to delete the offensive paragraph. Much to his dismay, a number of newspapers had obtained a copy and had already gone to print. In his annual message on December 3, Lincoln fully endorsed the conciliatory policy. "In considering the policy to be adopted for suppressing the insurrection," he announced, "I have been anxious and careful that the inevitable conflict shall not degenerate into a violent and remorseless struggle." McClellan must surely have approved. His conversations with those in power assured him that he was developing a military policy consistent with the aims of the government.[27]

While he was campaigning on the Peninsula, McClellan kept abreast of the political dimensions of the war, although he was not privy to their nuances and subtleties. On May 9, Gen. David Hunter, an avid abolitionist, issued a sweeping declaration of martial law in his department that abolished slavery in the states of Florida, Georgia, and South Carolina. Like Cameron and Frémont before him, Hunter had acted on his own, without consulting Lincoln and receiving his approval. On May 19, Lincoln rescinded Hunter's declaration and scolded the general. His order revoking Hunter's action, however, hinted that he might not be opposed to considering such a course in the future should the preservation of the Union require it. If, or when, that time came, he would be the one to issue the order. Conservatives applauded the president's action but may have

26. *OR,* vol. 3, 1:466–67; Basler, *Collected Works of Abraham Lincoln* 4:517–18.

27. Basler, *Collected Works of Abraham Lincoln* 4:48–49. On the same day Lincoln visited the Army of the Potomac at Harrison's Landing, McClellan wrote Stanton, alluding to the military policy he had urged in his letter to the president. Referring to the frequent conversation the two of them held during the past summer, McClellan informed Stanton that the letter "only expressed the opinions then agreed upon between us." See Sears, *Civil War Papers of George B. McClellan,* 347.

overlooked Lincoln's growing ambivalence over the whole issue of emancipation. McClellan, for one, was pleased to see that he and Lincoln remained in accord on the slavery issue. "I am very glad that the Presdt has come out as he did about Hunter's order," he wrote Ellen, "I feared he would not have the moral courage to do so."[28]

During the course of campaigning on the Peninsula, McClellan consistently waged war according to his strategic plan and his political understanding of the conflict. In attempting to avoid the "useless effusion of blood," McClellan strove to maximize opportunities while keeping casualties to a minimum. In his address to the soldiers of the Army of the Potomac at the outset of the campaign, he promised them he would seek the decisive battle with great care, and he hoped to "gain success with the least possible loss." Shortly after he arrived on the Peninsula, he contacted Stanton to receive approval for a general order he proposed to present to his army. "[The] general commanding deems it absolutely necessary for the protection of the inhabitants and their property and the good order of the army," McClellan explained, "to establish that unwritten code of law which civilization has provided for the exigencies of a condition of war." Having declared martial law, McClellan decreed that all crimes committed either by "soldiers . . . or by inhabitants" be punishable by a course of military commission. In addition to the obvious cases of rape, murder, and malicious personal injuries, McClellan added "arson, robberies, theft and wanton trespass" as crimes punishable under martial law.[29]

He repeatedly instructed his subordinates to keep a tight rein on their charges to prevent plundering that would both inflame the passions of the enemy and erode his own army's discipline. When Federal troops arrived at White House, the plantation of Lee's own son and the ancestral property of Martha Custis Washington, McClellan posted a guard around the house and prohibited the army from using it. Lee's wife had just vacated the premises in advance of the approaching Yankees and had moved to Edmund Ruffin's plantation on the Pamunkey River when the same Union army overran that site as well in June. That time she was trapped behind Federal lines. To avoid the potential embarrassment

28. Basler, *Collected Works of Abraham Lincoln* 5:219, 222–23; Sears, *Civil War Papers of George B. McClellan*, 274.

29. *OR*, vol. 11, 3:77.

of imprisoning a woman of such standing and to diffuse any ill will in the enemy, McClellan had Mrs. Lee escorted through enemy lines under a flag of truce.[30]

The end of the Seven Days' Battle marked a discernable shift in the administration's outlook on the nature of the rebellion and the means necessary to subdue it. To Lincoln's way of thinking, the "half defeat" on the Peninsula had spelled the end to the conciliatory policy. The long-anticipated swell of latent Southern Unionism had never materialized, nor had the expected collapse of rebel resistance. Now, Lincoln reasoned, Southerners had only become more convinced of the promise of ultimate victory. To date, he had resisted the demands for hard measures that were daily bombarding him from his own cabinet and party, as well as from the national press. He believed now that the nation would countenance bolder moves, and he was ready to try them. He told William Seward during the middle of the Seven Days' struggle that he was determined to "maintain this contest until successful, or until I die, or am conquered, or my term expires, or Congress or the country forsakes me." In the wake of his visit to the army at Harrison's Landing he contemplated the boldest of ideas–the emancipation of the slaves.[31]

Even before McClellan's retreating army reached the James in early July, Lincoln took practical steps to reinvigorate the war effort. On June 27, he named John Pope to command the newly created Army of Virginia. Pope, a Republican, was an old friend of the president's and was related to him by marriage into the Todd family. He was energetic and possessed the reputation as a no-nonsense hard fighter. Moreover, his radical views on the war had won him the ringing endorsement of the

30. Sears, *Civil War Papers of George B. McClellan*, 211; Sears, *To the Gates of Richmond*, 104, 162. It should be pointed out that Lee was a strong advocate of "civilized warfare" and strictly adhered to standard principles concerning the conduct of armies. In his two Northern campaigns, Lee issued strict orders against plundering, often to the despair of his hungry and destitute army. Proper conduct would demonstrate the Confederacy's legitimate right to independence. During the Pennsylvania campaign, one soldier wrote home with approval that the men were forbidden "even to pluck a cherry by the wayside." Quoted in Reid Mitchell, *Civil War Soldiers* (New York: Touchstone, 1988), 152.

31. McPherson, *Battle Cry of Freedom*, 500; Basler, *Collected Works of Abraham Lincoln* 5:291–92. On July 13, 1862, Lincoln informally informed Welles and Seward of his intention to issue a proclamation freeing all slaves in the South. See Howard K. Beale and Alan W. Brownsword, eds., *Diary of Gideon Wells, Secretary of the Navy Under Lincoln and Johnson*, 3 vols. (New York: W. W. Norton, 1960), 2:70–71.

emerging powerhouse in Congress—the Radical Republicans. His selection coincided with the passage of two laws that signaled a decided hardening of military policy. In particular, the confiscation act of July 1862 sanctioned the seizure of property, including slaves, that was deemed of military value to the rebels. The kid gloves were coming off.[32]

Assured of the support and good will of the president and the Republican party, Pope escalated his assault on McClellan's cherished policy of conciliation. In the customary first address to his new army, Pope, hoping to inspire its fighting spirit, spoke intemperately. "Let us understand each other," he began. "I have come to you from the West, where we have always seen the backs of our enemies; from an army who business it has been to seek the adversary and to beat him when he was found; whose policy has been attack and not defense." In what could only be construed as a critique of McClellan's Peninsula campaign, he admonished his soldiers to "study the probable lines of retreat of our opponents, and leave our own to take care of themselves . . . look before us, not behind . . . success and glory are in the advance, disaster and shame lurk in the rear." If Stanton did not have a direct hand in the drafting of that address, it is certain that Pope had his blessing and Lincoln's tacit approval.[33]

The address alone was sufficient to garner McClellan's enduring enmity. He certainly viewed Pope's braggadocio with disdain and was galled by the sarcastic references to the Army of the Potomac. But what really incensed McClellan were Pope's subsequent actions that threatened to reverse his diligent efforts to keep the war limited and relatively civilized. In a series of general orders, Pope authorized his officers to seize rebel property without compensation, to execute captured guerilla fighters caught firing on the army, to exile through enemy lines any civilians who refused to take an oath of allegiance, and to consider them spies if they attempted to return.[34] Worse, in McClellan's mind, Pope's bombast seemed to articulate a newly emerging policy on war, one that directly conflicted

32. Pope only enhanced his position with the radical members of the Joint Committee on the Conduct of the War when he told that assembly in an appearance on July 8 that he intended to "attack them [Rebels] at all times that I get the opportunity" and that had he been commanding McClellan's army he would have marched it clear to New Orleans. See *CCW* 1:278, 282.

33. *OR*, vol. 11, 3:472–74. A discussion on the authorship of Pope's address is found in Daniel Sutherland, "Lincoln, Pope and the Origins of Total War," *Journal of Military History* 56 (Oct. 1992): 576–77.

34. Nevins, *War for the Union* 2:150–56.

with his own. In the parting line of one of his letters to Ellen, he noted glumly that he "did not like the political turn that affairs are taking."[35]

McClellan quickly dug in his heels and initiated a campaign to counter Pope's influence. Receiving no intimations from Lincoln that policy changes were in the offing, he decided to make good on an earlier pledge to supply Lincoln with his views on the war. During their meeting at Harrison's Landing on July 8, McClellan handed Lincoln his now famous, or infamous, letter. "The time has come when the Government must determine upon a civil and military policy," McClellan declared. After acknowledging that the rebellion had now assumed the character of war, McClellan urged the president to conduct it "upon the highest principles known to Christian Civilization." He frowned upon any policy that sought to subjugate the people of any state. Rather, he suggested, the war should be directed against the "armed forces and political organization" of the Confederacy alone. His letter went on to condemn every practice currently being employed by Pope's army and specifically advised against using military power to "interfere with the relations of servitude," except in well-defined circumstances. Any "declaration of radical views, especially upon slavery," he vowed, would "rapidly disintegrate our present Armies."[36]

Uncertain as to what Lincoln's reactions were to his opinions, McClellan continued to pursue his conciliatory policies. When it came to his attention that soldiers had violated the property of a local plantation owner, Hill Carter, McClellan attempted to redress those injuries. McClellan was particularly upset in that case because he had been informed that the Carter family had taken care of many of his sick and wounded. For McClellan, Carter's kindness underscored the advantages of fighting the war along conciliatory lines. He extended the influential landowner his regrets that his property had been scarred by the ravages of war, since it had always been his "constant effort to confine the effects of this contest to armed masses and political organization" opposing him. His purpose was to maintain the Union, the Constitution, and the government's laws only; he assured Carter that he was not there to fight civilians, destroy property, or disrupt the "domestic institutions of the land." Even his formal exchanges with Lee over the matter of exchanging wounded prisoners was marked with kindness and gratitude for the civility Lee had

35. Sears, *Civil War Papers of George B. McClellan*, 369.
36. Ibid., 344–45.

demonstrated for helpless Union soldiers. Later, he ventured to send medical supplies to Richmond with the full knowledge and consent that the Confederates would need to appropriate some of them for their own use.[37]

July gave way to August, and with it, despite McClellan's constant urging to the contrary, went any hope of reviving the campaign on the Peninsula. During that time, Halleck, a well-known advocate of conservative policies, had been brought in by Lincoln to handle military affairs. McClellan immediately went to work on him in the hope that "Old Brains'" counsel would hold sway with the president, unaware that Lincoln was already contemplating escalating the stakes in the war with a complete change in civil policy. In his communication to Halleck on August 1, McClellan took the occasion to disparage the civil policies recently inaugurated by Pope. He condemned the confiscation laws recently enacted and argued against any "general emancipation" of the slaves. The actions of the Union army, as an extension of the government, should be what "we profess it to be, benign and beneficient." He deplored and viewed with "infinite dread any policy which tends to render impossible the reconstruction of the Union, and to make this contest simply a useless effusion of blood." Still viewing Pope's concept of the war as a possible aberration, he hoped that Halleck could explain the policy in effect so that he could "know what I am doing. We must have a full understanding on all points," he concluded with perspicacity, "and I regard the civil or political questions as inseparable from the military in this contest."[38]

Halleck agreed with McClellan, citing some of Pope's orders as "very injudicious." However, he countered by saying that the orders "were shown to the president before they were issued," and under such circumstances, he was unwilling to "countermand them." It must have begun to sink into McClellan's head that he was losing control over the policy issue. He was, however, not the only general to object to the changes. Among many, General Marsena Patrick resented the fact that Pope's order "gives a general license to pillage, rob & plunder—It has completely

37. Ibid., 352–53, 356, 368; McClellan to Lee, July 11, 1862, McClellan Papers, Manuscript Division, Library of Congress.

38. *OR*, vol. 11, 3:345–46.

demoralized my Brigade. . . . I am afraid of God's Justice, for our Rulers & Commanders deserve his wrath & curse."[39]

Despite their resentment over the change in policy, most officers decided to submit. If for no other reason, officers feared the deleterious impact portions of the new policy would have upon maintaining unit discipline. Although he decided to abide by his orders, McDowell, for one, attempted to circumvent them by ordering his staff to control the confiscation of property. He wanted no "indiscriminate marauding," and he enjoined his officers to keep their "men from strolling around the country." McClellan took the same approach upon hearing that Lincoln was planning to officially promulgate the confiscation act on August 9. On the evening of August 8, he vowed to Ellen that he would add an addendum to Lincoln's general order, thus striking Pope's policies "square in the teeth." Willing to accept the government's censure, he planned to forbid his army to contemplate pillage and plunder. "I will not permit this army to degenerate into a mob of thieves," he thundered, "nor will I return these men of mine to their families as a set of wicked & demoralized robbers." He remained true to his word. After directing the army's attention to the president's executive order, he added that the authorization to confiscate rebel property was not to be construed as a "pretext for military license." Rather than outrightly refuting the president's directive, he capitalized on Lincoln's caveats regarding any patent abuses in following those initiatives. Toward the close of his commentary, he reminded his soldiers that the war was to be conducted in a civilized manner; it was still directed at armed insurrectionaries and not the local inhabitants.[40]

Even as he was uttering those instructions, his army was preparing to evacuate the Peninsula. After repeated attempts to rejuvenate his campaign against Richmond, he now found himself ferrying his army back to the Potomac where it had all begun. He, too, would soon follow his army, uncertain as to his role in future command responsibilities. His military and political strategies lay in ruins. Others looked forward to fighting the war in earnest, freed from the shackles of a policy that

39. Ibid., 3:359; Marsena Patrick, *Inside Lincoln's Army: The Diary of Marsena R. Patrick, Provost Marshal General, Army of the Potomac,* ed. David Sparks (New York: Yoseloff, 1964), 115–16.

40. *OR,* vol. 12, 3:515; Sears, *Civil War Papers of George B. McClellan,* 387–88; *OR,* vol. 11, 3:362–64.

had patently failed. The conflict would take on a new appearance and would feature political and military dimensions that McClellan could not stomach.

Pope's monumental defeat at Second Manassas brought McClellan back to command. It would be but a brief stint. If his failure on the Peninsula had brought closure to the pursuit of his military and political strategies, his victory at Antietam ushered in entirely new ones. Armed with that triumph, Lincoln announced the general emancipation of slaves throughout the South. Whatever thoughts he might have harbored toward opposing the president's edict were quickly suppressed in favor of abiding with civil prerogative. He ordered his soldiers to respect the decisions of the chief executive and pointed out that the only qualified redress to this instruction was grounded in the democratic process. "The remedy for such errors, if any are committed," he observed, "is to be found only in the action of the people at the polls."[41]

McClellan's military strategy faltered for a variety and an abundance of reasons. The specific difficulties of a first campaign, the tactical errors of the commanding general, and the shortsighted decision making of the chief executive and war department have been discussed elsewhere in this study. In many ways, it would be unfair to say that McClellan's strategic perceptions were faulty since the limitations of time and the conditions necessary for implementation were never totally there. However, his conservative strategy of limited warfare was not out of step with national and political views on the nature of the rebellion and the appropriate means to curtail it. Throughout the first year of the war, McClellan's strategy was innovative, appropriate, and even brilliant in many respects. The amassing of an overwhelming military force, directed along the correct lines of manuever and brought to a selected battlefield, was both militarily sound and politically attuned to the national strategy. He was not an idiosyncratic doctrinaire.

Although McClellan had laid out the basics of his overall strategy in his memorandum to Lincoln on August 2, 1861, he was not in a position to implement it until Scott resigned. McClellan was undoubtedly opportunistic in his complaints about the general in chief, wanting, as he did, to acquire total control for himself. However, during the three months of his command in Washington, he exerted control only over the Army of the

41. Sears, *George B. McClellan: The Young Napoleon*, 325–27; OR, vol. 19, 2:395–96.

Potomac, and the period was marked by frequent disagreement between Scott and himself.[42] Upon assuming the overall command of the armies on November 1, he quickly understood that the other armies he hoped would operate in concert with his grand campaign were in no position to participate. Irrespective of the veracity of his postwar claim that the Army of the Potomac would have embarked on its mission had the other armies been equally prepared, the targeted date of December 1 was not the most opportune time to commence campaigning. His waterborne invasion plan for the spring of 1862 made excellent use of Northern resources and material advantages and carried with it every promise of success, especially since the western armies were in a position to collaborate. However, his role as general in chief of all Federal armies, thus far relegated to the quiescent winter months, was abolished by Presidential War Order No. 3 at the start of his campaign on March 11. His authority over other theaters of operation was removed, effectively destroying any unity in command and concert of action. Nor did he really control the forces allocated for his own army. The administration's exaggerated fears for the safety of Washington saw to it that his hope to overwhelm the enemy on the Peninsula was tampered with to the extent that he never commanded the numbers required for a successful execution of his strategy. The unified command structure scrapped on March 11 would not be restored until Grant came east in 1864. There is much to be said for Harsh's verdict that McClellan's strategy never actually failed because "it was abandoned and never tested."[43]

McClellan's cherished dream of fighting the war along conciliatory lines also fell by the wayside by July 1862, and it has been historically

42. Mark Grimsley, "Overthrown: The Truth Behind the McClellan-Scott Feud," *Civil War Times Illustrated* 19 (Dec. 1980): 20–29.

43. Harsh, "Lincoln's Tarnished Brass," 139. Harsh and Reed vociferously denounced that presidential order. Reed suggests that the moment McClellan was deprived of overall command, "the Union had no strategic plan for defeating the Confederacy. Each department commander was permitted to define his own objectives and all competed for the necessary resources." See Rowena Reed, *Combined Operations in the Civil War* (Annapolis: U.S. Naval Institute, 1978), 189. Despite McClellan's belief that he could "do it all," and the essentially correct opinions of Harsh and Reed, a strong case can be made that the complexities of commanding such a large and significant campaign in Virginia were enough for any one person to cope with. Perhaps McClellan's strategic principles might have been better served had he remained in Washington in overall command and another field general been assigned the Army of the Potomac.

deemed as unrealistic from the start. To a large degree, however, this assessment has been propagated and nurtured by presenting McClellan's views out of context. Moreover, those views suffer by invidious comparison to the strategic principles adopted by Grant and Sherman later in the war. In its time, however, McClellan's views were both appropriate and consistent with the national, political, and military perspective.

The death of the pure conciliatory policy can be attributed directly to McClellan's failure before the gates of Richmond. Success there would most likely have validated his strategy. It also failed because the assumptions upon which it was based were overly optimistic. Northerners attached too much importance to the slave power conspiracy and underestimated popular support for the rebellion, which mushroomed even more in the wake of the Southern victory at Second Manassas. Latent Unionist sentiment throughout the South could not be expected to gush forth with a single victory in only one sector of the Confederacy. Loyalist support could be counted upon only with outright Federal dominion or the exercise of raw military power in all sectors. Finally, that strategy had been predicated upon the quick and decisive defeat of the enemy army outside of Richmond. When that did not materialize, the passions generally aroused in warfare, especially in civil wars, gradually eroded the underlying restraint of conciliation. McClellan, despite all his efforts to control those passions, realized the inherent difficulties, and he acknowledged as much in his July 11 missive to Hill Carter. After apologizing for the depredations committed against Carter's property by his army, he confessed that "circumstances beyond my control have often defeated my purposes." Soldiers, and what they learn and do in the course of soldiering, helped undermine the effectiveness of the conciliatory policy.[44]

Nonetheless, the fact that the policies of conciliation and limited war ultimately failed does not mean that McClellan had developed a myopic strategy. Others, including Grant and Sherman, endorsed the same strat-

---

44. Sears, *Civil War Papers of George B. McClellan,* 352. Grimsley's "postmortem" on the failure of conciliation offers a fitting summary: "More than anything else, McClellan's failure on the Peninsula triggered the collapse of conciliation, because it dramatically increased the other pressures already at work: the Radicals who wanted to expand the war's goals, the troops who had never embraced the policy, and most importantly, the average Northern civilian, who saw a seemingly imminent triumph disappear into a stalemate whose duration no one could predict." See Grimsley, *The Hard Hand of War,* 94–95.

egy to varying degrees. Despite their exposure to guerilla warfare in Missouri that might well have accelerated their appreciation for harsher war measures, Grant and Sherman endorsed basic conciliatory policies throughout McClellan's tenure of command. Their evolution towards hard warfare[45] was a gradual one and was marked by considerably more restraint than is popularly held.

The Sherman of 1861–1862 was no more opposed to the conciliatory policy than McClellan was to harsher measures when the situation called for it.[46] Moreover, his path to adopting hard warfare was punctuated with episodes of self-doubt and remorse. Perhaps he was reminded of his pleasurable relationships with Southerners, many of whom he counted as friends. His fondest recollections of life before the war centered on his stint as superintendent of the military school in Louisiana. The same Sherman who, in July 1861, could counsel his daughter to spurn derogatory terms such as "rebels" was again writing in October 1862 that he still felt as though he were "fighting my own people, many of whom I knew in earlier years, and with many of whom I was once very intimate." As commander of occupied Memphis, he regretted that his army was looked upon as "invaders" and that he was perceived as a "brutal wretch." He did his best to assure Memphians of his peaceful intentions. "We tell them we want nothing they have . . . their houses . . . their farms, their niggers . . . ," he told Minnie, "but they don't believe us, and I fear that this universal feeling will cause the very result they profess to dread."[47] In truth, Sherman's kindness and fairness during his tenure in Memphis was such that it approached legendary status, in his brother's opinion. His brother thought that Sherman was falling far behind popular sentiment in the North, where people were clamoring for more punishment and less conciliation.

45. Grimsley is one with Mark Neely, Jr., in arguing that Grant and Sherman adopted a more "pragmatic" policy than the total war view that has often been attributed to their genius. At varying times throughout the war, they alternated between conciliatory and hard war policies as circumstances dictated. See Neely, "Was the Civil War a Total War?" 5–28; and Grimsley, *The Hard Hand of War,* 222.

46. McClellan, for example, ordered Brig. Gen. Thomas W. Sherman on the Sea Islands off the coast of South Carolina to seize "all the cotton and other property which may be used to our prejudice." The cotton would then be sold in the North and the revenue deposited in government coffers. Moreover, this cotton was to be loaded upon north-bound ships by the abandoned slaves who also were ordered to be used in military construction projects. See *OR,* vol. 6, 1:192.

47. Quoted in Fellman, *Citizen Sherman,* 139.

John informed William that the mounting criticism against him was a result of his "leniency to the rebels."[48]

Even with his army on the march, Sherman was meticulous in reminding the troops to conduct themselves with complete probity. Sherman's obsession with order compelled him to be on guard against behavior that would lead to a breach in discipline. In Marszalek's opinion, Sherman always believed that war had to be conducted along acceptable rules of conduct, or it would descend into anarchy and defeat. Throughout his 1862 campaigns, and well into 1863, Sherman repeatedly posted orders that banned wanton pillaging and liberal foraging. "Our mission is to maintain, not to violate laws, human and divine," he implored. He instructed his staff to assist him in "bringing to condign punishment the cowardly rascals who hang back when danger threatens, but are foremost in stealing, robbing, and plundering." The Sherman who waged relentless and destructive warfare upon the population of the South was still more than a year away. During his campaigns leading up to 1864, he practiced hard war only when guerilla activities provoked his wrath and called for a retribution that would discourage future depredations. If he ultimately evolved into the destructive warrior that Charles Royster portrays, he remained a very discriminate one up to then, and as Neely contends, he was not so great a revolutionary in his own mind.[49]

Grant contended that his conversion to a more punitive style of warfare occurred in the bloody aftermath of the battle at Shiloh. From that point forward, Grant forsook any hopes that the war could be won in any fashion other than the "complete conquest" of the Southern people.[50] His actions after Shiloh, however, betrayed his memory. Like Sherman, Grant, who had early exposure to the horrors of guerilla warfare in Missouri, continued to be selective in the way he turned Northern military

48. Fellman, *Citizen Sherman*, 138. As late as December 14, 1862, well after McClellan had been relieved of command, Sherman boasted to an old friend that his conciliatory approach toward the citizens of Memphis was paying off in big dividends. "Thousands of people who hated us with the deep hate of secessionists," Sherman declared, "now respect our authority and obey the laws of the United States from a sense of respect." This only confirmed an earlier message to his brother John: "I have a strong hold on the people here who admit that I am just and strictly legal in all my acts." See Fellman, *Citizen Sherman*, 139.

49. Marszalek, *Sherman: A Soldier's Passion for Order*, 195, 222–23; Royster, *The Destructive War*, 89; Neely, "Was the Civil War a Total War?" 20.

50. Grant, *Memoirs* 1:368–69; Ulysses S. Grant, "The Battle of Shiloh," in *Battles and Leaders* 1:486.

might against the resources and morale of Southerners. He proved decidedly more ambivalent in his application of hard war measures than he later claimed. Throughout the end of December 1862, Grant required officers to issue receipts for all goods taken from the local populations of Mississippi. Even as late as July 1863, after the collapse of Vicksburg, Grant practiced a pale version of the hard war policy in central Mississippi. "Impress upon the men," Grant instructed Sherman, "the importance of going through the State in an orderly manner, abstaining from taking anything not absolutely necessary for their subsistence while travelling. They should try to create as favorable an impression upon the people." He approved Sherman's request to provide battle-ravaged Jackson, Mississippi, with the necessities of life. He rationalized that kindness as simple justice. "I thought it only fair," he recalled, "that we should return to these people some of the articles we had taken while marching through the country." For Grimsley, his detailed study of Union military policy throughout the entire war revealed that in the western theater liberal foraging intensified as the war progressed, but it still remained selective. In the East, however, Grimsley concludes that "both official policy and actual conduct changed little from the days of McClellan."[51]

Sometimes a great principle develops into the promise of its own logic. More often, it does not. Such is the case with McClellan. His vision of a limited war with minimal casualties and little destruction of property foundered at the very gates of Richmond. His guiding strategy and policy, deemed unrealistic in hindsight, remained consistent with the views expressed by his own government and people at the time. Even after Antietam, his conservative principles still retained vitality and legitimacy as the results of the fall congressional elections of 1862 evinced.[52] Nevertheless, the day of limited warfare with its conciliatory thrust had passed at Antietam. If the attempts at policy making by Frémont and Hunter proved slightly premature in the months before the Seven Days' Battle,

51. *OR*, ser. 3, vol. 17, 2:336; Grant, *Memoirs* 1:577; Grimsley, *The Hard Hand of War*, 212.

52. A study of the fall elections in Illinois points out that the "Republican party fared poorly . . . especially in the North and Midwest." Displeasure with the administration's policies put thirty-four Democrats into the House of Representatives, cost the Republicans the gubernatorial posts in New York and New Jersey, and led to the Democratic capture of the state houses in Illinois, Indiana, and New Jersey. See Bruce Tap, "Race, Rhetoric, and Emancipation: The Election of 1862 in Illinois," *Civil War History* 39 (June 1993): 101.

then, McClellan's adherence to a vision of yesterday appeared archaic in the days after Antietam. By the fall of 1862, he most certainly had become a political liability to the adminstration. Lincoln's delay in removing him from command may well have been prompted by the passing of the elections rather than by the progress of his campaign into Virginia. McClellan's intransigence over the ascendancy of radical views by the fall of 1862 most likely made him a military liability as well. The administration needed commanders willing to fight the violent and remorseless struggle the Civil War had become.

5

Dodging the Albatross: McClellan and Grant and the Safety of Washington

ONE OF THE REASONS THE ARMY OF THE POTOMAC AP-
peared to experience less success than the western armies of Ulysses
S. Grant and William T. Sherman in the early part of the war was
its need to defend Washington from Confederate invasion. Robert E.
Lee parlayed that concern into strategies that both thwarted Federal
efforts to capture Richmond and hindered the Army of the Potomac from
making bold offensives across the Virginia landscape. Nowhere, and at no
other time, was fear for the safety of Washington a more determining factor in affecting a strategic outcome than it was in George B. McClellan's
drive up the Peninsula in the spring and early summer of 1862.

The strategic groundwork of the Peninsula campaign was shaped
by McClellan's February 3 memorandum in which he outlined in detail
the scope of the Urbanna plan. When General Joseph E. Johnston abandoned his defensive works near Manassas on March 9 and retreated to
the Richmond side of the Rappahannock River, McClellan was forced
to alter his plans accordingly. Shifting his focus south, McClellan decided that the army would be landed on the Peninsula. The options of
where to land the force quickly narrowed to one because the others
featured handicaps that could not be quickly surmounted. McClellan
would be compelled to land his gigantic force at Fortress Monroe, at the
tip of the Peninsula, and make his way up the sixty-odd miles to Richmond. One of the principal conditions Lincoln imposed upon McClellan's

plans was that he retain an adequate defense for the protection of the Federal capital.[1]

On March 17, Brig. Gen. Charles S. Hamilton's division of the Third Corps embarked from the wharves at Alexandria, en route to Fortress Monroe. That act initiated McClellan's prodigious task of bypassing the overland route to Richmond and taking a waterborne passage. The day before, McClellan had confidently written to his friend and mentor, Samuel Barlow, that he expected to "leave here on the wing for Richmond–which you may be sure I will take." A full week had not passed before news arrived that Confederate Maj. Gen. Thomas J. "Stonewall" Jackson was pressing Federal forces in the Shenandoah Valley under the overall command of Gen. Nathaniel P. Banks. At Kernstown, Brig. Gen. James Shields had fought Jackson stubbornly, even garnering a tactical victory, but he eventually was compelled to retreat down the Valley towards Winchester. Banks, fearful of Jackson's potential for trouble, suspended the forwarding of additional reinforcements for the Peninsula. One week later, on March 31, Lincoln notified McClellan that the situation in the Valley required the detention of Brig. Gen. Louis Blenker's division in order to beef up Banks's sagging fortunes.

The loss of Blenker's ten thousand troops, also known as the German division, was the beginning of what T. Harry Williams labeled the "decimation of McClellan's army." The most unfortunate aspect of that decision was the political motivation that prompted it. Frémont, the darling of the Radical Republicans, had been without an army or assignment since his removal from Missouri the previous November. On March 12, Lincoln had assured McClellan that he was opposed to detaching Blenker's Germans just to satisfy Frémont and his supporters. Nevertheless, three weeks later, Blenker was assigned to Frémont's newly minted Mountain Department, after the "Pathfinder" dangled the bait of a liberated East Tennessee in front of Lincoln's eyes. In a kindly gesture, the president wrote McClellan, informing him that it was a painful yet necessary decision. "If you could know the full pressure of the case," Lincoln confided to McClellan, "I am confident that you would

---

1. Portions of this chapter appeared earlier in somewhat altered form as Thomas J. Rowland, "'Heaven Save a Country Governed by Such Counsels!' The Safety of Washington and the Peninsula Campaign," *Civil War History* 42 (Mar. 1996): 5–17. The various options McClellan considered in his revised plans for the Peninsula campaigns are discussed in Harsh, "Lincoln's Tarnished Brass," 136–37.

justify it, even beyond a mere acknowledgement the commander-in-chief may order what he pleases."[2]

McClellan only issued a mild protest over Blenker's reassignment just before he set sail for the Peninsula. As it was the first tinkering with his plans, McClellan graciously promised to "use all the more activity to make up for the loss of this Division." According to Williams, Lincoln should have resisted both the pressure from the radical chieftains and Frémont's offer to take Knoxville. Frémont had enough troops to hold West Virginia, as well as to cooperate in the Shenandoah Valley, but nowhere near enough, even with Blenker's division, to take Knoxville. Blenker's soldiers ended up serving no one's advantage. While they might have been useful to McClellan in the early days of the Peninsula campaign, they were too exhausted from their long and rugged march in reaching Frémont to be of any use for days.[3]

While McClellan appeared to accept the loss of Blenker's division, he was not prepared for what was in store for him upon his arrival at Fortress Monroe. On the Peninsula he was greeted with the news that the secretary of war, Edwin Stanton, believing a sufficient host had already been raised and the army was on the move, had suspended recruiting efforts and disbanded recruitment stations throughout the Union.[4]

While that move did not adversely affect the initial operations as McClellan approached Yorktown, it would have a serious impact upon the government's ability to satisfy reinforcement requests as the campaign progressed. Reflecting upon that decision years later, McClellan noted that both common sense and military history dictated that when an army commenced a major undertaking it was imperative that every possible effort be enacted to "collect recruits and establish depots, whence the inevitable daily losses may be made good with instructed men . . . so that the fighting force may be kept up to their normal strength." McClellan continued to believe that Stanton's decision was prompted either by a desire to see the campaign flatly fail or by the secretary's sheer incompetence, and he rather wistfully added that "between the horns of this dilemma the friends of Mr. Stanton must take their choice."[5]

2. T. Harry Williams, *Lincoln and the Radicals*, 130; Basler, *Collected Works of Abraham Lincoln* 7:138; McClellan, *McClellan's Own Story*, 164.

3. Sears, *Civil War Papers of George B. McClellan*, 219–20; T. Harry Williams, *Lincoln and His Generals*, 77.

4. McClellan, *McClellan's Own Story*, 258.

5. Ibid., 258.

Later, in July, after the appalling casualties of the Seven Days' Battle had been tallied, Lincoln realized the mistake in allowing Stanton to suspend ongoing recruitment in the North the previous April. Lincoln feared, however, that a sudden call for massive volunteers would betray the government's panic, not to mention exposing the administration's earlier egregious error. At that critical juncture, the clever Seward came to Lincoln's rescue with an ingenious scheme. Rushing to New York, Seward convinced a meeting of Northern governors to allow him to draft an address on their behalf, urging the president to call upon the states to raise additional volunteers to "speedily crush the rebellion." By backdating the request appealing for recruits to June 28, Seward engineered it to look like the governors were prevailing upon Lincoln to resume recruitment. Pretending to comply, Lincoln on July 2 called for three hundred thousand new volunteers, thus allowing the president to save face.[6]

Of more immediate interest to McClellan was determining the best angle of approach and advance on the Peninsula. In most of the options, he hoped and thought, he had the navy's pledge of cooperation. McClellan's consideration of the James River as his base of operations, by far the most desirable of all the available options, was quickly dismissed by Flag Officer Louis M. Goldsborough's refusal to contest the waters of the James with the specter of the CSS *Virginia* looming over Hampton Roads. The second most attractive option also depended upon the navy's participation. In that scenario, the navy would assist McClellan in securing control of the York River by escorting part of his army, at least a corps, up to West Point on the Pamunkey River, roughly thirty-five miles shy of Richmond. The remainder of McClellan's army would land at Fortress Monroe and work its way up the Peninsula. That would place the Confederate army at Yorktown in a virtual vice grip. Its commander, General John Magruder would have to risk the capture of his entire force by remaining, or he would have to retreat quickly to Richmond, thus evacuating his fortifications at Yorktown. In either eventuality, McClellan's army would be able to climb the Peninsula with relative ease and haste.[7]

6. Basler, *Collected Works of Abraham Lincoln* 5:292–97.

7. Harsh, "Lincoln's Tarnished Brass," 137–38. See also "Narrative of Rear-Admiral Goldsborough, U.S. Navy," in *U.S. Naval Institute Proceedings* (Annapolis: U.S. Naval Academy, 1933), 59:1025.

That plan was immediately undermined by Stanton's failure to secure transport sufficient to carry any force larger than a division up to West Point. Revising his plans yet again, McClellan went ahead with the landing of the larger force at Fortress Monroe, with the idea that by the time McDowell's Corps, scheduled last to embark, was ready to move, the transport would be available. But his plans were thwarted once more. The navy, as in the case of the James, appeared equally unwilling to run the batteries overlooking the York River, thus forcing McClellan to put Yorktown to siege. His repeated efforts to induce Goldsborough and his subordinate, Captain J. F. Missroon, to assist in a combined operation met with refusal. The navy contended that the currents were too powerful for its gunboats to safely navigate and that the opposing batteries were too formidable. Moreover, Missroon argued, he did not have enough experienced staff officers to entrust with such an undertaking.[8]

Yet McClellan's greatest disappointment in the earliest days of the campaign would be reserved for Lincoln's decision to withhold the entire First Corps under Maj. Gen. Irvin McDowell that was to embark for the Peninsula on April 4. Bereft of naval support and beguiled by the ruses of Confederate Maj. Gen. John B. Magruder, McClellan had decided that Yorktown could be reduced only by investing it with a siege. The ink on McClellan's dispatch to McDowell, informing him of his role in assisting siege operations, had barely dried when he received word of Lincoln's command. To McClellan's thinking, McDowell's corps could be used to threaten Confederate positions at Gloucester Point, which lay opposite Yorktown on the York River. On April 5, McClellan begged the president to "reconsider the order detaching the first Corps from [my] command," as it would seriously imperil the expeditious reduction of Yorktown. His request was denied, although Lincoln did eventually release Maj. Gen. William B. Franklin's division of McDowell's corps for service on the Peninsula on April 22. According to Franklin's explanation to McClellan, McDowell claimed that Stanton's decision was "intended as a blow to you." Franklin also mentioned that McDowell had taken his case to the secretary of war, where he said that he "used all the arguments he knew of to convince Stanton that he was making a mistake." As a final measure, Wool's ten thousand-man force at Fortress Monroe was ordered to remain independent of McClellan's command. To McClellan's

8. *OR,* vol. 11, 3:80–82.

importuning for additional reinforcements, Lincoln responded that the general had better break the stalemate at Yorktown at once. "You must act," he implored McClellan.[9]

The restraint manifested in his objection to the government was not reflected in his private correspondence. To Ellen, he wrote that he had just begun to train his artillery at Magruder's fortifications when he "received the order detaching McDowell's Corps from my command–it is the most infamous thing that history has recorded. . . . [T]he idea of depriving a General of 35,000 troops when actually under fire!" Nor was McClellan the only one who objected strenuously to the president's decision. It even came from unlikely sources. Gen. Samuel P. Heintzelman, who had sided with the minority opinion against McClellan's Urbanna plans, viewed McDowell's recall as a "great outrage." Welles, another acerbic critic of McClellan's, believed the decision was part and parcel of the radicals' scheme to pressure McClellan into resigning so that a general of their own choosing could assume command. In a campaign retrospective, *Harper's Weekly* concluded that it was impossible "to exaggerate the mischief which has been done by division of counsels and civilian interference with military movements."[10]

The entire matter of reducing McClellan's campaign force was occasioned by the failure of the Federal command in and around the Shenandoah Valley to contain Jackson's striking force and unfortunate misunderstandings over the size and location of Washington's defenders. Historians, turned accountants, have worked up considerable lather in documenting the actual number of personnel McClellan assigned for the defense of Washington. McClellan, eager to depart the intrigues and complexities of headquartering in "that sink of iniquity," Washington, dashed a report off to the War Department, tallying the capital's defenders, on the very day he departed Alexandria for the Peninsula.[11] This was his one mistake in the ensuing ordeal; he should have taken more time to explain his arrangements to Lincoln and Stanton.

His figures reflected the total of all forces in and around Washington that could effectively rally for defensive purposes. By his reckoning, that

9. Ibid. 1:10, 3:66. Franklin's comments can be found in Sears, *Civil War Papers of George B. McClellan*, 231n.1; Franklin to McClellan, Apr. 7, 1862, McClellan Papers, Manuscript Division, Library of Congress; Basler, *Collected Works of Abraham Lincoln* 5:184–85.

10. Sears, *Civil War Papers of George B. McClellan*, 230; Heintzelman, *Diary*, Apr. 3, 1862; Beale and Brownsword, eds., *Diary of Gideon Welles* 1:349; *Harper's Weekly*, Aug. 9, 1862.

11. Sears, *Civil War Papers of George B. McClellan*, 223.

force totaled nearly seventy-four thousand. McClellan made allowance for
the fact that the city's actual defenders numbered only eighteen thousand
effectives by pointing out the available garrisons in Warrenton, Manassas,
the lower Potomac, and the Shenandoah. Moreover, he alluded to additional forces being collected for service in New York and to the fact that
Baltimore and the Eastern Shore of Maryland had nearly eight thousand additional defenders.[12] McClellan was convinced he had satisfied the
president's mandate for an adequate defense of Washington while he was
campaigning on the Peninsula. His allocations, moreover, satisfied the recommendations of all corps commanders in the Army of the Potomac.
Before he embarked from Alexandria, McClellan had taken pains to point
out to Brig. Gen. James Wadsworth, an aging politician-general appointed
for the defensive fortifications surrounding the capital, to "exercise vigi-
lance in your front, carefully guard the approaches in that quarter, and
maintain the duties of advance guards." He further recommended that
Wadsworth provide detailed weekly and monthly reports to both the war
department and army headquarters so that adjustments in the troop dispositions could address any exigency.[13]

Lincoln and Stanton, however, took a more rigid and static view of
the disposition of the capital's defenders. Shortly after Jackson's first foray
into the Valley, Wadsworth registered a formal complaint about the state
of the capital's defenses. Emphasizing that his force of 19,022 was in-
sufficient for the task at hand and that McClellan was even requesting
reinforcements from that number, Wadsworth highlighted the fact that
his command was the only one between Jackson and the capital since
Banks had been shoved far down the Valley.[14] Encouraged by Stanton and
several members of the Committee on the Conduct of the War, Lincoln
made inquiries into the troop allocations and decided that McClellan
had not arranged a suitable defense. That opinion led to the retention of
McDowell's corps in front of the capital.

The extraordinary concerns for the safety of the capital contrasted
sharply with the months of endless nagging for McClellan to assume the
offensive. Those fears also belie the initial ambivalence many politicians,
including the adminstration, had demonstrated toward defensive fortifications. For many, the focus on entrenchments was a demoralizing influence

12. *OR*, vol. 5, 1:60–61.
13. Ibid., 56.
14. Ibid., 61.

upon the army. Fortifications encouraged caution and robbed new volunteers of the initiative and verve needed to take the war to the enemy. During the winter hiatus in Washington, McClellan had been appalled by the resistance politicians and certain military advisors showed toward enhancing the capital's defenses. His hope to move an overwhelming force to destroy the enemy army was predicated on having a defensive structure in his rear to thwart any enemy feints toward the capital. Moreover, the very troops needed for his campaign army had to come from those forces that had heretofore provided the capital's defense. It was a basic strategic and tactical assumption for McClellan. Yet his attempts to employ engineering personnel to make Washington safe from attack were either rebuffed or ignored by an ill-informed Congress and president.[15]

The soundness of McClellan's plans for the defense of Washington has been endlessly argued by generations of historians. Unfortunately, the issue of appropriateness gets obscured in a maze of bean counting. Surprisingly, McClellan, normally reviled as overly cautious, had devised a more fluid defense structure than the political leaders could comprehend. McClellan's concept of a mobile defense force envisioned that any threat the Confederates might risk while the Army of the Potomac moved upon Richmond could easily be managed by the consolidation of Federal forces within easy marching distance of Washington. He immediately saw Jackson's plunge down the Valley for what it was—a diversion. It was intended only to frighten the Federal government into calling a halt to the massive concentration of force just outside their own capital.[16] It worked.

Washington's fears were exacerbated by the frightful performance of political generals assigned to deal with Jackson in the Valley. That concerns for the safety of Washington reached nail-biting proportions in May 1862 with Jackson's reappearance in the Valley can only be attributed to the sheer incompetence of Nathaniel Banks and John Charles Frémont, both of whom were entrusted with the security of that region. Actually, Lincoln and Stanton must be accorded some of the blame. It had not been necessary to appoint two separate commands in the Valley. Courtesy to the political sensibilities of either Banks or Frémont should have

15. Ibid., 678; T. Harry Williams, "The Attack Upon West Point during the Civil War," *Mississippi Valley Historical Review* 25 (Mar. 1939); and T. Harry Williams, *Lincoln and His Generals,* 224; Edward Hagerman, "The Professionalization of George B. McClellan and Early Civil War Field Command," *Civil War History* 12 (June 1975): 119.

16. Sears, *Civil War Papers of George B. McClellan,* 222–23.

been subordinated to the requirements of organization. Banks's force of nineteen thousand and Frémont's of sixteen thousand should have been consolidated into one command. Although hardly needed, McDowell's command, once retained, should have been merged with that command. Together, their coordinated movements could have stymied Jackson. As it was, all three forces operated independently and frequently at cross purposes. Frémont, who was known for finding new paths, was the most conspicuous in failing to respond with anything approaching alacrity to notices of Jackson's whereabouts. McDowell did a lot of marching but that was about it. The consequences of such folly played into Confederate hands. Structured as it was, Banks's equally numbered force could not contain the lightning thrusts of the professional Jackson at Front Royal and Winchester and was dispatched into a helter-skelter flight down the Valley to the banks of the Potomac by the last week of May 1862. Those who defend Lincoln's decision to retain McDowell's corps with the hope of snagging Jackson in the Valley need to admit that he mishandled the coordination of those forces.[17]

McClellan's insistence that the very presence of the Army of the Potomac on the outskirts of Richmond would serve as Washington's guarantee of safety was lost upon the shattered nerves of the government. Undoubtedly, Lincoln was correct in admonishing McClellan that the demoralizing loss of Washington, no matter how temporarily, would never be forgiven by the Northern people.[18] However, the lesson in political sensitivity, not only gratuitous in nature, missed the point. Washington was safe because the Confederates were not able and not inclined to mount an offensive with their own capital in peril. While Joseph E. Johnston had toyed with some strategic notions of assaulting Washington during the early days of the Peninsula Campaign, neither he, Jefferson Davis, or Robert E. Lee seriously considered those options once the size of McClellan's force became apparent.[19] Had the Confederates risked such a dangerous move, their progress would have been impeded by Johnston's own destruction of railroad lines and bridge crossings upon

17. Nevins, *War for the Union* 2:123–24. Two recent studies provide all the necessary details of Jackson's campaign in the Valley. See Robert K. Krick, *Conquering the Valley: Stonewall Jackson at Port Republic* (New York: William Morrow, 1996); and Robert G. Tanner, *Stonewall in the Valley* (Mechanicsburg, Pa.: Stackpole, 1996).

18. Letter from Lincoln to McClellan, Apr. 9, 1862, in John G. Nicolay and John Hay, eds., *The Complete Works of Abraham Lincoln*, vol. 7 (New York: Century, 1905), 141–43.

19. Long, *Memoirs of Robert E. Lee*, 151.

his retreat from Manassas. The resulting delays in reconstruction would have allowed the Federal government ample time to summon a formidable defensive force and would have left McClellan free to walk into Richmond. Indeed, the destruction of those transportation conduits conveyed to most military professionals, particularly McClellan, that the Confederates had no plans to seriously threaten Washington. Indeed, as Magruder delayed McClellan at Yorktown, Johnston was shuffling reinforcements to the front.[20]

Any preliminary thoughts McClellan might have had about using the James River as his supply base had been thwarted by the lingering presence of the CSS *Virginia* at Gosport Navy Yard in Norfolk. Consequently, he settled on the York River. It was hardly a difficult choice, as the York flowed into the Pamunkey, which allowed him to establish a base at the landing at White House. From White House the Richmond and York River Railroad could funnel supplies to the ever-expanding front on Richmond's outskirts and permit the transport of the heavy ordnance siege guns that increasingly became uppermost in McClellan's plans. Confederate dominance of the James River ended on May 11 when Norfolk was captured and the crew of the CSS *Virginia* were obliged to scuttle the ironclad. With that action, Federal control of both the James and York Rivers was complete.[21]

The significant drawback of the York River base was that both sides of the Chickahominy River, over which the Richmond and York River Railroad traversed, would have to be made secure. Under normal conditions, the Chickahominy River was a lazy, turgid stream that could be forded easily in the event one portion of the Federal army needed support from the other. The climate of May 1862, however, emerged as a meteorological curse to the Federal army. The area witnessed the heaviest amount of precipitation in local memory, and the Chickahominy became a raging torrent, forbidding simple fording and constantly threatening the structural integrity of its bridges.[22]

20. Sears, *Civil War Papers of George B. McClellan,* 220. On April 21, 1862, Lee notified Jackson in the Valley that Fredericksburg had already been abandoned, that bridges had been burned, and that the rear guard of Johnston's army was already fourteen miles south of the town. See Dowdy and Manarin, *Wartime Papers of Robert E. Lee,* 150.

21. *OR,* vol. 11, 1:634, 1163.

22. Weather observations can be found in numerous sources. McClellan's complaints about the weather and its impact upon operations between the Confederate evacuation of Yorktown and the beginning of the Seven Days campaign can be found in Sears, *Civil War*

On May 16, Johnston retired his entire force to the south side of the Chickahominy. On May 21 and 22, McClellan began to transfer the bulk of the Federal army from the north to the south side, closer to Richmond and on the heels of the retreating Confederates. He harbored no particular apprehensions for his supply lines nor for the only remaining corps left on the north side under the command of Brig. Gen. Fitz John Porter since on May 17, with the subsidence of activity in the Valley, McDowell's corps was aroused from its lethargy in Fredericksburg and ordered to advance towards Richmond and link with Porter's right.[23] That move would position two whole corps on the north side, which would secure the Federal right flank and would add to the pressure now building up against Richmond. To assist in linking the two corps, McClellan ordered Porter to extend his line northwestward and eliminate the remaining Confederate force at Hanover Court House on the Virginia Central Railroad. By May 29, Porter had destroyed all the railroads leading northward from Richmond and had removed the rebel menace at Hanover Court House.[24]

McClellan felt quite confident at that point. The enemy was offering little resistance, and the bulk of his troops were crossing the Chickahominy and forcing the Confederates to the outskirts of Richmond. His right wing appeared secure, particularly with the knowledge that McDowell would soon be joining it. He might not have felt as confident had he understood from the outset that Stanton's instructions to McDowell continued to reflect the wariness and indecision that had prompted the first recall. While encouraging McDowell to establish a "communication between your left wing and the right wing of General McClellan," Stanton applied the brakes by warning him to "hold yourself always in such position as to cover the capital . . . against a sudden dash of any large body of rebel forces."[25] As if on cue, Jackson launched his army against Banks in the Valley. Banks's retreat led to the revocation of McDowell's orders to join McClellan. On May 24, Lincoln telegraphed McClellan with the news that as a result of Banks's "critical position," he would be "compelled

---

Papers of George B. McClellan, 256–312. For corroborating testimony, see also Richard B. Sommers, "'They fired into us an awful fire': The Civil War Diary of Pvt. Charles C. Perkins," in William Miller, ed., *The Peninsula Campaign* 1:143–76. See also Heintzelman's pocket diary in Samuel P. Heintzelman Papers, Manuscript Division, Library of Congress.

23. *OR,* vol. 11, 1:637–38.

24. For Porter's version of the operations around Hanover Court House, see Fitz John Porter, "Hanover Court House and Gaines's Mill," in *Battles and Leaders* 1:319–23.

25. *OR,* vol. 11, 1:28.

to suspend Gen. McDowell's movement to join you." Moreover, Lincoln advised McClellan that he had better "attack Richmond or give up the job and come to the defence of Washington."[26]

McClellan was flabbergasted. "I have this moment received a dispatch from the Presdt [*sic*] who is terribly scared about Washington," he fumed in a letter to his wife on May 25, "& [he] talks about the necessity of my returning in order to save it. . . . Heaven save a country governed by such counsels!" After noting that Banks had been "soundly thrashed," and that "they are terribly scared in Washn. [*sic*]," he bitterly added that a "scare will do them good, & may bring them to their senses."[27] In responding to Lincoln's telegram, McClellan tempered his rhetoric and noted that he was fast approaching the point where he would be pressing the matter with the enemy. He returned to the subject of McDowell's recall in his telegram to the president on May 26, saying that he was undertaking the last of his preparations and would be "free to strike on the return of the force detached."[28] Two days later, Lincoln consoled his commander by promising to aid him to the extent he could, as long as it was consistent with his view on all theaters of operation. He also refuted McClellan's assessment that the rebels were concentrating against the Army of the Potomac, remarking that it "could not be certainly known to you or me."[29]

That McClellan would groan over the second suspension of the First Corps' marching orders surprised no one. McDowell's protest, however, commands greater respect because he was a disinterested barometer of military opinion on the wisdom of that order. Had Porter or Franklin issued vehement denunciations of the president's orders, it could have been dismissed as cronyism; the two of them were McClellan devotees and owed their rapid rise in the army to their commander's patronage. McDowell, however, was hardly one of McClellan's admirers. As Samuel

---

26. Basler, *Collected Works of Abraham Lincoln* 5:232, 235–36. McClellan might have underestimated Lee's capacity for leadership, but he respected Jackson's. On February 2, 1862, he had advised Gen. Frederick W. Lander to look out for Jackson, who he knew "to be a man of vigor and nerve, as well as a good soldier." See Sears, *Civil War Papers of George B. McClellan*, 162.

27. Sears, *Civil War Papers of George B. McClellan*, 275–76.

28. Ibid., 276–77.

29. McClellan, *McClellan's Own Story*, 373. McClellan had wired the president on May 14 that the "enemy lines were concentrating all their available force to fight this army in front of Richmond, and that such ought to be their policy." See McClellan, *McClellan's Own Story*, 343–44.

Chase's protege, he was held in high esteem in the Radical camp. He had been replaced by McClellan after the debacle at Manassas and had been the recipient of a number of slights at the hands of his successor. McDowell also suffered from McClellan's apprehensions that he was angling for his old post. Most importantly, he had initially opposed McClellan's waterborne strategy, preferring the overland route to Richmond via Fredericksburg.

If anyone would have liked to see McClellan's campaign falter, it certainly might have been McDowell. Yet, as a military professional, McDowell felt compelled to register his objections to the recall. Protesting that the decision played into the enemy's hands, McDowell wired the president that it was "a crushing blow to us." "I shall gain nothing for you there," McDowell argued in his reference to his summons to the Valley, "[and] shall lose much for you here."[30] To Wadsworth, whose actions had initiated the alarm, McDowell testily remarked that the government had better "try and get over the flutter into which this body seems to have thrown everyone," or the enemy would disrupt "all our plans." Taking his case to the secretary of war again, McDowell told him on May 28 that he did not "consider Washington City in any danger." Weeks later, he suggested to a friend that his well-equipped and high-spirited army of forty-one thousand should not have been detoured from its assignment to the Peninsula. And it should not, in his opinion, have been ordered to the Valley in a fruitless chase of Jackson. The exasperating conclusion he had reached was that nervous civilian leaders "were alarmed over the safety of Washington!"[31]

In the days following the Battle of Fair Oaks, when Johnston attempted but failed to dislodge the Federal force south of the Chickahominy, the Confederate high command became very anxious over the prospects of facing McClellan's siege force. On June 5, Robert E. Lee, Johnston's successor, opined that if Jackson could be reinforced, "It would change the character of the war." Suggesting that troops currently in North Carolina, South Carolina, and Georgia be added to the Valley force, Jackson would be free to threaten Maryland or Pennsylvania, compelling the enemy to abandon his offensive to meet the threat. That was the occasion upon which Lee soberly informed Davis that McClellan was

30. Basler, *Collected Works of Abraham Lincoln* 5:232–33.
31. *OR*, vol. 18, 1:268; Letter, Irvin McDowell to C. A. Hecksher, June 17, 1862, in S. L. M. Barlow Papers, Huntington Library.

about to "make this a battle of Posts," and that something had to be done quickly to untrack the methodical schedule, or he would not be able to successfully resist the enemy's overwhelming strength. While Lee's recommendation about stripping military units from the coastal states was largely ignored, Davis continued to support all efforts designed to prey on the fears of Washington. Jackson would never receive sufficient reinforcements to threaten either the capital or Maryland and Pennsylvania, but he did receive enough to continue making Washington squirm about his presence in the Valley.[32]

On June 8, the War Department once again ordered McDowell's corps to return to Fredericksburg from its futile mission in the Valley. The president, himself, admitted to a friend that the mission had ended disastrously. Naturally, McDowell's new orders instructed him to operate in the direction of Richmond but to cover all routes to Washington at the same time, and to McClellan's despair, McDowell's force was instructed to remain independent of his control.[33] That time, however, McDowell was much more sanguine about his reaching McClellan's army, observing that although that was the "third time" he had been ordered to join McClellan, he "hope[d] to get through." Pained by pointed inferences attributed to McClellan's friends, and the commanding general himself, that he was less than enthusiastic about moving to the Peninsula, McDowell wired that he was going "with the greatest satisfaction," and he planned to "arrive with my main body in time to be of service." As a measure of good faith, Brig. Gen. George A. McCall's division was dispatched in advance of the main force; the bulk of the corps would reach McClellan, by McDowell's estimation, within ten days.[34]

At about the same time McDowell was ordered to mobilize, Lee had decided that a concerted attack on Porter's Fifth Corps, while holding the Federal left wing in check, could relieve the pressure on Richmond and force McClellan to fight to preserve his supply line or retreat across the surging Chickahominy. He would eventually require Jackson's army to return surreptitiously from the Valley to assist in the pincer move.

32. Lee to Davis, June 5, 1862, in Dowdy and Manarin, eds., *Wartime Papers of Robert E. Lee,* 183–84.

33. *OR*, vol. 11, 1:216, 220; Orville H. Browning, *The Diary of Orville Hickman Browning,* eds. Theodore C. Pease and James G. Randall, 2 vols. (Springfield: Illinois State Historical Library, 1925), 1:548.

34. "Telegram, Irvin McDowell to George B. McClellan, June 8, 1862," *OR*, vol. 11, 1:220–21.

To determine the strength of the Federal right, Lee ordered Col. J. E. B. Stuart to reconnoiter Union outposts on the north side of the Chickahominy.[35] Prior to launching his attack upon the Federal right, he had to make certain that McDowell's large force was neutralized; it could not effect its merger with Porter. To wit, Lee removed a small force from the Richmond defenses on June 11 and forwarded them to Jackson's command in the Valley to frighten the Union government into withholding the release of McDowell's corps. The ruse succeeded. When Frémont and Banks reported a resurgence of activity in Confederate quarters, McDowell's forward progress was checked. McClellan never saw McDowell on the Peninsula and only received McCall's reserves as reinforcement.[36]

The vacillation of the administration over how to manage Jackson's potential, although improbable, threat to the capital reached ludicrous proportions in the critical last two weeks of June 1862. Exasperated with the divided counsels he was receiving, Lincoln even solicited the opinion of the retired general Winfield Scott at West Point. In his report to Lincoln, Scott validated McClellan's perception of the issue. He contended that both Frémont and Banks were strong enough and were strategically placed to negate any threat Jackson might pose. McDowell, Scott opined, was in no position at Fredericksburg to either ably contribute to the defense of Washington or render McClellan any effective assistance. The old general recommended sending McDowell by water to the York River where he could be put to good use. Unfortunately, the recommendation was dated June 24 and was obsolete before Lincoln could digest its import.[37]

Meanwhile, on the Peninsula, McClellan was growing quite exasperated himself. With his army divided by the unpredictable Chickahominy, McClellan continued to hope that McDowell would arrive to shore up his right wing. He had, after all, extended Porter's corps to the northwest as far and as thinly as he dared in order to link up with McDowell. On June 12, he expressed his concerns to Stanton about throwing Porter's force across the Chickahominy to effect the linkage with McDowell. "An extension of my right wing to meet him," McClellan said, referring to

35. Douglas Southall Freeman, *Lee's Lieutenants: A Study in Command,* 3 vols. (New York: Scribner's 1944), 1:277.

36. *OR,* vol. 11, 1:224, 590.

37. Report, Winfield Scott to Abraham Lincoln, June 24, 1862, in Basler, *Collected Works of Abraham Lincoln* 7:233–34.

McDowell's on and off again juncture, "may involve serious hazard to my flank and my line of communications and may not suffice to rescue him from any peril in which a strong movement of the enemy may involve him." More ominously, he warned Stanton that the enemy was massing troops on his front and "giving every indication of fight." On June 16, he notified Stanton that several corroborating reports had confirmed the concentration of Confederate forces he had earlier suspected. With growing urgency, he plaintively asked Stanton to let him know "when and [in] which direction McDowell's command will come."[38] Although he received no direct reply to his question, McClellan was informed by the president on June 20 that Gen. Franz Sigel, Frémont's successor, had reported that Jackson was probably being reinforced in the Valley, even though, in truth, Jackson had already received orders and was well underway in his return to Richmond to join the planned attack upon Porter's flank.[39] Compared to Lee's precision, Lincoln's remarks seem pathetically confused. While acknowledging the possibility that Jackson's reinforcements might only be a "contrivance for deception," he could not determine it for certain, adding that if he "knew it was not true we could send you some more force." Lincoln concluded the paroxysm of confusion with the consolation that reinforcements would be sent if improving conditions in the Valley permitted it.[40] Within days, Lee, reinforced by Jackson's quiet return from the Valley, began his attack upon McClellan's right wing. During that time, McClellan never mentioned McDowell's involvement again. He had most likely given up on the issue.

Many historians are quick to point to contrasts in the way Grant and McClellan conducted their respective campaigns in Virginia. With few exceptions those differences are employed at the expense of, and in disparagement of, McClellan's skill and determination. Yet, there were striking similarities and comparisons in both campaigns that normally are overlooked. And not included in these comparisons is the enfeebled argument that McClellan arrived at the same spot on the Peninsula as Grant,

---

38. Sears, *Civil War Papers of George B. McClellan,* 299; *OR,* vol. 11, 1:231.

39. Lee had written a dispatch to Jackson, ordering him to return to Richmond with all possible dispatch. See *OR,* vol. 12, 3:913.

40. *OR,* vol. 11, 1:236. Interestingly, at the same time Lincoln was admonishing McClellan to wait patiently for reinforcement, he was lecturing Frémont that Jackson's activity in the Valley was a mere deception. See *OR,* vol. 12, 1:661.

with none of the staggering casualties his comrade in arms experienced. For starters, both generals used the Peninsula as the pivotal location for their strategy to bring the Army of Northern Virginia to bay. For Grant, the slugfest from the Rapidan to Cold Harbor had failed to bring about the destruction of Lee's army, other than the attritional benefits attached to such methods. Grant did not inaugurate his final winning strategy until he marched across the Peninsula, crossed the James, and began to threaten Richmond from the south. Both men viewed a movement towards Petersburg as a means to revive their sagging fortunes. While Grant had hoped to annihilate Lee's army somewhere between the Rapidan and the northern environs of Richmond, he realized that Lee would not offer him such a conclusive battle. The movement on Petersburg maintained his initiative and salvaged his campaign. At Harrison's Landing, McClellan had given thought to resuscitating his stalled campaign by marching on Petersburg, but changes in the enemy's troop dispositions and the administration's lack of confidence in its commander foreclosed any serious consideration of the plan at that time. Finally, neither man shrunk from the prospect of conducting a siege. McClellan had just completed the preliminary preparations to begin the investment of Richmond when Lee went on the offensive and disrupted that initiative. Grant, despite his best efforts to smash Lee, settled in for a siege—one that would last for nine months and would ultimately prevail.[41]

The Seven Days' Battle marked the climax and denouement of McClellan's campaign on the Peninsula. With Lee's onslaught on his right flank, McClellan was forced to yield his supply lines to the York River, and Porter's corps was barely extricated from its predicament. Although McClellan imposed a positive spin upon his headlong flight to the James River by referring to it as a "change of base," it was a retreat by any other name. By the time McClellan repulsed Lee's injudicious assault upon Federal positions at Malvern Hill and retired to the protection of Union gunboats on the James, the Peninsula Campaign, for all intents and purposes, was over.

It would be misleading to suggest that the reason for the failure of the Peninsula Campaign was that it was completely ruined by the Lincoln administration's exaggerated concerns for the safety of Washington. McClellan deserves his share of the blame. He was overly cautious in his

41. Reid, "Grant's Crossing of the James," 297–99; Sears, *To the Gates of Richmond*, 351–53.

advance toward Richmond and appeared too meticulous in his reduction of Magruder's obstructions at Yorktown, where he wasted a month in the early stages of the campaign. His chronic overestimation of enemy forces frittered away prime opportunities to overwhelm them before their defensive perimeter became formidable, although the reasons suggested for that miscalculation beggar belief.[42] His miscalculations eventually backfired upon McClellan. Later, when he made desperate pleas for additional troops, the administration was able to point to his inflated estimates as proof that additional reinforcement requests were fruitless against such imposing odds. Lastly, he contributed greatly to the atmosphere of distrust and rancor that marked his relations with the president and the secretary of war.

Nonetheless, Lincoln and Stanton are as culpable as McClellan for the manifest failure at the gates of Richmond. Having acceded to McClellan's strategic plans, they repeatedly hedged their bets by holding back a significant part of the invasion force. They injected a serious degree of confusion at the most critical stage of the attack by alternately promising and then failing to support McClellan's extended right wing, which by design and necessity was isolated by the extraordinarily swollen Chickahominy River. Their decisions and mismanagement of the campaign demonstrated that they, too, were new to the ways of war. They may well have grown into capable civilian administration of the war as it progressed, but their records during the Peninsula campaign showed they were still well within the parameters of the training curve. McClellan was not entirely out of control when he penned Stanton those two infamous sentences, which a colonel in the telegraph office elected to suppress, and lambasted the administration for failing to sustain him. "If I save this army now, I tell you plainly I owe no thanks to you or to any other persons in Washington," he declared, and he added the mordant verdict, "[Y]ou have done your best to sacrifice this army.[43]

---

42. It has been speculated that McClellan was plagued by the unshakable conviction that the South was a military powerhouse and that he was vulnerable to inflated reports of Confederate troop strength. See Adams, *Our Masters the Rebels;* Edwin C. Fishel, "Pinkerton and McClellan: Who Deceived Whom?" *Civil War History* 34 (June 1988), and *The Secret War for the Union: The Untold Story of Military Intelligence in the Civil War* (Boston: Houghton-Mifflin, 1996), 581–87.

43. *OR,* vol. 11, 1:61.

In many respects, the failure of the Peninsula campaign was a result of divided command and counsels. Both military and political goals were obscured in the process. Lincoln failed McClellan by continually allowing Stanton and the war department to make decisions regarding troop dispositions that were both imprudent and undercut McClellan's strategy of overwhelming strength. McClellan, unaware that Lincoln was still willing to support him, felt that the Radical Republicans were undermining his position, and thus, he gave Lincoln numerous vague promises of action on the front that he never intended to initiate, so as to stall criticism of his campaign. Plenty of personal blame can be spread around for the poor partnership in command that emerged on the Peninsula. McClellan refused to appreciate the pressure being brought upon the president for action, and he was patently misleading in the timetables he established for assaulting the enemy. Stanton charged the atmosphere with criticism and invective, demonstrating that he was indeed the irascible character that most who made his acquaintance declared he was. Moreover, he frequently undermined the integrity of McClellan's strategy by implementing decisions that robbed McClellan of the force he needed to accomplish his mission. Lincoln also contributed to the ineffective command structure by assenting at first to McClellan's strategic designs, only to demonstrate his distrust of those plans once the campaign was underway. Although he showed an intuitive grasp of the military art, the critical blunders he made during the campaign earmarked him as a novice in the subject. And he shared with McClellan an unwillingness to be less than perfectly candid in his correspondence with his general.

Perhaps the most significant reasons why the Peninsula Campaign failed have less to do with the incompetency of the Lincoln administration and George B. McClellan than they do with the hurdles that faced McClellan and other commanders in the early part of the war. The Army of the Potomac, unlike its unfettered western counterpart, was saddled with the task of waging a war of conquest against a formidable opponent while constraining to protect their own capital at the same time. McClellan, himself, would be harried by that constraint throughout his next campaign in Maryland.

In the days following Pope's defeat at Manassas, inordinate fears for the safety of Washington were escalated by alarmists. Chief among them was the secretary of war. He ordered the Federal arsenal there emptied and sent to New York. Again, as in the days of the *Merrimac* crisis, he directed that a steamer be anchored in the Potomac to transport the president and cabinet to a safe place in the event the Confederates moved on the capital.[44] Halleck, who had the unenviable task of trying to get Pope and McClellan together at Manassas, totally collapsed on August 31, begging McClellan "to assist me in this crisis with your ability and experience. . . . I am utterly tired out."[45] After reorganizing and refitting the army and determining that Lee had begun to move into Maryland, McClellan advanced toward Frederick. To assuage concerns for the safety of the capital, McClellan left three corps behind. When combined with Banks's garrison force, the total number of troops positioned for the defense of Washington numbered 72,500.[46]

By the time McClellan was ready to move, Halleck's shattered nerves had settled enough to allow him to resume dispensing advice, something he was particularly good at, provided it did not include any responsibility. Unlike Stanton, Halleck did not initially entertain any fears for the safety of Washington. With uncanny prescience he had conjectured that Lee, who had been "baffled in his intended capture of Washington, will cross the Potomac and make a raid into Maryland or Pennsylvania." Yet, the moment McClellan went off in pursuit of Lee, Halleck became obsessed with the defense of the capital.[47] It is a small wonder, then, that McClellan advanced with caution and that any aggressive tendencies he might have possessed were clouded by an atmosphere of collective defensive-mindedness.

Despite the receipt of numerous reports that Robert E. Lee and his army were roaming throughout the Maryland countryside, Halleck continued to hamstring McClellan's northward advance. He had all but abandoned his opinion of September 3 that Lee was heading in force towards Maryland and Pennsylvania. On September 9, he telegraphed McClellan that "until we can get better advices about the numbers of the enemy at Dranesville, I think we must be very cautious about stripping too much the forts on the Virginia side." Surmising that it might be the "enemy's object to draw off the mass of our forces and then attempt to attack from the Virginia side of the Potomac," he advised McClellan to "think of this."

44. McClellan, *McClellan's Own Story*, 535–36; *OR*, vol. 12, 3:802.
45. Sears, *George B. McClellan: The Young Napoleon*, 258.
46. "Assignment of Regiments," ca. Sept. 7, 1862, McClellan Papers, Manuscript Division, Library of Congress.
47. *OR*, vol. 12, 2:169.

Two days later, he appeared to contradict himself by encouraging Mc-
Clellan to order troops from the commands of either Erasmus Keyes or
Franz Sigel to join him, since he now thought that the "main force of the
enemy is in your front." McClellan, who had been advocating the concentration of all available forces under his command all along, jumped on that
suggestion by asking for reinforcements. None were sent. Only Porter's
corps would be forwarded, arriving the day before the showdown on the
banks of the Antietam.[48]

As late as the morning of September 13, 1862, the very day McClellan
found the famous "Lost Orders" confirming Lee's troop dispositions, Halleck wired McClellan, reviving his previous anxieties over Lee's intention
to assault the capital:

> Until you know more certainly the enemy's force south of the Po-
> tomac, you are wrong in thus uncovering the capital. I am of the
> opinion that the enemy will send a small column toward Pennsyl-
> vania, so as to draw your forces in that direction; then suddenly
> move on Washington with the forces south of the Potomac. . . . In
> your letter of the 10th [11th?] you attach too little importance to
> the capital. I assure you that you are wrong. The capture of this
> place will throw us back six months, if it should not destroy us.[49]

Halleck's confusion is substantive testimony to the fact that at that
stage of the war, the art of estimating the strength and whereabouts of
the enemy was still in its amateurish splendor. Yet Halleck's telegram
of September 16 revealed that an overweening concern for the safety
of Washington superceded all other considerations. Despite the fact that
McClellan was peering across the fog-enshrouded fields of Sharpsburg,
directly at Lee's assembled army, Halleck advised him that he would find
that the "whole force of the enemy in your front has crossed the river."
Fearing that the enemy would cross the river near Harper's Ferry, Halleck
warned McClellan that Lee would "turn your left, thus cutting you off
from Washington." He glibly reminded McClellan that that "has appeared
to me to be a part of their plan, and hence my anxiety on the subject." He

---

48. McClellan, *McClellan's Own Story*, 554–55.

49. *OR*, vol. 19, 2:280–81. The letter that Halleck referred to was most probably Mc-
Clellan's September 11 missive in which he notified Halleck that Lee was in strength near
Frederick, Maryland. See *OR*, vol. 19, 2:254.

concluded his admonition by tossing McClellan the consolation that Lee might be confounded in his attempt to cross the Potomac, because a "heavy rain might prevent it." Even after the battle itself, Halleck renewed his concerns for the capital, claiming on September 19 that Lee's army, now across the Potomac, would make a bead on Washington while the Army of the Potomac remained at Sharpsburg. On September 26, Halleck attempted to pin down McClellan on his future plan of operations. Expressing his wish that McClellan would forego a planned crossing at Harper's Ferry in favor of one lower down the Potomac, "So as to cover Washington," Halleck expressed his opinion that "Washington is the real base of operations, and . . . it should not under any circumstances be exposed." So it was, and so it would be. The safety of Washington remained the paramount concern of the administration. It would compel McClellan and every other Federal commander through Grant to fashion strategic and tactical operations with that condition in mind.[50]

Some of the comparisons between the Virginia campaigns of McClellan and Grant have been highlighted earlier, but there are also a number of striking contrasts between them that historians tend to ignore. The most arresting ones can be seen in how the two generals dealt with the administration's concern for the safety of the capital, given the nature and extent of the existing threats and the relative strengths of the Army of the Potomac and the Army of Northern Virginia in 1862 and 1864.

To a degree there were some similarities in the perceived threats to the safety of Washington in 1862 and 1864. Both McClellan and Grant had the bulk of their armies to the east and southeast of the Confederate capital of Richmond. McClellan was just about to begin his siege in 1862, and Grant was barely a month into his long siege at Petersburg. Both Confederate forays into the Shenandoah Valley were devised by Lee to divert the attention of the enemy away from their grip on his army and Richmond. And both of the Confederate armies unleashed into the Shenandoah numbered near fifteen thousand.

50. McClellan, *McClellan's Own Story,* 556; *OR,* vol. 19, 2:319, 330, 339, 342, 353, 360. During Lee's next invasion of the North, Halleck advised Meade to pursue cautiously so as to keep all routes to Washington covered. See A. Wilson Greene, "Meade's Pursuit of Lee," in Gary Gallagher, ed., *The Third Day at Gettysburg and Beyond* (Chapel Hill: Univ. of North Carolina Press, 1994), 185.

Like McClellan, Grant wanted all available forces directly under his supervision to maintain the maximum pressure against the armies of the enemy. Consequently, Grant took a most cavalier approach to the safety of Washington. Aware that a great deal of money had been lavished on the fortifications encircling Washington to ensure its protection from attack, Grant believed that the garrison could fend for itself. As the casualties mounted during the Wilderness campaign, Grant began to borrow liberally from the garrisons, snaring the most experienced troops and leaving the recent arrivals to man the defenses. Moreover, the defensive works that McClellan had labored so hard to perfect had been neglected over the years and were, in the opinion of the chief engineer's assistant, Lt. Col. Barton S. Alexander, in eroded condition in July 1864.[51]

Grant also enjoyed the confidence of the president, who made no serious attempts to question the actual numbers of soldiers assigned to the defense of the capital. Lincoln was also mindful of his pledge not to interfere with Grant's decisions, knowing that he had been criticized for interfering before, especially in the case of McClellan in 1862.[52] Grant had, in fact, adopted a course of action similar to McClellan's. Included in his tally for the defense of Washington were troops stationed in the Shenandoah Valley, Harper's Ferry, Baltimore, and Harrisburg. The war department counted upwards of seventy-five thousand troops "arrayed from West Virginia to the northeast as protection for the capital region." In reality, hardly half that number were available for immediate concentration in the event of a quick strike by the enemy.[53] Unfortunately for Grant, like McClellan in 1862, part of that force was commanded by generals of dubious distinction. Weeks after Early's troops had departed the Petersburg lines on June 16, Halleck wired Grant, telling him he needed to remember that the "three principal officers on the line of the road are Sigel, Stahel, and Max Weber." Thus, Grant could judge for himself "what probability there is for a good defense if the enemy should attack the line in force."[54]

51. John Gross Barnard, *Report on the Defenses of Washington* (Washington, D.C.: GPO, 1871), 123; *OR*, vol. 37, 2:83–85.

52. Donald, *Lincoln*, 518.

53. Benjamin F. Cooling, *Jubal Early's Raid on Washington, 1864* (Baltimore: Nautical and Aviation, 1989), 37.

54. Cooling, *Jubal Early's Raid*, 37.

Grant had, in fact, weakened the defenses of Washington to a significantly greater degree than McClellan had in 1862. When the crunch came, and Early's forces were bearing down on Washington from the Mococacy Halleck was forced to issue arms to invalid soldiers and government clerks and order them to the fortifications. In fact, had it not been for General Lew Wallace's sacrifice on the Monocacy that stalled Early's advance, Washington might well have been overrun by the Confederates, as Grant confessed in his memoirs. Halleck and Stanton had once again become distraught over the safety of the government. Stanton was reported to have implored one of his own clerks, E. H. Johnson, to take his own $5 thousand in cash, as well as Mrs. Stanton's gold, and hide it in Johnson's own home. Panic spread elsewhere as well. Lincoln was embarrassed and annoyed when he heard that Welles's assistant, Gustavus V. Fox, had ordered a naval steamer made available in the Potomac in the event that Lincolns needed to escape. It may well have reminded him of Stanton's excessive alarm during the *Merrimac* and Stonewall Jackson scares of 1862. All of that was occasioned by a ragged force of fifteen thousand men under the command of Jubal Early. That reality has not escaped the notice of one historian, Benjamin F. Cooling, who flatly concluded that "Old Jube was no Jackson." These were not the "same men who followed the gallant Jackson two years before," Cooling observed. "These were weary, ill-clothed, malnourished, undisciplined troops who were possibly more interested in plunder and liquor than maintaining discipline necessary for total victory."[55]

Grant pressed on with his affairs at Petersburg with a nonchalance and disregard for the government's concern that made McClellan's attitude in 1862 pale by comparison. For the longest time, Grant was totally unaware that Early had vacated his front. But Early did so on June 16. On July 3, Grant tried to assuage Halleck's concern over reports of increased resistance in the upper Shenandoah Valley near Lynchburg against Federal forces under General David Hunter's command. Actually Hunter had already been chased, somewhat willingly, right out of the Valley and into West Virginia by that time. "Early's corps is now here," Grant trumpeted. "There are no troops that can now be threatening Hunter's department, except the remnant of the force W. E. Jones had, and possibly Breckinridge." On that very day, July 3, Early was pushing Sigel across the

---

55. Grant, *Memoirs* 2:304–06; Cooling, *Jubal Early's Raid,* 88, 249–50; Donald, *Lincoln,* 518.

Potomac and was preparing to swing southeast towards Washington. It was not until July 8 that Grant was finally persuaded that Confederate activity near the Potomac was more than a small cavalry raid. It took confirmed reports of skirmishing, preliminary to the battle at the Monocacy River on July 9, to rattle Grant from his lethargy.[56]

Lincoln, who had forced himself to remain silent on the sidelines of the unfolding drama, now leapt into action. He seized upon Grant's half-hearted offer to come to the capital himself to supervise its defense. Lincoln took him at his word. "Now, what I think is that you should provide to retain your hold where you are, certainly, and bring the rest with you personally, and make a vigorous effort to destroy the enemies [sic] force in this vicinity," the president advised Grant. Although he couched this advice in the form of a suggestion rather than an order, there was no doubt that he wanted Grant in Washington. Given that outlet, Grant quickly decided to remain at his City Point, Virginia, headquarters, and he turned down the president's overture by remarking, "I think, on reflection, it would have a bad effect for me to leave here." In his place, Maj. Gen. Horatio Wright's Sixth Corps was shipped to the capital to join an assortment of troops from other departments that were directed to Washington.[57]

The most significant contrast between the Virginia campaigns of Grant and McClellan is that Early's offensive did not accomplish its ultimate objective—to relieve the pressure on Lee's army at Petersburg. Jackson's campaign in the Shenandoah Valley did. Unlike McClellan before him, Grant would not be forced to alter his designs on the James River one iota. Moreover, Grant was facing an army totally incapable of resuming the offensive. Grant enjoyed a manpower advantage over Lee that would have made McClellan envious. Throughout the entire 1864 campaign, after juggling the fluctuations caused by staggering casualty rates and the fresh infusion of reinforcements, Grant always enjoyed a clear two to one superiority over Lee. Contrary to popular mythologizing, Grant was intensely concerned about receiving a steady, uninterrupted flow of

56. *OR,* vol. 37, 2:15. Grant remained so unconcerned about the impact of Early's raid that Charles Dana felt compelled to warn John A. Rawlins, Grant's most trusted aide, of the negative backlash against Grant in the government. Many in Washington, Dana pointed out, were beginning to judge Grant's campaign and control of military matters as failures. See Simon, *Papers of Ulysses S. Grant* 11:353–54.

57. Lincoln to Grant, July 9, 1864; Grant to Lincoln, July 10, 1864, *OR,* vol. 37, 2:134, 155–56.

fresh troops, initially to maintain his fighting edge, finally to permit him to continue his strategy of exhaustion. The major difference between McClellan, who is oft maligned for his constant whining over reinforcements, and Grant is that Grant did not have to worry as much about asking. Nor did Grant ever have to deal with Stanton's tinkering with the recruitment stations in the North. A draft was firmly in place, and although Grant's extravagant use of manpower in the Wilderness made draft officials concerned over a possible revolt, it continued to churn out the men necessary to fulfill Grant's purposes.

In the middle of July 1864, after the incredible bloodbath in the Wilderness had seriously depleted his ranks, Grant advised Lincoln that an additional three hundred thousand men needed to be called up. He predicted that the "greater number of men we have the shorter and less sanguinary will be the war." He offered that advice by way of suggestion and not demand. Grant could afford to be coy. He knew full well that the men could be supplied. If that capability was not Shelby Foote's proverbial "other arm" coming out, it most certainly demonstrated that the "one arm" was rippled with abundant muscle. Lincoln acknowledged Grant's request for three hundred thousand men with the pithy rejoinder, "I suppose you have not seen the call for 500,000 made the day before, and which I suppose covers the case." Grant's feigned humility must have caught Lincoln's approving notice, and the president concluded his response to Grant's request by remarking, "[A]lways glad to have your suggestions."[58]

Every Federal commander in the East, including Grant, was hindered by the government's concern for the safety of Washington. It hovered like the legendary albatross, over the heads of all of them, refusing to go away. The difference is that by the time Grant, who had actually pared down the capital's defenses more than McClellan, came along, he was fighting an opponent badly depleted in force and morale and incapable of launching a significant counteroffensive. Even so, the Confederates never came closer to waltzing into Washington than they did during Grant's watch. Like many of his predecessors, Grant was caught up in the fog of war and was entirely in the dark as to Early's departure from his front. Shaken from his ignorance, Grant was able to rush a spare corps to the

58. Grant to Lincoln, July 19, 1864, *OR*, vol. 37, 3:384; Lincoln to Grant, July 29, 1864, ibid. 2:400.

defense of Washington without the slightest loosening of his grip on Lee's army in the siege lines at Petersburg.

McClellan's Peninsula campaign, the first major Federal offensive in the East, experienced serious difficulties associated with being the first. It also experienced problems uniquely its own, not the least of which was the administration's failure to sustain the plans they had, however reluctantly, agreed to support. Except for a brief period at the very beginning of the campaign, McClellan never enjoyed the overwhelming strength he considered necessary to wage an offensive campaign against the enemy. He was ultimately deprived of a full third of the force he was counting upon and was denied the reinforcements required to replenish casualty losses in the field. At the crux of the campaign, when the enemy army was equal to his own force, he was not sustained in the one thing he absolutely required—sufficient force to repel an assault upon his vulnerable right flank.[59]

McClellan has been verbally pilloried by historians for his excessive caution and timidity. In the main, this criticism has been justified. James M. McPherson, decidedly more balanced in his evaluation of McClellan than others, divined McClellan's failure as a good commander by noting that "military success could be achieved only by taking risks," and that "McClellan seemed to shrink from the prospect."[60] The stunning irony in the Peninsula Campaign, however, is that it was McClellan, not Lincoln and Stanton, who was willing to take acceptable risks concerning the safety of the capital. Lincoln and Stanton are the ones who blinked.

59. Much like the debate over the number of men McClellan left for the defenses of Washington, troop estimates for both Federal and Confederate armies on the Peninsula have fallen victim to great controversy. Numbers fluctuate depending on particular dates during the campaign itself and in the bias historians bring to their narratives. I have elected to go with McWhiney and Jamieson, who based their estimates on the classic study undertaken by Thomas L. Livermore in his work, *Numbers and Losses in the Civil War in America: 1861–1865* (Bloomington: Univ. of Indiana Press, 1957). Moreover, McWhiney and Jamieson do not have any particular bias to exploit in this work (for or against McClellan). Their estimates for the number of men engaged in the Seven Days campaign are: Confederate army, 95,481; Union army, 91,169. See Grady McWhiney and Perry D. Jamieson, *Attack and Die: Civil War Military Tactics and the Southern Heritage* (Tuscaloosa: Univ. of Alabama Press, 1982), 11.

60. McPherson, *Battle Cry of Freedom*, 365.

6

·· ❦ ··

On to Richmond:
Illusion of Easy Victory,
1861–1862

T
HROUGHOUT THE FIRST TWO YEARS OF THE WAR, MANY
Northerners harbored the illusion that government forces would
quickly and decisively dispatch Confederate armies, bringing a summary end to the rebellion. Similarly, the great illusion perpetuated by
many Civil War historians is that the vision of a timely victory was reasonable, and it was not achieved because early military commanders were
not equal to the task. For many historians the arrival of Grant in the East
and Sherman's ascendancy in the West signaled an end to that frustration. Finally, the North had the leadership capable of living up to popular clamor and expectations. While the naivete of those caught up in
the war itself is understandable, the endorsement of historians that the
war could have been speedily won by the North and that Federal commanders, particularly George B. McClellan, erred in ignoring political
pressure to assume offensive campaigns is more difficult to comprehend.
Nothing in the American experience of war, both prior to and following
the Civil War, suggests that an early triumph should have been anticipated in a struggle on the scale that emerged in 1861. And it is precisely
that phenomenon that needs to be acknowledged and integrated in any
assessment of the military performance of George McClellan and other
early Civil War commanders.

Even a cursory review of the American experience of war dispels
the notion that the outbreak of any major conflict has ever been a quickly
concluded matter. In fact, America's other wars offer parallels to the scope,

nature and progress of the Civil War. The French and Indian War of the mid-eighteenth century pitted American colonists and the powerful British Empire against the French and their assorted allies in a struggle that lasted nine years. In that conflict the British and their colonial allies initially suffered crippling setbacks, and only a resolve to mobilize to the fullest extent reversed fortune's momentum. Once focused and determined, the British were able to sweep the increasingly demoralized and disinte-. grating French armies from the North American continent.[1]

The American Revolution, whose legacy was shared by both North and South in the Civil War, reminds historians that a war requiring even a first rate military and naval power to conquer vast amounts of territory, as well as to suppress an armed rebellion, is no easy matter. Despite obvious material and professional advantages, the British army could not occupy the length and breadth of colonial America, nor could it restore control by destroying the American will to resist. Nowhere was that inability to triumph better illustrated than in Lord Cornwallis's aggressive but futile southern campaign of 1780–1781. In the end, British determination collapsed, thus ensuring American independence. The struggle, beginning with the armed resistance on Lexington Green and concluding with the effective surrender of British efforts at Yorktown, lasted over six years. When news of Cornwallis's defeat reached London, the compliant ministry of Lord North collapsed, ending George III's reign of personal rule and limiting further British campaigning in America. War officially came to an anticlimactic close in 1783, when an exhausted Britain signed the Treaty of Paris and removed the remaining British garrison at New York.[2]

The Napoleonic Wars, frequently believed to have supplied the theoretical framework for strategy and tactics during George McClellan's

1. A tidy summary of the war's progress and British efforts to overcome early failures can be found in Douglas Leach, *Arms for Empire: A Military History of the British Colonies in North America, 1607–1763* (New York: Macmillan, 1973), 415–77. A more recent and focused study can be found in Fred Anderson, *A People's Army: Massachusetts Soldiers and Society in the Seven Years War* (Chapel Hill: Univ. of North Carolina Press, 1984), esp. 142–64. Warren W. Hassler, Jr., *With Shield and Sword* (Ames: Iowa State Univ. Press, 1982), esp. 3–19, remains useful.

2. An excellent analysis of the difficulties the British faced in subduing the American rebellion can be found in Russell F. Weigley, *The American Way of War* (Bloomington: Indiana Univ. Press, 1973), 18–39. See also Sylvia R. Frey, "British Armed Forces and the American Victory," in John Ferling, ed., *The World Turned Upside Down* (New York: Greenwood, 1988), 165–83. See also John S. Pancake, *This Destructive War: The British Campaign in the Carolinas, 1780–1782* (Tuscaloosa: Univ. of Alabama Press, 1985).

Civil War, spawned the War of 1812. Emerging as a peripheral and relatively minor conflict for the beleaguered British government, that struggle reinforces the argument that waging war to a decisive conclusion against determined opposition is likely to prove a very long and arduous task. Conflicts like the Napoleonic Wars, entailing the conquest of large tracts of territory, the destruction of enemy armies, and the suppression of national will were hardly effortless tasks, even in cases where monumental battles with conclusive outcomes were fought. The war-weary British hoped to punish the United States for its interference in their European struggle. The opportunistic Americans schemed to steal British Canada. Both found decisive victory elusive.[3]

Whereas the war with Mexico in 1846–1847 and the Spanish-American War of 1898 proved to be decisive and expeditious in their execution, they also differed greatly from other American conflicts in both scope and nature. While the Mexican War may well have served as the paradigm for skewed northern war expectations in 1861,[4] it did not pit against each other two nations desperately committed to total victory, nor did it require widespread occupation of enemy territory or the subjugation of every army. American war aims were geared toward forcing Mexican recognition of United States annexation of Texas, along with a few additional territorial perks, to satisfy President James K. Polk and other expansionists. Moreover, the Mexican armed forces under Gen. Antonio Lopez de Santa Anna were a poor match for American might. With virtually no navy or industrial power, Santa Anna presided over an army that, though united in its contempt for Yankee aggression, had little investment or interest in the outcome. After shifting his army by sea to the port of Vera Cruz, Gen. Winfield Scott was able to roll up the Mexican army on his march inland toward the capital of Mexico City. In virtually every confrontation with the Mexican army, Scott's flanking manuevers led to its general panic and rout. Having determined that the destruction of the Mexican army was unnecessary to accomplish his strategic goals, Scott

3. Hassler, *With Shield and Sword*, 70–104. See also J. C. A. Stagg, *Mr. Madison's War: Diplomacy and Warfare in the Early American Republic, 1783–1830* (Princeton: Princeton Univ. Press, 1983).

4. Weigley, *The American Way of War*, 66–68, 76. See also Robert W. Johannsen, *To the Halls of Montezuma: The Mexican War in the American Imagination* (New York: Oxford Univ. Press, 1985), 108–43.

convinced Santa Anna of the futility of protracted opposition. The demoralized dictator sued for peace.[5]

The war with Spain featured a decadent and tottering Spanish imperial force attempting to stem strong indigenous opposition in Cuba. Luckily, the Cubans were supported in their bid for independence by an emerging imperial power in the United States. Aided by its virtual contiguity to the major theater of operations, the Americans defeated the Spaniards handily. A quick and painless victory had been anticipated; anything less would have been surprising. Nonetheless, the American army's effectiveness, like the Union army in the early years of the Civil War, was undermined by lack of preparation and coordination and faulty logistical support. That "splendid little war" escaped stretching into a protracted guerilla conflict only by the "incredible ineptitude of the Spaniards and the phenomenal luck of the Americans."[6]

American involvement in significant wars of the twentieth century buttresses the argument that it is difficult to vanquish formidable foes. In August 1914 the armies of Europe all marched to the battlefront, confident that the war would be short and that they would return home as glorious conquerors by Christmas. However, as historians have noted, those illusions were quickly extinguished, and the war increasingly became a testimony to the limits of human endurance. The ultimate victors merely succeeded in outlasting Germany's resolve and ability to resist. It should be stated, however, that the German, British, and French high commands could not be disabused of the notion that a quick and decisive victory was imminent. Consequently, for four long years, thousands upon thousands of young soldiers, like their Civil War predecessors, were

5. T. Harry Williams, *The History of American Wars from 1745 to 1918* (New York: Knopf, 1981), 161. Believing that the capture of the Mexican capital alone would paralyze the country and compel Santa Anna to save himself by suing for peace, Scott recalled that "to compel a people, singularly obstinate, to sue for peace it is absolutely necessary . . . to strike effectively at the vitals of the nation." See Scott, *Memoirs* 2:404.

6. Quoted in Frank Freidel, *The Splendid Little War* (Boston: Little, Brown, 1958), 3. See also Walter Millis, *The Martial Spirit* (Boston: Houghton-Mifflin, 1931); and Graham A. Cosmas, *An Army for Empire* (Columbia: Univ. of Missouri Press, 1971), 295–314. Albert Nofi's recent study credits the Spanish army as a well-equipped and tactically sophisticated force. See Albert Nofi, *The Spanish-American War* (New York: Combined Books, 1996). An insight into the demands placed upon the American military in mobilizing for the Cuban expedition can be found in George C. Reinhardt and William R. Kintner, *The Haphazard Years: How America Has Gone to War* (Garden City: Doubleday, 1960).

sacrificed to that dream, thrown, as they were, into futile open assaults upon fortified entrenchments. Even as late as 1918, Gen. Erich von Lu- dendorff pinned final hopes of German victory upon smashing the Allies into submission before the Americans arrived in great numbers. For their part, the Americans were slow in coming to the aid of their allies. Despite early protestations of absolute neutrality, the United States had long been immersed in a war-preparedness campaign. Notwithstanding that preparation, Gen. John J. Pershing refused to expose the American Ex- peditionary Force to the front lines until it completed a lengthy period of mobilization and training. American forces did not begin relieving British and French units at the front until the spring of 1918.[7]

Although it featured the wholesale destruction of cities and the deaths of countless soldiers and civilians, the Second World War pro- vides yet another example of the chimera of instant victory. Irrespective of the ease with which the Axis Powers initially overpowered Allied forces, replete with the capture of whole armies and the conquest and occupa- tion of immense land masses, Germany and Japan fell short of the global domination they sought, and they failed to neutralize Allied perserver- ance in the process. The Allies, though stunned by enemy aggression and grossly ill-prepared for offensive operations initially, were able over the course of four bitterly contested years to reverse the tide of defeat. In time, the Allies were able to harness their military, naval, and logistical advan- tages to the point of breaking the Axis Powers' ability and willingness to wage war.[8]

Parallels to the American experience in the Civil War can even be found in the more limited American engagements in Korea and Vietnam.

7. A concise summary of European frustration in surmounting the difficulties of trench warfare can be found in Marc Ferro, *The Great War, 1914–1918* (London: Routledge and Kegan Paul, 1969). Excellent studies of the American war effort continue to be found in Edward M. Coffman, *The War to End All Wars: The Military Experience in World War I*, rev. ed., (Madison: Univ. of Wisconsin Press, 1986); and David Kennedy, *Over Here: The First World War and American Society* (New York: Oxford Univ. Press, 1980). See also Timothy K. Nen- ninger, "American Military Effectiveness in the First World War," in Allan R. Millet and Wil- liamson Murray, eds., *Against All Enemies: Interpretations of American Military History from Colonial Times to the Present* (New York: Harper Collins, 1989), 24–27. A useful discussion of the United States's rush to preparedness can be found in Meirion and Susie Harries, *The Last Days of Innocence: America at War, 1917–1918* (New York: Random House, 1997).

8. Weigley, *American Way of War*, 242–359. The progress of the war against the Empire of Japan can be found in Ronald H. Spector, *Eagle Against the Sun* (New York: The Free Press, 1985).

Those struggles demonstrated that a first-class military power cannot be assured of success against committed foes that have a strong investment in the outcome. Vietnam, in particular, vividly showed that inhospitable terrain can amply substitute for expansive territory in rendering hopeless expectations for a fast triumph. Facing an enemy with immense indigenous support, long inured to war, the powerful United States war machine sputtered to a most inglorious defeat. Despite nearly sixteen years of continued political involvement and nine years of concentrated military intervention, popular support for prosecuting the war eroded in the United States, and defeat, no matter how honorable a spin attached to it, was finally admitted in 1973.[9]

If the American experience of war evinces any enduring insights, it is that one battle does not a victory make, nor one victory a war won. Irrespective of numerical or material superiority, the outcomes of wars are more likely to be decided by the degree to which those impressive advantages are either marshalled or squandered. A victor must also be governed by an unshakable sense of purpose in order to weather internal crises of morale. Conversely, the apparently weaker foe still has a reasonable chance to triumph if able to sustain a resolve while the moral fiber of the opposition disintegrates. Historians looking at the two major wars of the twentieth century have been able to identify that the key to success rested much more with endurance and organization rather than raw power. Both Germany and Japan in World War II, impressively powerful in 1939, were not able to outlast their opponents in the contest of logistics and organization. The ultimate outcomes of wars can also be influenced by a host of other contingencies, such as the ability to manipulate political or diplomatic intervention or the ability to deny offensive initiatives to the opposition. Good leadership, and even good fortune, are variables that can negate the strengths and weaknesses of opponents, leading one to victory and the other to defeat.

All the same, it is hard to fault the various generations of Americans for thinking that their commitment to fight would translate into instant

9. Excellent analyses of the performance of U.S. arms in Vietnam are abundant. For an insightful study of the failure of U.S. war aims and flawed political assessments, see Guenter Lewy, *America in Vietnam* (New York: Oxford Univ. Press, 1978). To appreciate the negative impact upon the American will to resist, stemming from one campaign alone, see Ronald H. Spector, *After TET: The Bloodiest Year in Vietnam* (New York: The Free Press, 1993). See also Stanley Karnow, *Vietnam: A History* (New York: Viking, 1983); and Daniel C. Hallin, *The "Uncensored War": The Media and Vietnam* (New York: Oxford Univ. Press, 1986).

victory. American colonials marching with Braddock were as cocky as their commander in believing they would push the French out of the Ohio Valley. The cadre of American heroes in the American Revolution, though less confident of success than other generations of American soldiers, found their pledge to fight seriously strained by eight years of struggle and sacrifice, marked by periods of despair and defeatism. The war hawks of 1812 discovered that wresting Canada from British control was a lot more difficult than originally imagined. The great wars of the twentieth century, like the American Civil War, taught Americans that only a huge expenditure of energy and human life would ensure victory and avert defeat. The Korean experience revealed that a first-rate military power, handicapped by serious political constraints, could not achieve any level of mastery over the foe without incurring a great loss of life. And in a clear reflection of the Civil War, the American experience in Vietnam went to great lengths in dispelling the illusion that a show of force by a nation blessed with logistical largesse would necessarily compel an obstinate and determined foe into submission. Nonetheless, it is not difficult to comprehend why Northerners were convinced that a quick and decisive thrashing of the Rebel army would defeat the Confederacy in 1861. What is difficult to understand is why many historians, despite their professed conviction that the war would be long and bloody, continue to insist that the rebellion would have been snuffed out had certain Northern commanders delivered a severe drubbing to the Confederate armed forces early in the war. Yet, as we shall see, that is exactly what they do.

Irvin McDowell, George McClellan's immediate predecessor, was the first of a series of Federal commanders to fail the Union cause. Although most historians condone his performance at Bull Run in July 1861, they are quick to excoriate his role as John Pope's principal lieutenant at the second meeting of Union and Confederate forces on the same battlefield. In truth, McDowell was the first to fall victim to Northern expectations of a quick rout of rebel forces. A West Point graduate and career officer, with no previous field command experience, McDowell was pressed into the role as commander by virtue of default. As an officer on the staff of the aged and debilitated general in chief, Winfield Scott, he was promoted by his patron and fellow Ohioan, Salmon P. Chase, secretary of the treasury. Furthermore, he was present in Washington at the time the earliest volunteers responded to Lincoln's call. When Northern public opinion, expressed in strident tones by the press,[10] urged a quick advance on the Confederate capital of Richmond, Lincoln abandoned Scott's strategy of enveloping the rebellious states with a naval blockade in favor of an assault on a Rebel force assembled at Manassas. Scott's thinking had been influenced by the prevailing sentiment that support for secession would be undermined by Southern Unionists who would not long endure the ravages of economic isolation. Any destructive movement against the Confederate states would violate Southern Unionist good will and would jeopardize the requisite spirit of reconciliation. For his part, Lincoln endorsed a limited war concept but was keenly aware that that policy alone would not succeed in restoring the Union within an acceptable time frame. Northern newspapers reviled Scott's strategy as the "Anaconda Plan" and urged the government to move on the Confederate capital. Popular clamor, fueled by a jingoistic press, and political pressure were too formidable for Lincoln to ignore. He ordered a movement in the direction of Richmond, and Scott and McDowell were asked to supply a plan. At the same time, a Rebel army began to concentrate in the vicinity of Manassas Junction where the Orange and Alexandria and Manassas Gap railroads converged. McDowell developed a plan of attack to flank the Confederate position.[11]

Despite devising a feasible plan of operations, McDowell was not sanguine about the prospects of leading a volunteer army with virtually no training. Lincoln appreciated McDowell's predicament, but he could offer only the consolation that the general's opponents were as green as his own force. So it was, then, that McDowell filed out of Washington on July 16 with a force of thirty thousand men. He headed out on the road to Manassas to face a force of nearly twenty thousand Confederates under the command of Pierre G. T. Beauregard. A vital ingredient to McDowell's plan for turning the rebel flank at Manassas was that Beauregard not be reinforced by Joseph Johnston's force in the Shenandoah Valley. Ostensibly, McDowell and Scott made plans assuming that Union forces in

10. Perhaps the most quoted newspaper headline in the days before McDowell's advance upon Manassas appeared in Horace Greeley's *New York Tribune*. Responding to the announcement that the Confederate Congress intended to hold its first meeting in the new Virginia capital on July 20, 1861, the paper boldly exhorted it readers, "Forward to Richmond! Forward to Richmond!" Other papers quickly took up the call.

11. Scott to McClellan, May 3, 1861, *OR*, vol. 6, 1:369–70.

the Valley, under the command of Gen. Robert Patterson, would prevent Johnston from linking up with Beauregard. Unfortunately for the Union cause, Patterson misunderstood his instructions, and instead of engaging Johnston, maneuvered his force completely out of the campaign. Informed by Confederate spies and sympathizers within the Federal capital, and aided by the ponderously slow march of McDowell's army, Beauregard was prepared to meet the onslaught. At the same time, Johnston slipped out of the Valley and headed to Beauregard's position by use of the Manassas Gap Railroad.

On July 21, 1861, McDowell launched his long-awaited attack. At first, his flanking maneuver against the Confederate left caught the Rebels off guard, and McDowell pressed his numerical advantage by sweeping aside the forward units of the Confederate army. However, as the hours passed, Johnston's reinforcements began to fall into the battle line. Buoyed by the additional firepower, Beauregard's ranks stood firm. By the close of day, Federal forces began an orderly withdrawal from the field, which soon developed into hasty retreat. When a well-aimed shell overturned a Federal wagon on one of the bridges and blocked the passage of Federal troops, the rout degenerated into an absolute panic. The frenzied pace of retreat did not subside until the exhausted army was safe within the defensive works of Washington.[12]

According to a story that circulated around Washington at the time, Lincoln visited McDowell in Arlington two days after the battle. To Lincoln's blandishment that he had not "lost a particle of confidence" in the general, McDowell somewhat priggishly responded, "I don't see why you should, Mr. President." McDowell was largely justified. He had not wanted to advance his raw troops against entrenched positions until they had been adequately trained. His own staff had not acquired sufficient experience to move troops in enemy territory, let alone plan and conduct a battle. Bereft of accurate maps and proper reconnaissance, the march towards Manassas was marked by unnecessary delays. Ironically, the Federal defeat might have been averted had McDowell been able to initiate action on July 20. But the hapless McDowell was a day too late. Johnston's timely arrival from the Valley on the afternoon of the following day proved to be the deciding factor. Despite giving his reassurance to the

12. W. Glenn Robertson, "First Bull Run, 19 July 1861," in Charles E. Heller and William A. Stofft, eds., *America's First Battles, 1776–1965* (Lawrence: Univ. of Kansas Press, 1986), 98–108.

beleaguered general, Lincoln clearly did not envision McDowell as capable enough to reinvigorate the Union war effort. The day before his consoling conversation with McDowell, Lincoln had the war department wire George B. McClellan in West Virginia to relinquish his command there and "come hither without delay."[13] McDowell was discarded very quickly, and his defeat at Bull Run virtually destroyed his career. He would remain in active service in the East for another year, but he became so associated with failure that his very name was equated with defeat and cowardice.[14]

For reasons that would be echoed repeatedly during the Civil War, Johnston and Beauregard were incapable of pursuing and destroying the routed Federal army as it streamed toward the safety of Washington. Nor were they able to mount an assault upon the defenses of the Northern capital, even though many believed it in their power to do so. Nonetheless, McClellan inherited a situation upon his arrival in Washington in late July that was both as precarious as it was thoroughly disorganized. He immediately threw himself into the tasks of shoring up the defenses of Washington and reorganizing the Union army. By most accounts he acquitted himself well in those efforts.[15]

13. Quoted in T. Harry Williams, *Lincoln and His Generals*, 23; *OR*, vol. 2, 1:753. For a highly favorable review of McClellan's western Virginia campaign strategy, see Clayton R. Newell, *Lee vs. McClellan: The First Campaign* (New York: Regnery, 1996), 58–83.

14. After his role in the Union defeat at Second Manassas in August 1862, in which his performance invited justified criticism, McDowell was vilified unmercifully by the rank and file as well as by the Northern press. He was portrayed as a traitor and idiot. Perhaps the most outlandish accusation leveled at McDowell concerned his hat. In a war that did not promote sartorial uniformity, McDowell wore something resembling a pith helmet during the hot months of summer campaigning. Stories circulated that whenever McDowell and his "traitor's hat" appeared on the front, it was a signal for a better opportunity to attack. See D. M. Perry, "Gen. McDowell's Hat," *National Tribune*, Dec. 1, 1892.

15. T. Harry Williams, *Lincoln and the Radicals*, 29; McPherson, *Battle Cry of Freedom*, 349. Even Sears in his scant coverage of this topic admits that McClellan restored order and confidence. He also claims that officers like Sherman, Franklin, and Burnside were on hand to prevent troops from "cowering on the riverbank half a dozen days after the battle," as McClellan claimed. See Sears, *George B. McClellan: The Young Napoleon*, 96–97. This observation overlooks the fact that many regiments of the ninety-day enlistment stripe were disbanding and departing the capital with raw replacements arriving at the same time. Moreover, commanders like Sherman were itching for reassignment to the West, and Burnside had actually marched the 1st Rhode Island regiment out of Washington on the morning of the same day (July 26) that McClellan arrived from West Virginia. See Sherman, *Memoirs* 1:192; Marvel, *Burnside*, 31.

McClellan's first priority was the reorganization of the army. He charged his provost marshal, Brig. Gen. Andrew Porter to direct military police to comb the city, forcing officers and rank and file out of saloons and hotels and back to their regiments. Incompetent officers were released and strict discipline was imposed. He was responsible for assimilating thousands of new soldiers who responded to Lincoln's call for volunteers in the wake of the Bull Run debacle. It was essentially a thoroughly new and untrained army, not unlike that which responded to the initial call and came to Washington in May and June 1861, only to be led unprepared into battle by McDowell in July. McClellan was very disappointed and critical of McDowell's premature offensive, for he was convinced that its failure had only emboldened Rebel resolve. In a memorandum to the president shortly upon his arrival in Washington, McClellan ventured that had the Federal army been successful at Manassas, the Southern people might have abandoned their "governing aristocratic class" and appealed for reunion with the North. Now he was convinced that only a vastly superior armed showing by the North would defeat the South. Moreover, that force would need to be better trained and disciplined to assume another offensive if a repeat of Bull Run was to be avoided.[16]

McClellan succeeded in imbuing the Army of the Potomac with pride and confidence, and he shaped it into a well-disciplined fighting organization. His frequent reviews and parade ground inspections, a subject of considerable derision by late fall 1861, maintained discipline and instilled an esprit de corps among the soldiers. Hailed by most historians as his greatest contribution to the war effort, McClellan's creation of the Army of the Potomac into an efficient fighting force provided a cohesion that sustained it for the entire length of the war. At the same time he was implementing those reforms, McClellan expended great energy in completing the outer defenses of Washington. He assigned Gen. John G. Barnard the architect and engineer of the fortifications to ring the capital city. By the close of 1861, construction was essentially completed on forty-eight forts and batteries. Nearly 480 guns were in position, requiring 7,200 artillerists to man them. That force could be augmented by infantry and would be fluid enough to adjust to changing circumstances in the operational field. Interestingly, Barnard felt considerably more comfortable with

16. George B. McClellan to Abraham Lincoln, Aug. 2, 1861, in Sears, *Civil War Papers of George B. McClellan,* 71-72.

the army's ability to defend the capital at the close of 1861 than he did in July 1864 when General Jubal Early gave Grant the slip in Petersburg and threatened Washington during his celebrated raid.[17] Although it eventually became a sarcastic sobriquet for McClellan's perceived inactivity, the verse, "All Quiet on the Potomac," was composed as a tribute to the restoration of order and security in the Northern capital. The real significance of McClellan's handiwork there was that fears of a Confederate surge against the city would not necessarily complicate or suspend future offensive campaigning by the Army of the Potomac.[18]

McClellan addressed his concerns for a well-trained army by implementing required schools of instruction on a scale never permitted to McDowell. Volunteers who streamed into Washington during the month of August were given basic training under the direction of Gen. Silas Casey, a veteran officer known for his strict adherence to drill and discipline. Following that instruction, they were assigned to brigades and divisions for additional training. Once the transfer to the brigade level had been made, McClellan ordered his general officers to personally supervise the instruction of the rank and file. More importantly, however, McClellan was dismayed by the atrocious deficit in trained officers at both the regimental and company levels. Accordingly, he initiated training programs for both field and noncommissioned officers, ranging from tactical drills and recitation in army regulations to minute instructions regulating the posting of sentinels and the implementation of field marches. The corps of officers were in an equally lamentable condition in the late summer of 1861. On September 20 McClellan created two boards of inquiry to examine the qualifications of officers sent as provisional commanders by the state militias. By the end of the month, nearly 170 officers, including two regimental colonels, resigned rather than defend their credentials. Most of these would-be officers lacked fundamental military knowledge or were incapable of establishing and maintaining discipline. If McClellan was viewed as failing to delegate authority and responsibility in the early months of his tenure in Washington, it

17. John G. Barnard to Joseph G. Totten, December 10, 1861, in *OR,* vol. 5, 1:683; Benjamin F. Cooling, *Symbol, Sword, and Shield* (Hamden, Conn.: Archon Books, 1975), 93.

18. McPherson, *Battle Cry of Freedom,* 349; T. Harry Williams, *Lincoln and His Generals,* 29. Kenneth P. Williams, however, downplays the prevailing disorganization in the capital and denies McClellan credit for securing the safety of the city, See Kenneth P. Williams, *Lincoln Finds a General* 1:113–21.

was those military considerations that compelled him to do so, not an inability to place trust in anyone.[19]

Notwithstanding those serious handicaps, the initial patience and understanding extended to McClellan by the Congress and the Northern press was beginning to wane by October. On October 21 McClellan ordered an engagement with the enemy, although he soon regretted the decision. Rebel forces occupied the town of Leesburg, Virginia, on the Potomac River. McClellan enjoined Gen. Charles P. Stone to make a "slight demonstration" from the Maryland side of the river while shifting a larger force to cross upriver and flank the Rebel position. Stone assigned Col. Edward Baker, a former Illinois politician and good friend to Lincoln, the task of holding the attention of the Confederates on the river near Ball's Bluff. Unwisely and rashly, Baker deployed most his force in charging across the river where they were greeted by a hail of fire. When the sad affair ended, Baker was struck dead and his force was thoroughly routed. Many in the command were drowned trying to swim back to the Maryland side. When Congress convened in December, it established the Joint Committee on the Conduct of the War to investigate the reasons for the defeats at Bull Run and Ball's Bluff. Although Stone eventually became the scapegoat for the latter disaster, McClellan accurately perceived that he, rather than Stone, was the Committee's actual target. Ball's Bluff and the continued inactivity of the Army of the Potomac added to the mounting criticism aimed at McClellan. The Northern press began to critique his lethargy and suggested that winter was an excellent time to campaign in the South. Scheduling McClellan as its first witness, the Committee leadership prepared to lay into him. They had to wait for McClellan's testimony, however, for he was stricken with typhoid fever shortly before Christmas, which laid him low until the middle of January. When he did appear on January 15, the Committee had already determined that McClellan had no plans to advance on the enemy, that he was not to be

---

19. George B. McClellan to General Officers, Division of the Potomac, Aug. 4, 1861, in Sears, *Civil War Papers of George B. McClellan*, 76–77; *OR*, vol. 3, 1:382–83. Glatthaar asserts that as a consequence of his deep distrust of everyone, McClellan was incapable of "delegating responsibilities sensibly." See Glatthaar, *Partners in Command*, 62. Of course, it should be noted that many West Point commanders acted in a similar way. Part of the reason why Sherman overworked himself into a frenzy in Kentucky was that he felt there was no one else competent to attend to the details. See Sherman, *Memoirs* 1:200. Grant, too, did not always believe in his subordinates "as having the capacity for independent judgment." See McFeely, *Grant*, 102.

inherently trusted as one would a Napoleon or Wellington, and that Mc-
Dowell should be reinstated as head of the Army of the Potomac.[20]

Many Civil War historians treat that period of inactivity during Mc-
Clellan's command with circumspection and balance yet hold him responsible for the unsettled feeling in the North. In general, they con-
cede that there were great obstacles to launching a successful offensive in
1861. T. Harry Williams noted that after Bull Run Northerners forgot the
"cheering crowds and hopes of easy victory . . . and began to buckle down
for a long war." The first months of the war, Williams asserts, represented
a time of testing and trial for both sides, and both governments looked to
mobilizing land and sea forces. Neither side "was prepared to undertake a
major effort." Allan Nevins underscores the lack of preparation by describing that tentative period of the war as the "improvised" stage. McPherson
acknowledges the difficulties facing McClellan but is inclined to think that
he shrank from taking appropriate risks. Sensing that McClellan might
have suffered from a "Bull Run syndrome," he concludes that the general
hesitated to make any movement against the rebels until his preparations
were completely and perfectly finished.[21]

Other historians, while admitting to Northern ill-preparedness, down-
play the need for extensive preparation. With considerable vitriol, Kenneth P. Williams condemned the fall of 1861 as a period of inexcusable
delay. He scoffed at the "big reviews" staged by the commander and con-
temptuously gloated over McClellan's discovering "Quaker guns" at Mun-
son's Hill and later at Manassas. More recently, Stephen Sears suggested
that McClellan was willfully stubborn, even insubordinate, in refusing to
divulge his operational plans to Lincoln and the committee. He is particularly critical of McClellan for appearing to court the *New York Herald* as
the means to announce his upcoming campaign. For Sears, McClellan was
beginning to manifest the glaring latent psychological deficiencies long ingrained in his difficult personality.[22]

McClellan's unwillingness to assume the offensive in 1861 was dictated by prudence and not excessive caution. The sheer folly of Mc-

20. For Benjamin Wade's verdict on McClellan, see *CCW* 1:155. See also, David
Donald, ed., *Inside Lincoln's Cabinet: The Civil War Diaries of Salmon P. Chase* (New York:
Longman's Green, 1954), 56–58.

21. T. Harry Williams, *History of American Wars,* 259; McPherson, *Battle Cry of Freedom,* 359.

22. Kenneth P. Williams, *Lincoln Finds a General* 1:122–51; Sears, *George B. McClellan:
The Young Napoleon,* 139–46.

Dowell's expedition marching off unprepared to do battle in July 1861 suggested that greater preparation and organization was required. Lincoln's folksy rejoinder to McDowell that the Confederates were as unprepared as his Federal force ignored the fact that offensive operations were much more difficult to conduct than defensive ones. Though no absolute guarantor of success, a better trained Federal force would have probably performed better than the one hastily slapped together and precipitately rushed to battle.

McClellan inherited in August a situation similar to the one that faced McDowell in May 1861. He was greeted by the arrival of new volunteers, except the number and variety of forces far exceeded what McDowell had handled. To a large degree, McClellan's impressive host was comprised of the "paper armies," as Sherman called them; the numbers did not always represent the effective strength of the army. The Union failure at Bull Run demonstrated that a significant offensive campaign could flounder when conducted by troops and officers with barely two month's training. Perhaps, McDowell's repeated pleas for additional time were rooted in common sense and should have been heeded. In October McClellan implored Lincoln to refrain from forcing him into taking the field before he was prepared, to which the president replied, "You shall have your own way in the matter, I assure you." McClellan was adamant that he would not consider offensive action until he created an army that was well trained and led by competent officers. By nearly all accounts, McClellan successfully addressed that need, and if nothing else can be said in his favor, that accomplishment alone rightly earns him praise. It seems patently unfair, then, in light of Bull Run, to criticize McClellan for failing to assume the offensive before the onset of winter.[23]

Attention to Washington's fortifications commanded a great deal of McClellan's time throughout the fall of 1861.[24] The priority Lincoln and the government placed upon the safety of Washington throughout the war underscores its importance. McClellan's campaign on the Peninsula was compromised by Lincoln's fear of Confederate armies making a rush on Washington. John Pope, to whom McClellan was ordered to rush rein-

23. Mark DeWolfe, ed., *Home Letters of General Sherman* (New York: Scribner's, 1909), 316; Tyler Dennett, ed., *Lincoln and the Civil War Diaries of John Hay*, 33.

24. Kenneth P. Williams, *Lincoln Finds a General* 1:124–25; T. Harry Williams, *Lincoln and His Generals*, 31; McPherson, *Battle Cry of Freedom*, 349; Sears, *George B. McClellan: The Young Napoleon*, 116; Hattaway and Jones, *How the North Won*, 87.

forcements, was under orders to consider the safety of the capital as he manuevered his army in northern Virginia. When he blundered badly at Second Manassas and retired toward Washington, the administration reluctantly called upon McClellan to secure the city. When ordered to pursue Lee's army and bring it to battle, McClellan was hamstrung by reminders to cover routes that converged on the capital. Subsequent commanders like Ambrose Burnside, Joseph Hooker, and George Meade were all encouraged to display aggression but to advance on Lee's position by movements that would prevent any northward thrust by the enemy. Even Grant at Petersburg was distracted by concerns for protecting Washington, although his having stripped the fortifications of some of its artillery and veteran force warranted that distraction. Slow to comprehend the destination of Jubal Early's raiding army, he narrowly missed sending reinforcements to Washington in time. It would seem that McClellan's decision to delay offensive operations until a formidable defense perimeter was established was not without justification.[25]

Adulation greeted McClellan's early achievements in turning about the demoralized state of affairs in the wake of McDowell's defeat. By October, however, pressure surfaced from Radical Republicans and certain elements of the northern press to resume campaigning in the field. When November rolled around, the pressure began to swell. Still, Lincoln continued to support McClellan's decision to delay. Although McClellan hinted that he was nearly prepared to take the field, it would appear that he was not sincere in that regard. He did not believe that preparations were completed, and he was contemplating a movement to circumvent the army's employing the overland route through Virginia. Moreover, that movement was predicated upon simultaneous and coordinated operations in the West. Halleck was not prepared to move along the Mississippi, nor was Don Carlos Buell, who had recently relieved the unnerved Sherman in November and was ready to make a push through Kentucky. Besides, with winter approaching, the season for campaigning was coming to a close. While the relatively warm and dry days of November 1861 proved to be agreeable for campaigning, December was hellish. It rained incessantly, and the Virginia roads quickly became quagmires, inhibiting the

25. William L. Barney, *Flawed Victory: A New Perspective on the Civil War* (Lanham, Md.: Univ. Press of America, 1982), 13–14; Hennessy, *Return to Bull Run*, 8; Cooling, *Jubal Early's Raid*, 199. A complete discussion of the administration's security interests during the Civil War is in Cooling, *Symbol, Sword and Shield*.

movement of a large army. McClellan's claim that the army was unprepared to campaign was underscored by the humorous fact that many
of his soldiers had not received their issues of overcoats, and others who
not possess even trousers, were forced to drill and parade with only their
drawers. Despite the preparations required to move an army, McClellan is
criticized for allowing the year to end without advancing upon the enemy,
almost as if he could have delayed the arrival of winter.

No uniform policy or practice regarding the cessation of active
campaigning emerged during the Civil War. McClellan's decision to go
into winter quarters was a natural consequence of his feeling that the
army was only approaching the point of being adequately prepared. In the
West, neither Halleck nor Grant felt adequately prepared to launch campaigns after the Battle of Belmont. In fact, Grant declared that until he was
more adequately provisioned, his force would remain inactive. After the
misdirected aggressiveness of Gen. Nathaniel Lyon led to a Federal rout at
Wilson's Creek in August 1861, efforts in the Trans-Mississippi languished
until the following spring. In 1862, operations in both western and eastern
theaters began well before the advent of spring. Grant and Sherman broke
off campaigning for the year after the desultory assault at Chickasaw Bluff
faltered at the end of December, while Rosecrans stopped fighting after
his victory at Stones River, just as the new year of 1863 dawned. Burnside, pressured to produce a battle after the administration had sacked
McClellan for dallying, rashly assaulted Confederate entrenchments up
the snow-covered hills at Fredericksburg before calling it a season days
before Christmas 1862.[26]

Subsequent Federal commanders only continued the trend established by their predecessors. Hooker waited to launch the Army of the
Potomac's campaign season until early May 1863, and Meade concluded
it in November of that year. Grant and Sherman remained active during
the winter of 1862–1863, but most of that activity involved efforts to cut
navigable canals off the Mississippi as a way to approach Vicksburg successfully. Their efforts proved fruitless, and Grant began fighting in earnest
with the arrival of spring. That season proved to be a lengthy one as fighting did not come to a halt until January 1864. The last full campaign season saw Sherman refusing to step off for Dalton, Georgia, until his supply

26. Oddly enough, Burnside had assumed command from McClellan during a raging
snowstorm outside Warrenton, Virginia, in early November. See Hassler, *General George B.
McClellan: Shield of the Union*, 315.

line was firmly established in May. In the East, Grant fixed the start of his campaign for early May, "When the season should be far enough advanced . . . for the roads to be in a condition for the troops to march." Except for minor skirmishing, he concluded active operations well before the month of October was over. Even had McClellan not envisioned the Peninsula strategy, his decision to complete the Army of Potomac's training and provide for the defense of Washington before assuming the offensive foreclosed any realistic opportunities for a massive campaign in the fall.[27]

McClellan, however, was not prudent in one important aspect of his preparations during the fall of 1861. He should have taken Lincoln into his confidence concerning his campaign plans. The president had obligingly assured McClellan that he would not compel him to move the army until the general felt ready. He did, however, reveal that the pressure to strike a blow at rebeldom was overwhelmingly real and could not be ignored. As commander in chief, Lincoln had every prerogative to be apprised of his subordinate's intentions as well as to play a part in suggesting alterations in light of political imperatives. After all, Lincoln would ultimately be held responsible for the success or failure of Union war efforts. McClellan's intransigence in the matter was inexcusable. He failed to understand that his occasional rude and arrogant behavior directed at Lincoln was inappropriate. It could only compromise a viable relationship with his superior and would undermine his credibility. Moreover, he gave the impression that he might not want to use the magnificent army he had molded. It was not unusual that a military professional like McClellan disdained civilian meddling in operational concerns. However, McClellan's gratuitous belittling of Lincoln's military acumen was unwarranted and foolish, for it may well have eroded the president's willingness to protect and sustain his charge from the rising popular and political tempests.[28]

McClellan's justification for his reluctance to provide the administration with details of his plans was inadequate. True, he was genuinely concerned about confidentiality. It was evident that Southern spies and

27. William L. Shea and Earl J. Hess, *Pea Ridge: Civil War Campaign in the West* (Chapel Hill: Univ. of North Carolina Press, 1992), 2–3; George Washington Adams, *Doctors in Blue: The Medical History of the Union Army during the Civil War* (New York: Macmillan, 1961), 186. Grant is quoted in Grant, *Memoirs* 2:208.

28. Sears, *George B. McClellan: The Young Napoleon,* 134; Glatthaar, *Partners in Command,* 64.

sympathizers had forewarned Beauregard of McDowell's impending advance upon Manassas, and droves of Northern reporters were snooping around military camps, looking for the latest scoop. That was a sensible consideration. Other Federal commanders felt the same as McClellan. At about the same time McClellan was coming under fire for his secrecy, Sherman had elements of his conversation with Simon Cameron leaked to the press, leading to the first reports of his "insanity." From that point onward, Sherman curbed reporters' access to military camps and retained his own counsel. Grant, too, preferred to divulge as little as military necessity permitted. In his memoirs he recalled that during the Vicksburg campaign he suffered charges that he was "idle, incompent and unfit to command men in an emergency" because he refused to discuss military affairs. At one point, he purposefully informed no one, not even an officer on his staff, of his plans to bypass Vicksburg along the Mississippi for fear of public disclosure. Therefore, it is not surprising when McClellan, summoned to a cabinet meeting in January 1862 announced his reluctance to detail his plans to any panel he thought either incompetent or unreliable. He would gladly inform the president and secretary of state of all details if they made that request in writing and assumed responsibility for secrecy.[29]

In a meeting with the cabinet and several of his corps commanders, McClellan is said to have remarked that he preferred not to inform Lincoln of his plans because the president was an incurable talker; he even told military secrets to his son Tad. It was not uncommon for cabinet members to leak specific self-serving pieces of information to the press. Called east in 1864, Grant patiently listened to Lincoln's ideas for the Virginia campaign before he kindly rejected them. Remembering that Stanton and Halleck had warned him that the president "was so kind-hearted, so averse to refusing anything asked of him," he declined to communicate his campaign plans to Lincoln, or Stanton and Halleck, for that matter. Where McClellan erred in dealing with Lincoln is in his failure to assuage the president's concerns and anxieties in the early days of the war and to defer to his position. He also was inconsistent in his policies, frequently seizing opportunities for self-promotion. Although he did not provide explicit details of his upcoming Peninsula campaign, McClellan appeared interested enough in cultivating a good public impression with the help of the *New York Herald* that he exchanged full disclosure on oper-

29. Sherman, *Memoirs* 1:203–6; Grant, *Memoirs* 1:458–59; McClellan, *McClellan's Own Way*, 156–58.

ations elsewhere. On other occasions, he was candid and informative with Stanton and Chase, particularly when he felt they were championing his cause.[30]

McClellan's shortcomings in his relationship with Lincoln obscure his accomplishments during the latter part of 1861. He assumed command of a disorganized and routed mob and transformed it into a well-disciplined and confident army, commanded by efficiently trained officers. He provided a solid defensive structure and quelled fears for the safety of the capital. Plans for an offensive strike at the enemy, predicated upon supporting movements in the West, were prudently shelved with winter approaching and the inability of all Union commanders to participate in the fall. While inactivity in the West was easily overlooked, popular and political demands for action in the East were based upon unrealistic expectations. Because it seems as valid to argue that another ineffective campaign similar to McDowell's would have had greater demoralizing results than the stationary position of McClellan's army, many historians assert it as gospel truth. Many remain ambivalent about McClellan's ability to launch a successful campaign. They acknowledge existing limitations by paying lip service to them, but they lament the lost opportunities by accenting them in their judgments at the same time. Instead, historians have preferred to focus on McClellan's personality. They link his unwillingness to campaign and his silence on his plans in 1861 with paranoia, political grandstanding, dishonesty, and cowardice. For many of them, McClellan was a failure even before he launched his campaign in the spring of 1862. Before Grant assumed command in the East in 1864, there would be lots of campaigning, attended by considerable death and destruction. Still, no decisive, war-ending blow was delivered to the Confederates. Many historians have judged those campaigns as failures, the result of ineffective and flawed Federal leadership.

Early Federal commanders in the East are criticized because they were inclined, in the opinion of many historians, to embrace excessive caution as their byword. Eschewing aggression, those generals were incapable of dealing a crushing blow against Confederate armies. Of those, McClellan, and occasionally Meade, is the chief culprit for advocating cautious advances, and he is severely censured for forfeiting the best

30. Sears, *George B. McClellan: The Young Napoleon*, 141; Grant, *Memoirs* 2:123; George B. McClellan to Randolph Marcy, Jan. 29, 1862, in Sears, *Civil War Papers of George B. McClellan*, 160.

chance at destroying Lee's army. Pope and Burnside are reprimanded for misguided aggression, while Hooker has the unique distinction of becoming unnerved after initially displaying promising aggression. Like McClellan and Meade, Hooker also missed a prime opportunity to decimate the Army of Northern Virginia. Western commanders, such as Buell and Rosecrans, simply pale in comparison with Grant and are generally dismissed as too cautious. As is often the case, the long shadows of Grant and Sherman have loomed to dwarf those cast by their predecessors, and they have shaded most appraisals of early Federal command.

While a more detailed review of McClellan's Peninsula and Maryland campaigns will be conducted later, a general assessment reveals that historians have critiqued them as models of excessive caution. Believing that McClellan embarked upon the Peninsula only by Presidential edict,[31] historians have criticized his unwillingness to storm the undermanned defenses of Yorktown. He is condemned for his cautious pace up the Peninsula, and many believe he failed to inflict serious damage to the retreating Confederate army at Williamsburg. Then, upon arriving in view of the church spires of Richmond, McClellan surrendered the initiative to a reinforced Rebel force by electing to prepare for a siege. Thus, he placed the Army of the Potomac at risk by allowing Johnston and Lee to steal the tactical offensive.[32] Similarly, many historians believe McClellan mismanaged the campaign leading up to the Battle of Antietam. He was slow in galvanizing the Federal forces into action following Second Manassas, and he moved at a glacial pace towards Frederick to intercept Lee. McClellan compounded his tardiness by failing to move swiftly against the scattered elements of Lee's army in the wake of discovering his adversary's plan of operations. Once upon the battlefield, he became timid and committed his attacking force piecemeal, dooming any chance for success. He refused to commit the army's sizeable reserve corps, which might have broken Lee's line, and declined to offer battle the following day. Finally, he failed to contest Lee's retreat across the Potomac and lost a ripe opportunity to destroy him in a precarious position.[33]

On the other hand, John Pope was anything but timid, and his misdirected aggression proved his undoing. Fresh from his successes in the

---

31. Sears, *To the Gates of Richmond,* 11.
32. Ibid., 162.
33. A. Wilson Greene, "'I Fought the Battle Splendidly,'" 59.

West, where he was most known for his capture of Island Number 10 on the Mississippi, Pope was given command of all Federal forces in the Washington area, including those in the Shenandoah Valley. He was instructed to screen any Confederate feint towards the Union capital while maneuvering his force toward Richmond, where he could converge with McClellan in an assault upon Lee's sandwiched army. With McClellan at a standstill at Harrison's Landing, Lee sent Jackson northward. At Cedar Mountain, Federal forces were able to blunt Jackson's thrust sufficiently, allowing Pope time to consolidate his army. Jackson, however, veered into the Valley, leaving Pope to pull back in the general direction of Manassas Junction. By early August, McClellan accepted the fact that the administration would no longer support his plans to resume the initiative, and he began to siphon his forces away from Harrison's Landing by transport. Lee was now free to slip away from Richmond and hurl his entire force upon Pope.[34]

Unknown to Pope, Jackson's forces had already filed through the Bull Run Mountains and eventually settled behind an unfinished railroad bed just northwest of the original site of First Manassas. In the late afternoon of August 28, 1862, the brigades of General Rufus King's division were slammed by Jackson's hidden artillery, and the fight was on. Although not compelled to attack, John Pope spent the entire day of August 29 launching a series of frontal assaults at Jackson but failed to produce any favorable effect. Falsely encouraged by the dust generated by Longstreet's advancing corps, and seeing it as a sign that Jackson was in retreat, Pope ordered further assaults; however, those proved as barren in result as those on the prior day. When McDowell, Pope's senior corps commander, realigned his divisions, to the detriment of the Union left, Longstreet exploited the mistake and caved in the Federal flank. Pope had no recourse but to fall back. Although Second Manassas was a "severe defeat," Pope was not routed, and the army "retreated in good order."[35]

Pope's defeat was avoidable because the battle itself was unnecessary. Pope erred by offering battle when he should have awaited the arrival of McClellan's army, and he should not have expected that reunion to have been effected speedily. He had the option of either entrenching at Manassas, inviting Jackson to fall upon his works, or withdrawing to a defensible position at Centreville, where McClellan could have reinforced him in a

34. Hennessy, *Return to Bull Run*, 28–252.
35. John Codman Ropes, *The Army under Pope* (New York: Scribner's, 1881), 141.

timely manner. Pope may have been a "vigorous, active, resolute man," possessing the military virtues of courage, persistence, and self-confidence, but those characteristics alone did not guarantee success in the East against the likes of Lee, Jackson, and Longstreet.[36]

Pope's defeat and hasty departure from command after Second Manassas underscored the concerns Federal commanders shared in aggressively pursuing Lee's army. Irrespective of whatever presidential assurances were given to generals who risked battle,[37] defeat in the East generally presaged dismissal from command. Pope, at least, learned that lesson firsthand. Pope was also seduced by the illusion that Southern forces could and should be beaten decisively in the field. To some extent, Pope victimized himself by proclaiming he was a "Western man," accustomed only to seeing the backs of his enemies. He was puffed up by relatively easy victories in the West and was convinced that aggressive action would alleviate the torpor into which Eastern armies had fallen. Even if he had not deluded himself in that regard, Pope knew he had been summoned East to deliver quick and decisive victories. That vision blinded him to the strategic and tactical realities imposed upon him on the plains of Manassas. Consequently, he served the remainder of his Civil War career suppressing the Indian uprisings on the Minnesota and Iowa frontiers.[38]

Ambrose Burnside, McClellan's reluctant successor, mirrored Pope in his predicament. Keenly aware that his predecessor had been sacked for his excessive caution and failure to demolish Lee's army, Burnside wasted little time in bringing on an engagement, even though the winter season was well upon him. Hoping to steal a march before his adversary could entrench, Burnside, after expressing an interest in resuming McClellan's

36. Ropes, *Army under Pope*, 171.

37. While McClellan and Meade were constantly counseled and goaded to be more aggressive, other commanders received assurances that the administration would support them if they sought battle. Such assurances did not, however, prevent their dismissal from command, as Pope, Burnside, Hooker, and Rosecrans discovered. See, *CCW* (Pope's Report, supplement) 2:189; Pope to Halleck, and Halleck to Pope, Sept. 5, 1862, *OR*, vol. 12, 3:812–13; Pope to Stanton, Dec. 25, 1864, Stanton Papers, Library of Congress; *CCW* 1:718–19; Lincoln to Hooker, Jan. 26, 1863, in Nicolay and Adams, *Complete Works of Abraham Lincoln*, 206–7; Lincoln to Hooker, May 13, 1863, *OR*, vol. 25, 2:474; Halleck to Buell, Oct. 19, 1862, in Nicolay and Adams, *Complete Works of Abraham Lincoln* 8:63–64; Lincoln to Rosecrans, Aug. 22, 1863, *OR*, vol. 51, 1:439.

38. *OR*, vol. 13, 1:617.

Peninsula strategy, agreed to an overland approach to Fredericksburg. However, Halleck failed him by neglecting to requisition and transport the necessary pontoon bridges required to cross the Rappahannock above Fredericksburg. By the time the pontoons arrived, Lee had entrenched himself firmly on the hills rising to the west of the town. To even the untrained eye, an assault under these unfavorable conditions was both prohibitive and indefensible. Undeterred by the daunting prospects, Burnside launched a rather unimaginative attack against Confederate positions on the heights. It was a slaughter. Longstreet was said to have remarked to Lee that if the Federals persisted in their assault, he "might kill them all." As the afternoon of December 13 wore on, Burnside became so distraught and panicky that he had to be talked out of personally leading one last desperate rush up the hill. When considered as a single and total battle plan, Fredericksburg was unparalleled in Federal efforts during the war for its sheer stupidity.[39]

Burnside was clearly not as cocky as John Pope. He also lacked the confidence of his predecessor, McClellan, and his successor, Hooker. Twice he had spurned offers to replace McClellan and finally accepted when informed that command would otherwise go to Hooker. His insistence that he was not qualified for overall command does not seem so much an expression of humility, as his most recent biographer contends, as it was an assertion of candor.[40] Desperate to find a commander who would press the issue with the enemy, Lincoln chose poorly in Burnside. For his part, Burnside was determined to draw Lee's army into battle before winter's lock precluded campaigning. Lee obliged him. However, the battle was on ground of Lee's choosing and was so forbidding that Burnside should have declined fighting and retired to winter quarters. The pressure to fight the decisive battle obscured Burnside's better judgment. Within weeks of the battle, Burnside joined McDowell, Pope, and McClellan on the scrap heap of discarded commanders.

The era of Joseph Hooker was ushered in with Burnside's downfall in late January 1863. A self-serving and scheming insubordinate, Hooker had achieved acclaim as a hard-fighting division and corps commander, leading to the haunting nickname of "Fighting Joe." In the same letter in which he stated he would risk dictatorship, Lincoln requested his newest charge to "give us victories." Perhaps chastened at having goaded Burnside

39. Longstreet is quoted in *Battles and Leaders* 3:81.
40. Marvel, *Burnside*, 1–2.

into his ill-fated attack on Fredericksburg, Lincoln softened his vigor by admonishing Hooker to "beware of rashness."[41] Hooker used the remaining winter season to revive the morale of the army, which had sunk considerably since the departure of McClellan, the bloodbath at Fredericksburg, and the ignominy of Burnside's failed Mud March earlier in January. On April 29 the Army of the Potomac was on the move again. Hooker succeeded admirably in swinging the bulk of his army far up the Rappahannock, which he forded, and he arrived in Lee's rear by the evening of April 30. The remainder of his army was left under Gen. John Sedgwick, who was commanded to keep Lee's attention riveted at the river crossings near Fredericksburg.

Hooker was ecstatic with the progress of his deception and gave vent to the braggadocio that afflicted so many Civil War commanders when he announced, "The rebel army . . . is now the legitimate property of the Army of the Potomac. They may as well pack up their haversacks and make for Richmond. I shall be after them."[42] The words had barely passed his lips when he suddenly lost his nerve and began to issue commands to pull back and entrench near Chancellorsville. The remainder of the story is well known. Lee responded to the threat in his rear with alacrity, sending his able lieutenant, Jackson, by circuitous march beyond Hooker's right flank. Before nightfall on May 2, Jackson crashed through the Union lines and sent the Federals reeling. The following day, Hooker was knocked unconscious by a wooden column splintered by a Confederate shell. Although he regained control of his senses later in the day, he lost his final reserve of nerve and placed exaggerated importance upon Sedgwick's advance from the east. When Sedgwick was checked at Salem's Church, Hooker despaired of victory. During the late night hours of May 5, he decided to withdraw his army across the Rappahannock, using the need to defend Washington as a pretext for the movement. The Battle of Chancellorsville had come to an inglorious conclusion. Although Lincoln was thoroughly distraught by yet another setback, he decided to retain Hooker's services. Lincoln compared Hooker to a gun that had once misfired: Rather than remove Hooker from command, "He would pick the lock and try it again." However, Hooker exasperated Lin-

41. *OR*, vol. 25, 2:4.
42. Quoted in William Swinton, *Campaigns of the Army of the Potomac* (New York: Charles B. Richardson, 1866), 275.

coln and Halleck to a degree surpassing even McClellan, and he was relieved on June 28. Command passed to George Meade.[43]

Meade was an excellent choice. For two years he had served as
both a division and corps commander, and, unlike Burnside or Hooker,
he held the respect and confidence of both officers and soldiers in the
Army of the Potomac. He assumed control of matters only days before
the army collided with Lee in Pennsylvania, where he fought a creditable
fight at Gettysburg and secured an important, even critical, Union victory. While Lincoln was pleased with Meade's performance at Gettysburg, he was gravely disappointed with the general's failure to pursue the
retreating Confederates, noting that he was "distressed immeasurably
because of it." Lincoln remained disturbed by Meade's cautious advance
into Virginia and his desultory campaigning in the late summer and fall
of 1863. To Lincoln, Meade was McClellan revisited. When Meade settled into winter quarters, north of the Rappahannock, Lincoln's thoughts
drifted to finding for the Eastern army a leader willing to fight. It was
during that winter respite that Lincoln found his general and summoned
Grant to Washington. While Meade would continue to command the
Army of the Potomac, Grant would direct the campaign and issue Meade
the orders.[44]

Meanwhile in the West, early Northern commanders fared little
better than their Eastern counterparts. While Halleck and Grant enjoyed
some success along the Mississippi and its various tributaries, the commanders of the Department of the Cumberland, operating along the
interior lines of Kentucky and Tennessee, were off to a slow start. Don
Carlos Buell, once described as "a McClellan without charm or glamor,"
was sent in mid-November 1861 to relieve Sherman of command. Sherman, who had eagerly accepted a western assignment after his experience at Bull Run, had originally requested a subordinate position. He was
obliged. He arrived in Louisville, Kentucky, in September to serve under
Gen. Robert Anderson. Within weeks, Anderson requested to be relieved,
citing poor health as his reason. His resignation elevated Sherman to a
position he had wished to avoid. It was not long before he began to utter
dark forecasts for Union hopes in Kentucky unless he was immediately

43. Meade, *Life and Letters of George Gordon Meade* 1:385.
44. Lincoln to Meade, July 14, 1863, in Nicolay and Adams, *Complete Works of Abraham Lincoln* 9:29–30.

and heavily reinforced. He also ruled out any idea of advancing upon Confederate positions until he received a force of two hundred thousand men. Increasingly rattled, Sherman drew the attention of high command, leading to McClellan's supplanting him with Buell.[45]

During Buell's entire command he was constantly under pressure to drive the Rebels not only out of Kentucky but East Tennessee as well. Ironically, it was McClellan who first applied that pressure, since his own operational plans called for simultaneous activity in the West. In addition to severing Confederate transportation and communication lines, Lincoln also favored a movement into East Tennessee in order to provide protection to the sizeable Unionist enclave in that part of the state. He did not, however, take into account the real, not imagined, logistical handicaps that faced Buell in effecting that movement. Buell was at pains to impress the administration with how he would not be able to supply an army through the mountainous terrain, harrassed by Confederate bushwackers. He presented a sound plan of operations that moved his army in the direction of Nashville, which would force the Rebels to confront him or risk capture by a flanking movement. T. Harry Williams claims that McClellan vetoed the plan because only a movement upon East Tennessee would directly assist him in his forthcoming campaign against Richmond. That is not entirely true. McClellan appreciated Lincoln's concerns for the Unionists, and facing pressure to begin campaigning himself, he felt obliged to support one of Lincoln's greatest desires in the early part of the war: the liberation of East Tennessee.[46]

Buell was caught between what one historian has described as an "immovable object of intractable logistics and the irresistable force of a determined president pushed by an impatient public." After making a feint towards East Tennessee that actually resulted in a Union victory at Mill Springs, Kentucky, in January 1862, Buell was eventually spared the rigors of marching into the mountains when Grant's victories at Forts Henry and Donelson presented Nashville for the taking. Once Nashville was secured, Buell, now in a subordinate position to Henry W. Halleck, was diverted from returning to eastern Tennessee towards a movement in support of Grant's approach on Corinth, Mississippi. At Shiloh in

45. T. Harry Williams, *Lincoln and His Generals*, 48.

46. Buell to McClellan, Nov. 27, 1861, *OR*, vol. 7, 2:450–51.; T. Harry Williams, *Lincoln and His Generals*, 47–48, 54–55.

April 1862, he provided timely support to Grant in checking Confederate initiatives of the first day's battle and then shoving the enemy back to Corinth.[47]

Both Buell and Grant joined Halleck in the lumbering advance upon Corinth, a trudge that proceeded at a one-mile clip each day. Finally, after seven weeks of inching along the short distance towards Corinth, the Federals dislodged the rebels from that city.[48] Buell was then ordered to march upon the vital Confederate nerve center of Chattanooga, an objective that would appease the administration's wish to secure East Tennessee. This optimistic and ambitious movement, however, attracted the attention and alarm of the enemy. Under the direction of Generals Kirby Smith and Braxton Bragg, the Confederates acted upon Buell's worst nightmare by marching into northern Tennessee enroute to Kentucky. Bragg and Smith put themselves athwart Federal communication and supply lines, forcing Buell to retire north to deal with the threat. Bragg not only turned Buell out of middle Tennessee but was found threatening the outskirts of Louisville on the Ohio River by August 1862.

Buell and Bragg collided on October 8, 1862, at Perryville, Kentucky. It was a battle plagued by strange, acoustical anomalies, rendering both Buell and Bragg unaware of the full extent of the forces engaged. Although a tactical draw, the Confederates were compelled to retire from the field, largely unmolested, to the safety of eastern Tennessee. Buell declined pursuit because he felt that the "limited supply of forage which the country affords is consumed by the enemy as he passes." He speculated that even the enemy could not remain long in the area before available forage was used up. "For the same reason," he argued, "We cannot pursue in it with any hope of overtaking him, for while he is moving back on his supplies as he goes consuming what the country affords we must bring ours forward." Buell's unwillingness to follow Bragg into

47. Hattaway and Jones, *How the North Won*, 62.

48. While Halleck's ponderous progress in the Corinth campaign invites comparison to Grant's aggressive style of fighting, it should be noted that Grant approved of Halleck's approach. Claiming that it was difficult "to get a large Army over country roads where it has been raining for the last five months," Grant recognized the logistical problems in supplying the vast Federal army. Moreover, he noted that the presence of the enemy forced the army to remain compact and that "we do well to approach a few miles everyday." See Ulysses S. Grant to Julia Dent Grant, Apr. 15, May 4, May 13, 1862, in Simon, *Papers of Ulysses S. Grant* 5:47, 110, 117–18.

eastern Tennessee exhausted Lincoln's patience and brought about his swift removal from command.[49]

The first full calendar year of the war came to an inglorious close for the North in December 1862. Since the first major defeat upon the plains of Manassas in July 1861, a host of Union generals had passed through the turnstile of command. In the West, Buell was the most signifcant casualty of northern impatience with failure to deliver victory. His predecessor, Sherman, had collected his wits during a furlough in Ohio following his dismissal, and he soon joined Grant in an adjutant capacity. Grant, himself, discovered that his early victories had earned Halleck's enduring jealousy, and after his questionable performance at Shiloh, he was placed under the yoke of "Old Brains'" tutelage. Fortunate was he when Halleck was summoned to Washington to assist Lincoln in directing the war's progress; it resurrected another command position for him.

There was no cohesive command in the East as the year 1862 came to a close. Unlike the western theatre, the public and political expectations held for Federal commanders in the East were intense, and their every decision and move were the subjects of intense scrutiny. McDowell, who had been sacrificed upon the altar of First Manassas, was thoroughly humiliated as Pope's chief lieutenant in the second encounter there. He spent the last weeks of the year defending his own actions and castigating Fitz John Porter's reputation at Second Manassas in a formal court of inquiry. He would sit out the next two years of the war in an administrative post in Washington before being banished to the Pacific coast to a relatively insignificant position.[50]

Pope's meteoric rise to prominence was shot down at Manassas, and he, like McDowell, was pushed into the background with no chance of redemption. Within a scant two weeks of his crushing defeat, he told an audience of well-wishers gathered outside his Chicago hotel how ecstatic he was to once again breathe the "pure air of Illinois." "God Almighty only knows," he intoned, "how sorry I am I ever left it." He was on his way to a new assignment in Minnesota to quell a recent uprising of the Sioux—tantamount to military exile.[51]

49. Buell to Halleck, Oct. 16, 17, 1862, *OR*, vol. 16, 2:619–22.

50. The text of McDowell's tortured testimony during the court of inquiry appears in *OR*, vol. 12, 1.

51. *New York Tribune*, Sept. 18, 1862.

Of all the Federal commanders in the early going, none, most likely, experienced a more miserable New Year's Eve (1862) than Ambrose Burnside. Not only had he been forced to stare across the frigid Rappahannock at the site of his monumental blunder, but he found himself traveling to Washington that day to meet with his commander in chief. A cabal of high-ranking officers had gone over his head to express their utter lack of confidence in their commander, and Burnside was there to explain the matter. For all intents and purposes, Burnside was used up, although he maneuvered to compel either Lincoln, Stanton, or Halleck to expressly authorize any fresh assaults upon the entrenched Confederates. Despite Lincoln's assurance that neither the country nor the government was driving him into another campaign, Burnside's days were numbered. The ill-starred Mud March in the middle of January was his swan song, and Lincoln, almost mercifully, relieved him of command on January 24.[52]

Yet, of all early Federal commanders, McClellan was most conspicuous for failing to live up to the expectations of a quick victory. To paraphrase an axiom, McClellan was the one to whom great trust was extended; thus, great things were expected. In that regard, McClellan was both the greatest failure and the greatest victim of the early part of the war. And modern Civil War history has inked thousands of words in judging him to be the greatest disappointment of the war. To T. Harry Williams, McClellan was Lincoln's "auger" that proved "too dull" to take hold. The other Williams, Kenneth P., vouched that McClellan had demonstrated in countless failures that he had always lacked the "capacity to command."[53] More recently, Sears has concluded, as mentioned earlier, that based upon the record, McClellan was indisputably the worst of all commanders, and that is truly saying something. When Glatthaar describes the scene of McClellan turning over command of the army to Burnside, he notes that that was merely the capstone to a "long line of failures with authority figures." As for Lincoln, Glatthaar maintains that that incident marked the culmination of "sixteen months of frustration."[54]

52. *CCW* 1:730–46; Halleck to Burnside, Jan. 7, 1863, in Nicolay and Adams, *Complete Works of Abraham Lincoln* 8:179–81.

53. T. Harry Williams, *Lincoln and His Generals,* 177; Kenneth P. Williams, *Lincoln Finds a General* 1:257.

54. Sears, *George B. McClellan: The Young Napoleon,* xii; Glatthaar, *Partners in Command,* 52.

Throughout the last fifty years of academic and popular writing in the Civil War, the verdicts of these scholars have found fertile ground.[55]

The fact of the matter is that 1862 was not an exclusively successful year for any major Federal commander, with the possible exception of Halleck, who would take the remainder of the war to prove he was not especially useful to the war effort. That complete success proved elusive was the case even for Grant and Sherman. Sherman, it should be recalled, was hesitant from the onset of secession even to get involved in the war, feeling, as he did, that Northerners were not taking the state of affairs seriously.[56] After years of professional and personal frustration, Sherman did not want to become part of an enterprise he believed certain to fail. Although his participation in the debacle at First Manassas confirmed his worst suspicions, it did not deter him from further involvement, provided he left the eastern theater of the war and avoided a top command position. He got his wish, but it did not work out according to his plan.[57]

Assigned as second in command to Gen. Robert Anderson, the unlikely hero of Fort Sumter, Sherman was in fine mettle for a few weeks.

55. The list of names is prohibitively long but a few deserve mention. James M. McPherson, perhaps today's preeminent Civil War scholar, found McClellan lacked the "mental and moral courage required of great generals," and his greatest failure was his fear of risking failure. See McPherson, *Battle Cry of Freedom*, 365. Nevins speculated that while many of McClellan's earlier shortcomings could be forgiven, his actions following Antietam "seemed to presage continued failure." See Nevins, *War for the Union* 2:331. In more popular avenues, Bruce Catton summarized years of writing of the Civil War by identifying the reason for McClellan's failure: "He did not like to fight." See Catton, *Reflections on the Civil War*, 82. Murfin's unheralded study of the Antietam campaign is introduced by the full chapter title "McClellan: Lincoln's Dilemma." See Murfin, *The Gleam of Bayonets*, 35–62. And, most recently, Waugh has suggested that while no general in the Civil War was as charismatic as McClellan, he "failed so utterly to use it to stir his soldiers to win battles." See Waugh, *Class of 1846*, 518.

56. In his memoirs, Sherman recalled his first meeting with Lincoln in March 1861 as a disaster. Introduced to the president by his brother John, a senator from Ohio, as newly arrived from Louisiana, Sherman was shocked by Lincoln's casual concern for the impending crisis. To Sherman's pointed reference to the South's "getting along swimmingly–they are preparing for war," Lincoln breezily replied, "Oh well, I guess we'll manage to keep house." Sherman was stunned into silence but managed to warn his brother that the politicians had managed to get things into "a hell of a fix and you may get them out as best you can." Sherman, *Memoirs* 1:168.

57. When McClellan assumed command in the wake of First Manassas, he recalled finding Sherman anxious and depressed about the Union's fortunes. See McClellan, *McClellan's Own Story*, 69–70.

Then, Anderson took leave on medical grounds, leaving Sherman in command. His dread of failure soon became a self-fulfilling prophecy. Within a couple of months, he had completely unravelled, prompting stories of his utter and complete insanity. The same instability cropped up again in his next assignment in Missouri. Sherman was lucky, however, for it is unlikely that others would have been coddled during such a critical period. Halleck was Sherman's mentor, and he saw to it that Sherman was nurtured until he could regain his composure. Sherman's confidence was not restored until he was assigned to Grant's command in February 1862.[58]

Sherman, himself, would always point to Shiloh as the moment of his recovery. Yet, the victory there was, in fact, a tainted one. Grant and Sherman were not properly prepared for the Confederate onslaught of the first day of battle. It is all the more difficult to ignore that oversight since there seems to be ample evidence to suggest that they had received reliable intelligence of a Confederate massing on their front. While it would appear that Grant stemmed the Confederate advance on his own, Buell's arrival on the evening of the first day certainly buttressed Grant's forces and allowed for a concentrated counterattack the following day.[59]

Sherman spent the remainder of 1862 in a wide range of assignments. Most noteworthy was his stewardship over the captured city of Memphis, and in this task he proved to be an efficient procurator of the government's presence there. Yet, Grant and Sherman continued to be stymied when it came to their significant mission of securing control of the Mississippi so that penetration of the deep South could be facilitated. The conquest of Vicksburg emerged as the key to accomplishing the task. In what would be but one of several sputtering steps to force the capitulation of Vicksburg, Sherman spent the last month of the year in a costly and weakly conceived offensive against entrenched Confederate positions northeast of the city. That attack culminated in the disastrous assault at Chickasaw Bluffs. The parallel to Burnside's failure in December at Fredericksburg can hardly escape notice. Not only were both battles fought in the same month and year, but they both featured similar elements of topography, similar infatuous planning, and similar results. The most

58. For Halleck's role in aiding Sherman's recovery, see Fellman, *Citizen Sherman,* 100–102.

59. Like nearly all memoirs, both Grant's and Sherman's were self-serving and selective in their memories. For their remarks concerning preparations at Pittsburg Landing, see Grant, *Memoirs* 1:357–58; and Sherman, *Memoirs* 1:229–30.

significant difference was that Burnside lost his job, while Sherman, though criticized somewhat in the press, was perceived as at least trying, something most Eastern commanders shunned.[60]

Sherman's new mentor, Grant, would have to wait until 1863 to enjoy unsullied adulation. The year 1862 was one of mixed reviews for Grant. He started off the year in grand fashion by capturing Forts Henry and Donelson on the Cumberland River. The aggressive qualities he displayed attracted the attention of Lincoln and others in Washington and contrasted favorably to McCellan's apparent languor. In reality, however, the victory at Fort Henry was a naval one, since the poorly constructed fortification was pounded into submission by the gunboats of Flag Officer Andrew Hull Foote. Moreover, like McClellan later at Malvern Hill, Grant was absent during the major Confederate sally out of Donelson against his works.[61]

Initially hailed as the great victor of Shiloh, Grant was stung even more than Sherman by the mounting criticism of his poor preparation. Again, he was absent at the start of the battle, even lulling Sherman into believing that the enemy had no intention of going on the offensive. He had just reported to Halleck that "I have scarcely the faintest idea of an attack (concerted one) being made upon us." He also violated basic tenets of military logic by refusing to have his men build trenches and leaving his army divided by the Tennessee River. And, like in many Civil War victories, Grant felt unable to implement an organized pursuit of the fleeing foe. Yet the most stinging accusation was that the reason he was so grossly unprepared was because he had been drinking once again. Halleck had already reprimanded him, however unfairly, on that subject after his victory at Fort Donelson. When Halleck, who not yet been called to Washington, descended upon Pittsburg Landing to take control of the offensive against Corinth, Grant was forced to assume a secondary role, one that turned out to be virtually uninvolved. His fortunes had sunk so low that he confided to Sherman his intention to leave the army, only to be dissuaded by his friend.[62]

60. For a discussion of the folly of attacking the enemy at Chickasaw Bluffs, see Royster, *The Destructive War*, 110–14.

61. As Hattaway and Jones illustrate, Halleck was the architect of the strategy at Forts Henry and Donelson and Grant followed his chief's instructions to the letter. See Hattaway and Jones, *How the North Won*, 65–77.

62. Grant to Halleck, Apr. 5, 1862, in Simon, *Papers of Ulysses S. Grant* 5:13. Sherman did not exactly persuade his chief that an attack was imminent, despite hearing of an in-

Although he was restored to command when Halleck left for Washington in July, Grant remained largely inactive during that period. The only two significant actions in his theater were commanded by Buell's eventual replacement, William S. Rosecrans, at Iuka and Corinth. Both were partial victories, and Grant, perhaps jealous of the good press Rosecrans received, criticized his subordinate for failing to go over to the offensive. As William S. McFeely has suggested, it took a rival, John S. McClernand, to arouse him from this dormancy and set his sights on Vicksburg. The year 1862 came to a close with Grant returning to Memphis after bogging down in the overland route to Vicksburg. He was humiliated and disgusted. His supply camp at Holly Springs had been surprised and destroyed by Confederater raiders, and his wife, Julia, had almost been captured by another party. To round off the year, he was informed of Sherman's repulse at Chickasaw Bluffs.[63]

In late 1862, Philadelphian Charles Janaway Stille published a pamphlet, *How a Free People Conduct a Long War.* Citing the example of Britain during the Napoleonic Wars, Stille exhorted his northern compatriots to steel themselves for a bitter and protracted contest with the South. He clearly recognized that the illusion of a quick and painless war had been shattered, no matter how much the public and political forces had wished it so. In fact, that illusion had hampered the war effort, for it had not compelled the North to make the adjustments necessary for a long war.

The shattered careers of several Federal commanders who, themselves at times, beheld the vision yet chafed under its heavy demands, bore witness to the disillusionment that had settled over the North in 1862. The illusion did not vanish on the plains of Manassas, as is frequently suggested in melodramatic tones, for it kept resurrecting itself

---

crease in activity at his front and receiving such confirmation from his pickets. The evening before Johnston's horde overran his position, Sherman assured Grant, who was several miles downstream, that he did not "apprehend anything like an attack" in the offing. See *OR,* vol. 10, 2:93–94. By Halleck's order, Grant even lost temporary command of the Army of the Tennessee. Sherman's account of his dissuading Grant from resigning appears in Sherman, *Memoirs* 1:255. A tidy summary of Grant's predicament following Shiloh can be found in McFeely, *Grant,* 111–21.

63. McClernand was a volunteer officer from Illinois who had persuaded Lincoln and Stanton to allow him to raise an army for the purpose of taking Vicksburg and opening up the Mississippi River. See McFeely, *Grant,* 122–27. Grant's abilities were again questioned, and the following spring Stanton sent Charles A. Dana to spy on him.

in places like the Peninsula, Antietam, Nashville, and Shiloh. But it most certainly disappeared by the end of 1862.[64]

With hindsight, it should not come as a surprise that the conflict that emerged during the Civil War did not end in a matter of weeks or months. Nothing in the American military experience prior to the Civil War had come close to matching it in scale and complexity. Despite a number of impressive advantages, the North faced serious obstacles at the onset of hostilities. The sheer landmass that needed to be conquered and subdued was a daunting prospect alone. As an army of conquest, the North would need to establish and maintain an elaborate logistical system that would guarantee supply and communication, both in front of a respectable foe and in the midst of a hostile people. The host of men who would need to be armed, supplied, and trained was unprecedented in national memory. And from where would experienced officers to direct those offensives come? These were but a few of the issues the North would have to address before it would bring the war to a successful conclusion.[65]

64. Lincoln was quite depressed at the end of 1862. The few victories in the West were clearly overshadowed by the disappointments and failures in the East. With all eyes riveted on the fortunes of the Army of the Potomac, little elsewhere mattered much. See Gallagher, *Antietam: Essays on the Maryland Campaign,* 2–3.

65. The magnitude of the difficulties facing the North in restoring the Union had convinced Winfield Scott at the onset of hostilities to opt for his blockade of the South. *OR,* vol. 51, pt. 1, 387.

7

The First Will Be Last
and the Last Will Be First

THE POPULAR CLAMOR TO PRODUCE A QUICK AND DECISIVE
victory was not the only thing that affected George B. McClellan's
chances for success at the beginning of the war. He was also plagued
by myriad complexities attendant to the command of a large volunteer army that was committed to the offensive. The pressure of meeting
public demands for an advance on Richmond actually complicated the
pressing organizational needs McClellan faced when he arrived in Washington in the wake of the defeat at First Manassas. Commanding, training,
supplying, and coordinating the strategic maneuvers of a massive army of
hastily gathered civilian soldiers was without precedent in the American experience of war. On one hand, many historians of the Civil War
readily acknowledge those challenges as a matter of fact. They do not,
however, use that recognition to temper their criticisms of McClellan.
Generally, little attention is paid to the context in which McClellan dealt
with the difficulties that faced the Federal army in the first fifteen months
of the war. Yet, in great measure, his early tenure deprived him of the
advantage of leading matured and seasoned civilian soldiers, adapted to
the demands of a new age of warfare, that later commanders of the Army
of the Potomac had. In studying the pressing need for staff organization
in the first year of the war, Edward Hagerman has astutely observed that
McClellan "suffered the frictions and frustrations of being first."[1]

---

1. Edward Hagerman, *The American Civil War and the Origins of Modern Warfare*
(Bloomington: Indiana Univ. Press, 1988), 47. This study is, perhaps, the most underrated

Grant and Sherman, themselves, were not without sympathy for McClellan's plight. During his celebrated world tour of 1877–1879, Grant gave periodic audiences to John Russell Young, a reporter for the *New York Herald*, who was part of the entourage. Russell compiled his recordings into a handsomely illustrated, lavender bound, two-volume set entitled, *Around the World with General Grant*. Toward the end of the tour, perhaps on the deck of a steamer in the India Ocean, Grant was asked to render his opinion of George McClellan. After supplying the often-cited quote, "McClellan is to me one of the mysteries of the war," Grant acknowledged that, although he had not taken time to study his campaigns, he was still favorably impressed with McClellan. More importantly, however, Grant divined from the mystery that the "test which was applied to him [McClellan] would be terrible to any man, being made a major-general at the beginning of the war." In response to the swirling controversies of the day that surrounded McClellan, and strangely prescient of future debates, Grant advised critics of McClellan that they had not considered "this vast and cruel responsibility–the war, a new thing to all of us, the army new, everthing to do from the outset, with a restless people and Congress." McClellan's unique disadvantage, according to Grant, was that he "was a young man" when the responsibility devolved upon him, and "if he did not succeed, it was because the conditions of success were so trying." Had he entered the war as Sherman, Thomas, or Meade had, Grant opined, there would have been no reason why "he would not have won as high a distinction as any of us."[2]

Although it has been argued that Grant's remarks reflected an unwillingness to denigrate a fellow officer who was still alive, Grant held a high regard for McClellan and many other professional officers during the war. And he expressed that respect at times when their personal fortunes had already taken a turn for the worse. Traveling east to his new command in 1864, Grant held lengthy conversations with Sherman concerning former eastern commanders who might benefit Sherman in his campaign in Georgia. "They are soldiers and good ones," Grant reportedly said, "and

---

work in Civil War literature, as it provides an excellent context for understanding why early Federal commanders were frustrated in producing the victories needed to defeat the Rebels and salvage their jobs.

2. Young, *Around the World with General Grant* 2:210–11. Some have attempted to deflate Grant's assessment, chalking it up to supreme magnanimity. Waugh called it "mitigating kindness." See Waugh, *Class of 1846*, 519.

we must not let them go under if we can help them in any way." Sherman agreed. Among the select number of specific officers mentioned was the name of George McClellan. Grant soon learned that political considerations would prevent him from employing the talents of those discredited officers. At the height of the crisis precipitated by Jubal Early's advance on Washington in July 1864, Grant suggested that Gen. William B. Franklin be appointed to the defense of the capital. In fact, when he did not receive a response to his first request, he asked a second time. At that point, Halleck enlightened Grant as to the true political nature of his suggestion. Franklin was an unacceptable choice because he was a member of the old McClellan clique and would not be tolerated by the radicals in Congress.[3]

Sherman, too, was understanding in his judgment of McClellan, and under circumstances less compromising than Grant's. Nearing the end of his occupation of Atlanta, with the election of 1864 a scant two weeks away, Sherman responded to his wife's inquiries concerning McClellan. Noting with amusement that her request was but one of several sought, including his brother John's, related to a report that he had pledged the army's support to McClellan, Sherman sharply rejected that canard. He did, however, refuse to join those who hoped to smear McClellan's military career for political profit. "At the time the howl was raised against McClellan, I knew it was in a measure unjust, for he was charged with delinquencies that the American people are chargeable for," Sherman argued. Referring to his own circumstances, in which the government's troop estimates fell far below the actual number, Sherman suggested that the Federal armies were "merely paper armies," and "so it was with McClellan . . . he had to fight partly with figures."[4]

More than any other, Sherman could readily understand the problems that faced McClellan in 1861. He, himself, had assiduously avoided those challenges in that year, knowing that in his case, he would have met with certain failure and disgrace. After his disappointing meeting with Lincoln in March, Sherman repaired to St. Louis where he observed the growing secession movement with despair and gauged the government's

3. John Y. Simon, ed., *Personal Memoirs of Julia Dent Grant* (New York: Putnam's, 1975), 128–29; *OR,* vol. 37, 2:373–74, 384–85, 400.

4. De Wolfe, *Home Letters of General Sherman,* 314–16. Sherman's views on McClellan are more revealing than Grant's, for he was aware of his wife's antipathy toward her husband's former commander. Ellen Sherman had blamed McClellan as one of the conspirators responsible for undermining Sherman's position in Kentucky in November 1861. See Marszalek, *Sherman: A Soldier's Passion for Order,* 167.

actions to stem it with scorn. He refused offers to command volunteer troops, noting to his brother, John, that until "professional knowledge will be appreciated, I will bide my time." It was not until June that he finally accepted the colonelcy of the Thirteenth Regular Army Regiment, a newly organized unit.[5]

Given the dearth of experienced West Point officers, it was not long before Sherman was elevated to command of the Third Brigade of Daniel Tyler's First Division. The assignment, which he accepted, brought with it the responsibility of training several volunteer regiments. Although he pitched into the work with great zeal, he was wary of leading the raw troops in battle. His apprehension was confirmed when public pressure prematurely pushed McDowell to lead the army into the Virginia countryside to do battle. Horrifed with the lapses in discipline and the poor showing of the volunteers, Sherman regretted he had agreed to get involved. The battle on the banks of Bull Run only confirmed his conviction that the Union was not yet prepared to subdue the rebellion. Asserting that Napoleon had taken three years to build an army, Sherman groaned that "here it is expected in ninety days, and Bull Run is the consequence." Consequently, if the government was going to rely on untrained and undisciplined civilian volunteers, he was not going to remain in a command position. "Not until I see day light ahead," he moaned to his wife, "do I want to lead." He made good on that conviction by leaping at Anderson's invitation to serve under his command in Kentucky. Within weeks he found himself commanding again, and his failure in Kentucky is the stuff of which legends are made.[6]

In the early weeks of the war just about anybody, provided he had sufficient connections, could present himself at the White House and expect to receive an appointment to command. In many cases, political considerations were of paramount importance, prompting Lincoln to choose candidates based on their abilities to bond one interest group or political faction to the national cause. In a democratic government, the selection of political generals and prominent spokesmen was an essential part of the process. But such leaders sometimes produced military disas-

5. William T. Sherman to John Sherman, Apr. 18, 1861, in Papers of William T. Sherman, Manuscript Division, Library of Congress.

6. De Wolfe, *Home Letters of General Sherman*, 214. Sherman's second letter is quoted in Marszalek, *Sherman: A Soldier's Passion for Order*, 155.

ters. One of the most amusing anecdotes to surface regarding the practice recalled the selection of the colonel for the Seventy-Fourth Pennsylvania, Alexander Schimmelfennig, one of several Prussian refugees who found their way into the Union army. Supposedly, Lincoln and Stanton were reviewing an appointment list, looking for qualified candidates to command one of the many German-American regiments being raised. To Stanton's objection that Schimmelfennig did not come highly recommended, Lincoln riposted: "No matter about that. His name will make up for any difference there may be, and I'll take the risk of his coming out all right." Then with a chuckle, he pronounced each syllable of the name distinctly, accenting the final one, "Schim–mel–fen–*nig* must be appointed." That was only a mildly exaggerated example of a practice that continued throughout the war. It was, however, felt more acutely in the beginning of the war when so many appointments were available. In time, many of those appointees resigned their commissions or developed into acceptable officers, or failing that, they were shunted to insignificant commands out of harm's way.[7]

Ordinarily, dubious military virtues in colonels could be offset by firmer hands on the brigade and division level. Yet, the same process was frequently enacted for both appointments and promotions to those important command posts. "It seems but little better than murder to give important commands to such men as Banks, Butler, McClernand, Sigel, and Lew Wallace," growled the professional West Pointer Halleck, "yet it seems impossible to prevent it." To military professionals it must have seemed that an almost carnival-like atmosphere prevailed in Washington, as promotions to high commands were handed out like so many candied apples. Underscoring the incredible nature of the situation was an encounter on the steps of the White House between Sherman and McDowell.

"Hello Sherman," McDowell called. "What did you ask for?"
"A colonelcy," Sherman replied.

7. Quoted in Carl Sandburg, *Abraham Lincoln: The War Years*, 4 vols. (New York: Harcourt, 1939), 2:60. In fairness, it should be noted that his incident is cited as an example of Lincoln's mastery over the delicate political dimensions of fighting the war. In any event, Schimmelfenning had a respectable, if not spectacular, career during the war. He gained some notoriety at the Battle of Gettysburg, where, upon stumbling behind enemy lines, he sat out most of the conflict hidden in a woodshed.

"What?" McDowell implored, "You should have asked for a
brigadier general's rank. You're just as fit for it as I am."
"I know it," Sherman shot back.

Yet, here was a frequently duplicated case in which two men, one of
whom having long resigned his commission, were vaulted to sensitive
leadership roles. Both of them, but McDowell in particular, were selected
for posts way out of proportion to their experience.[8]

And so it was with McClellan, too. Notwithstanding his boast that
he could "do it all," his very selection to succeed McDowell to command
in Washington was somewhat presumptuous and only underscored how
totally unprepared the northern army was to restore the seceded states
to the Union. Fresh from his victorious campaign in the mountains of
western Virginia, McClellan was a mere thirty-four years of age when
he assumed command in 1861. His early success was more significant in
its political outcome than spectacular in its execution. Yet who was there
to be tapped for such an exalted command position? For that matter, who
was prepared to even lead a brigade, let alone a division? One of the
heroes of the War with Mexico, Zachary Taylor, was long dead. Older
career officers, like Joseph Mansfield, Edwin Sumner, and John Wool,
with experience in the Mexican War, were found wanting. Robert Patterson, who along with Winfield Scott was an old relic of the War of 1812,
had already proven himself a liability in command, for it was he who
allowed Johnston to rendezvous with Beauregard at Manassas.[9]

The general in chief, Scott, had himself never commanded more
than ten thousand men at any time. Moreover, he no longer commanded
the public's confidence as a warrior. At the ripe age of seventy-four, his
immense frame had become saddled by an almost comical obesity. Barely
able to walk, the general had done himself and every horse within grasp a
favor by generally opting to travel by carriage. Between gargantuan meals,
he frequently napped and conducted most of his business reclining on
a divan. While he was still capable of supplying intelligent advice, he was
hardly capable or expected to take to the field. Then again, McClellan's
predecessor and Scott's eventual choice to command the first call of volunteers, McDowell, did not exactly possess impressive credentials. While

8. Quoted in Shelby Foote, *The Civil War: A Narrative*, 3 vols. (New York: Random
House, 1958–74), 1:59.
9. Sears, *George B. McClellan: The Young Napoleon*, 79–94, 125.

older than McClellan, he had nothing in his background to suggest that he could capably direct an army of thirty-five thousand raw troops to do battle.[10]

As we have already seen, McClellan proved extremely capable in addressing the basic military needs in the wake of First Manassas. Despite the exaggerated fears of a Confederate assault upon Washington following McDowell's rout, McClellan quickly took measures to complete the construction of a formidable defense perimeter around the city. He implemented a rigorous selection process to screen new officer applicants, and he weeded out the existing ineffective ones. He launched an unprecedented training program that whipped a mass of raw civilian recruits into a highly skilled fighting force—the greatest army ever assembled on the North American continent. He accomplished all of those things within a political structure that had always frowned upon maintaining large standing armies and that could not provide an organizational framework to develop a fighting force rapidly.

That conservative course of action was seconded by both Sherman and Grant in late 1861. In Kentucky, Sherman was paralyzed by the thought of even conducting an offensive campaign, since he believed he was scarcely capable of holding his own against his opponent. Grant, fresh from his first taste of battle at Belmont, hunkered down in Cairo, Illinois, and did "little except prepare for the long struggle."[11]

To a generation of officers who had little in their career portfolios to prepare them for a modern war of conquest, the challenges of the first two years of the war were staggering. The tactics, logistics, intelligence, and medical services that would be required in the conflict had outstripped the needs embodied in an earlier age of limited wars those men had studied at West Point. The introduction of technological advancements, such as the railroad, telegraph, and a vast array of new weapons of destruction, had far eclipsed their tactical imaginations. The innovations in waging war made the burden of the offensive a most difficult task. And in the early years of the war, many Federal commanders struggled, and often failed, in resolving those difficulties. Such was the case with McClellan, Sherman, and Grant.

10. Useful descriptions of the officers available for command in 1861 can be found in Davis, *Battle at Bull Run*, 4–14.

11. Sherman wrote directly to Lincoln on the subject of his unpreparedness. See *OR*, vol. 4:300, 306–7; Grant, *Memoirs* 1:168.

Logistical considerations were the bane of offensive campaigning, making it difficult at best and perilous at worst. Unlike a defensive force that has its back to its communication and supply lines, the attacking force is compelled to extend further from its base with each passing mile. Extended supply lines invite attack from enemy raiding parties and disruption from hostile populations. Examination of the logistical problems in the early part of the year makes it understandable why early Federal commanders were frustrated in their offensive designs. That was the case not only with McClellan and Buell, but with Grant and Sherman as well.

Of all the early Federal commanders, Buell faced the greatest challenge in addressing the offensive goals laid out for him when he replaced Sherman in November 1861. Sherman had not initiated even the first steps in his assignment, as he felt the task was too daunting to consider. After pacifying Kentucky, it was hoped that Sherman would lead his force into eastern Tennessee to rescue the large Unionist population from Confederate control. Moreover, a move into eastern Tennessee was envisioned as part of an overall concert of action directed against the Confederacy, enabling each sector to assist the other and use the overwhelming numbers to squash the rebellion in piecemeal fashion. Like McClellan would do in the East, Sherman magnified the strength of the opposing force under General Simon Buckner Bolivar. He refused to move from his defensive works and initiated a series of requests for massive reinforcements to maintain his position in the face of an overwhelming foe. At one point, he refused to guarantee the safety of Louisville and proclaimed he would need a force of two hundred thousand to make an advance.[12]

Buell inherited Sherman's dilemma, although his superior organizational skills and calming influence quieted concerns for the safety of northern Kentucky. His attempts to divert the government's fixation on eastern Tennessee in favor of controlling Bowling Green and Nashville were rebuffed by Lincoln's insistence that the main focus remain where it was. When his subordinate, Gen. George H. Thomas, gained a victory at Mill Springs over an enemy force under impetuous Gen. Felix Zollicoffer,

12. McClellan's plan for the Army of the Cumberland was outlined in his strategic memorandum to Lincoln on August 2, 1861. Once Kentucky was "cordially united" to the Union, McClellan proposed that the army would move toward eastern Tennessee in order to assist local Unionists and seize the "railroads leading from Memphis to the East." See Sears, *Civil War Papers of George B. McClellan*, 71–75. For Sherman's view of his predicament, see William T. Sherman to Lorenzo Thomas, Oct. 8, 1861, Sherman Papers. See also Thomas's reply of October 10, 1861 in *OR*, vol. 4:299–300.

Buell was expected to cross the Cumberland River and advance into east-ern Tennessee. Thomas, however, advised Buell that he could not advance any further, as he would be unable to find forage within a fifteen-mile radius of his army and that the roads were in such dreadful condition that "by the time the wagons reach here the teams have nearly consumed their loads." In a route without any railroad lines, Buell's attempts to corduroy the muddy paths in the region proved a Sisyphean mission. Fortunately for him, Halleck's designs on Confederate forts guarding the Cumberland and Tennessee Rivers in the western part of Tennessee saved him from his useless labors.[13]

As we have already seen, Buell entered Nashville after the Confeder-ate collapse at Forts Henry and Donelson. Then he moved in support of Grant at Shiloh and participated in Halleck's advance upon Corinth. Following Corinth, Buell was instructed to move towards Chattanooga; however, he was first slowed by supply and communication problems and later by Bragg's and Morgan's flanking movements into Kentucky. He eventually stymied Confederate ambitions in Kentucky at Perryville in Oc-tober 1862, but he discovered he could not pursue the enemy into eastern Tennessee for the same reasons he faced at the beginning of the year when Halleck called him away. Buell was back to square one. While his opportunities looked "particularly promising at a distance," according to Alan Nevins, they were "particularly difficult at near view." That time, however, Halleck was in Washington and seconded Lincoln's impatience with Buell. Buell was sacked and replaced by Rosecrans.[14]

Meanwhile, back East, McClellan shared some of the same diffi-culties Buell experienced—and a few uniquely his own. In preparing for his grand campaign on the Peninsula, McClellan had to provide sup-plies for an army that would hover somewhere between 90,000 to 110,000 men. The magnitude of that unprecedented need alone was perplex-ing. In his final campaign, following the battle of Antietam, he had to

13. Although he appreciated Buell's difficulties, McClellan commanded him to pro-ceed to East Tennessee, noting that "you have no idea of the political pressure brought to bear upon the Government for a forward advance." See OR, vol. 7:564. Earlier, Halleck had declined to assist Buell in his proposed move upon Tennessee, observing that he was thor-oughly disorganized and unprepared for activity. Halleck cautioned McClellan that "the 'On to Richmond' policy here will produce another Bull Run disaster." See Halleck to Mc-Clellan, Dec. 26, 1861, OR, vol. 8, 462–63.

14. Buell to Halleck, Oct. 16, 17, 1862, OR, vol. 16, 2:619, 622; Nevins, War for the Union 2:11.

contend with an exhausted supply system that confounded an immediate pursuit of the enemy into Virginia.

Ironically, of all the potential flaws that might afflict the opening of a first major campaign, supply problems were not among them. McClellan's selection of a waterborne passage to the Peninsula bypassed the dangers of maintaining overland supply lines by relying on the Union's superior naval presence. Despite its eventual vulnerability, the supply depot at White House Landing, except for periodic shortages and the actual distribution of goods, kept the Federal army in fighting trim. McClellan's meticulous preparation, the source of much criticism among both his contemporaries and today's historians, had at least paid off in that one vital regard. "The supply bureaus," in one historian's estimation, "managed to supply what for the time was equivalent to the population of a large American city."[15]

The Peninsula Campaign, the first major Federal offensive in the East, was plagued by difficulties inherent in novel undertakings. While the measure of a good commander is the degree to which he can manage the unexpected, the aggregate number of obstacles McClellan faced was astounding. Admittedly, his excessive caution and his inflation of enemy strength played a significant role in the progress of the campaign. However, those limitations did not necessarily doom the campaign to failure. An array of factors beyond his control had an even greater adverse impact.

The army, unprecedented in its size and needs, marched with maps that defied accuracy. Two years later, Grant would benefit from the handiwork of McClellan's surveyors and cartographers. The task of supplying an immense army strained the considerable talents of the army's quartermaster service. Attempts to coordinate combined operations with the Union navy were undercut by interservice jealousies and a dearth of experience. The navy was reluctant to deal with the Confederate ironclad menace at Hampton Roads, declined McClellan's invitation to help turn the Confederates out of Yorktown, and failed to assist in making the James the army's offensive left wing in the initial approach to Rich-

---

15. Hagerman, *The American Civil War*, 46. Not only were supply needs prodigious, but, as Quartermaster General Montgomery Meigs observed, "a few weeks only have been allowed for the outfit of expeditions which other nations would spend months in preparing." See *OR*, vol. 11, 2:797.

mond. Incessant and prodigious amounts of rain turned the few roads into quagmires and limited the ability of the army to maneuver through forested and swampy areas.[16]

Breakdowns in communication, the result of an inadequate development in staff organization, stalled offensives by disrupting the necessary coordination of movements. At the time, few realized that the demands of modern warfare needed to be addressed by an overhaul of the army's staff departments. Most early commanders simply improvised with the structures they had inherited. Unglamorous as such an undertaking might have been, the benefits of reorganization would have been enormous. The first steps in staff organization were taken under McClellan's tenure, but they functioned imperfectly even until the end of the war. For example, the army's reliance on civilian agents for reconnaissance and intelligence gathering underscored the amateurish character of making war in 1862 and the folly of inadequate staff development. Finally, the entire campaign on the Peninsula was affected by a series of untimely decisions on the part of the administration. They effectively eroded the integrity of McClellan's strategy and alienated the military commander from his civilian superiors, who, of course, had only grudgingly assented to his plan of operations in the first place.[17]

McClellan's second campaign that climaxed at the battle of Antietam, only to sputter in his reluctance to pursue Lee into northern Virginia, was beset by logistical problems. In the wake of Second Manassas, Lee compounded Pope's inglorious retreat to the hills of Arlington by turning northwards into Maryland with the intention of sacking Harrisburg, Pennsylvania. McClellan, recently restored to command the capital's defense, was now ordered to pursue Lee's army. Again, he faced the difficult task of reorganizing a routed force and integrating it with newly mustered

16. An excellent study of one of the most difficult obstacles and most underestimated factors in conducting offensive operations—the terrain of Virginia—is developed in Mark E. Neely, Jr., "Wilderness and the Cult of Manliness: Hooker, Lincoln, and Defeat," in Boritt, ed., *Lincoln's Generals*, 51–77.

17. For a discussion of the difficulties surrounding operations in the Peninsula campaign, see Reed, *Combined Operations in the Civil War.* Hagerman emphasizes the woeful lack of development in staff organization in his sympathetic treatment of McClellan's problems, although he contends that this "blind spot" in McClellan's professional education reflected West Point's emphasis on tactics and technological technique to the detriment of strategic organization. See Hagerman, *American Civil War,* 51.

volunteer regiments that had been hastily summoned to Washington. Wasting little time, the army moved out to seek immediate battle with an illusive foe.[18]

Without the advantage of preparation or the security and consistency afforded by water routes, supplies had to catch up with the army on the move. In the main, the army remained sufficiently supplied throughout the course of the campaign leading up to the battle on the banks of the Antietam. Pursuit of Lee's retreating army, however, was another matter, despite the acrimonious debate between McClellan and Lincoln over fatigued horses. The continued growth and constant turnover in the Army of the Potomac outmatched the ability of the supply service to provide for more than a day's march. Both McClellan and Meigs ascertained that the Virginia countryside in which the army would be campaigning and foraging was barren of supply, having been "ravaged by the repeated passage of armies." Translated into concrete terms, the army could not effectively campaign twenty to twenty-five miles beyond the terminal depots of only two railway lines. His adversary, Lee, understood McClellan's predicament. Allaying his own commander in chief's fears for the safety of the Army of Northern Virginia, Lee noted that he believed McClellan "is yet unable to move, and finds difficulty in procuring provisions more than sufficient from day to day."[19]

Despite supply shortages,[20] McClellan's unwillingness to cross the Potomac into Virginia was exasperating the government's patience, and

18. Although it attained legendary status for its heroic role at Gettysburg, the 20th Maine was one of many regiments that arrived just in time to see the wounded return from Second Manassas. It was so green that its inability even to march in step drew sneers from veteran soldiers and jeers from spectators. See Alice Rains Trulock, *In the Hands of Providence: Joshua L. Chamberlain and the American Civil War* (Chapel Hill: Univ. of North Carolina Press, 1992), 64–65.

19. In response to a report from McClellan that his mounts were "absolutely broken down from fatigue and want of flesh," Lincoln lashed out with the sharp inquiry: "Will you pardon me for asking what the horses of your army have done since the battle of Antietam that fatigues anything?" Unknown to Lincoln, an epidemic of foot and mouth disease had broken out among the army horses. See *OR*, vol. 19, 2:485–86, 798. According to Hagerman, both Meigs and McClellan based their estimates upon the Napoleonic equations for supply standards that were inadequate for Civil War armies. See Hagerman, "The Professionalization of George B. McClellan," 130; Lee to Davis, Oct. 2, 1862, *OR*, vol. 28:644.

20. On October 20, 1862, Meade wrote his wife: "I have hundreds of men in my command without shoes, going barefooted, and I can't get a shoe for man or beast." See Meade, *Life and Letters of George Gordon Meade* 1:320.

suspicions concerning his desire to crush the rebellion resurfaced in Washington. Towards the end of October, McClellan began to move the army onto Virginia soil. Once across the Potomac, he moved with surprising vigor. By November 6, he had brought the bulk of the army to the area surrounding Warrenton. He had effectively divided Lee's army into two widely separated halves, intending to drive between them. The celerity of those moves alarmed Lee, as he noted in his report to Davis on November 6: "[McClellan] is also moving more rapidly than usual, and it looks like a real advance." Longstreet was equally taken aback, recalling that McClellan's movement between his corps and Jackson's was exactly that with which the Confederates "felt serious apprehension." Unknown to Lee and Longstreet, McClellan would never realize the outcome of his general advance, for the axe had already fallen on his career.

On November 5, Lincoln had drafted the order to relieve McClellan of command. Fearing that McClellan would refuse to give up his command, his inveterate detractor, Stanton, called Brig. Gen. Charles P. Buckingham to his office on the evening of the sixth with detailed instructions for handling the matter. After convincing Burnside that he must accept command of the army, Buckingham was instructed to deliver the news of the change in command to McClellan, in person. McClellan, ordered to repair to Trenton to await further instructions, never again saw active duty in the Civil War.[21]

Sherman, Buell, and McClellan were not the only commanders at the beginning of the war to experience difficulties adjusting to realities of a new age of warfare. Grant, too, had his full share of problems that frequently sidetracked him from his offensive impulses. Shortly after taking command in Cairo, Grant complained to the War Department that

---

21. Lee to Davis, Nov. 6, 1862, *OR,* vol. 28:697. Longstreet's comments can be found in "The Battle of Fredericksburg," *Battles and Leaders* 3:85. Rufus Ingalls, McClellan's chief quartermaster and outspoken critic, noted in his official report that McClellan's advance after crossing the Potomac "was a magnificent spectacle of celerity and skill." See *OR,* vol. 27:96. Gideon Welles, too, was surprised by McClellan's rapid movement. See Beale and Brownsword, *Diary of Gideon Welles* 1:183. Burnside, McClellan's successor, was the victim of a supply system that was not clicking on all cylinders. Halleck and the War Department failed to deliver the pontoon bridges Burnside ordered well in advance. The Federal army, having stolen a march on Lee, was forced to wait on the river bank opposite Fredericksburg. Although some suspect that Halleck, Burnside, and Stanton were all at fault, T. Harry Williams pins the bulk of the blame at Halleck's doorstep. See T. Harry Williams, *Lincoln and His Generals,* 196–97.

"[There] is a great deficiency in transportion. I have no ambulances. The clothing received has been almost universally of an inferior quality and deficient in quantity. The arms in the hands of the men are mostly the old flint-lock repaired. . . . [The] Quartermaster's Department has been carried on with so little funds," he wailed, "that Government credit has become exhausted."[22]

Grant drew first blood at Belmont in November 1861. It went well until his force overran the enemy camp, whereupon the evident lack of discipline induced his troops to rummage for trophies instead of pursuing their foe. That lapse allowed the routed Confederate force to manuever itself between Grant's force and their transports on the river, compelling the Federals to fight their way through the enemy. In Grant's case, his undisciplined troops nearly cost him his life, as he found himself the last man between the rebel army and the departing boats. Luckily, the captain of the last transport to shove off noticed him courageously, but frantically, riding in his direction. A gangplank was run out to rescue the general. It is no wonder that his troops "did little but prepare for the long struggle" before taking to the field again.[23]

When he ventured out again, Grant engineered the victories at Forts Henry and Donelson. The reduction of those two fortifications alone forced the entire collapse of the Confederate defensive system on the Cumberland and Tennessee Rivers, compelling the Confederate general, Albert S. Johnston, to retreat into northern Mississippi. Although those were triumphs of great strategic importance, they were accomplished with relative ease. And they were not managed without mishap or without the cooperation of incompetent Confederate leadership. Flag Officer Andrew Hull Foote was the actual victor at poorly constructed Fort Henry, as his gunboats pounded it into submission. The remaining officer and artillery regiment that had not fled to the safety of Fort Donelson quickly surrendered as Grant's host began arriving. In fact, the fort was built so low to the river that, at the time Foote's naval officer arrived to

22. *OR*, vol. 7:442.

23. Grant, *Memoirs* 1:278–79. Grant was shocked to learn that this battle "was severely criticized in the North, as a wholly unnecessary battle, barren of results, or the possibility of them from the beginning." He consoled himself with the thought that had he not fought at Belmont, another Federal force under one of his subordinates would have been destroyed. Caught in an impossible dilemma, he wagered that had his subordinate been crushed, he "should have been culpable indeed." See Grant, *Memoirs* 1:281.

accept its surrender, his boat crew sailed clear through the main portal into the very fort itself. Attempts to repeat the naval pounding of Fort Henry proved unsuccessful at Fort Donelson, although its structural integrity was only slightly better than Fort Henry's. To Grant's credit, he refused to be cowed by the Confederate repulse of the Union gunboats. He dug in and proceeded to invest the rebel stronghold. Many of his soldiers, who had previously discarded their coats and blankets during an earlier winter's thaw, must have regretted their commander's resolve, as the weather abruptly turned fiercely cold.[24]

Like McClellan at Malvern Hill on the Peninsula, Grant used the respite in action to confer with Foote about the future use of the navy's gunboats. While he was absent from his troops, the Confederate force attacked. Scurrying back to the front, Grant noticed that his force was greatly demoralized by the enemy's obvious determination to stay and fight. Moreover, he recalled that although there was an abundance of ammunition lying around the Federal camp, many officers did not know how to keep the troops continually supplied during battle conditions "at that stage of the war." The Federals sufficiently rallied to both stem the enemy advance and push them back to their fortifications. Having failed to sever the Federal encirclement of the fort, the Confederate commanding officers knew that capitulation was inevitable. Grant had already taken advantage of the poor executive ability exercised by the former United States secretary of war, John Floyd, first in command at Donelson.[25] Now, the bungling Confederate leadership, inept in its best showing, took a farcical twist. Floyd, fearful of his very life as a high-ranking traitor, turned over the responsibility of surrendering to his second in command, Gen. Gideon Pillow. Described by Grant as "conceited," Pillow had no more relish for the task than Floyd had shown. In turn, he handed the honor of surrendering Donelson over to Simon Bolivar Buckner, Grant's friend from the old army. Donelson fell on February 16, 1862, but not before Floyd and Pillow had fled across the Tennessee River. Also making

24. Grant, *Memoirs* 1:282–87; Benjamin F. Cooling, *Forts Henry and Donelson: The Key to the Confederate Heartland* (Knoxville: Univ. of Tennessee Press, 1987), 101–6.

25. For the misappropriation of national property and violation of public trust, Floyd had every reason to fear capture. During the closing months of the Buchanan administration, Floyd had authorized the transfer of Federal arms and munitions to state arsenals in the South. He had also scattered the national forces in such a way as to aid the South during the secession crisis.

his way to freedom was Nathan Bedford Forrest, commander of a battalion of cavalry, and perhaps the only one of the three fugitives whom the Confederates would have otherwise missed.[26]

Following the battle at Shiloh, where his ostracism at the hands of Halleck almost prompted his resignation from command, Grant received permission to move his headquarters to Memphis. He regained his former command position in July when Halleck was called to Washington. Before leaving, however, Halleck had scattered the huge force under his command at Corinth, leaving Grant with little option other than to remain on the defensive. In September and October, Grant's subordinate, Rosecrans, fought two fierce actions at Iuka and Corinth, Mississippi. Rosecrans successfully repelled the Confederate advance, but his pursuit of the retreating enemy was hampered by his unfamiliarity with the terrain and his outdistancing his own supply lines. At that point, Grant began to turn his attention to Vicksburg.[27]

In recalling the faltering steps in the early stages of the Vicksburg campaign, Grant wrote that "[Up] to this time it had been regarded as an axiom in war that large bodies of troops must operate from a base of supplies which they always covered and guarded in all forward movements." So it was, then, that Grant began his overland approach to the fortress of Vicksburg by establishing a supply line. Meanwhile, Sherman was sent down the Mississippi with the expedition that would at first wallow in the swamps of Steele's Bayou and then falter on the slopes of Chickasaw Bluffs. At Holly Springs, Mississippi, Grant established his principal forward supply depot. From there, he continued his march south to Oxford with the hope of swinging westward towards Vicksburg as part of the pincer movement upon that bastion. The ease of the march deep

26. McPherson describes the performance of Confederate leadership at Donelson as an "opera bouffe." See McPherson, *Battle Cry of Freedom*, 401. Grant admitted that had Buckner been in command from the outset that Donelson would not have fallen so easily. See Grant, *Memoirs* 1:308–10.

27. Grant was particularly upset with Rosecrans's inability to follow up his success on the battlefield. However, at Iuka, Grant, who was poised to rush reinforcements to Rosecrans, never heard the sounds of the battle because the wind swept the noise away from his direction. By the time Rosecrans's courier reached Grant over nearly impassable roads, the enemy was well into their retreat. Grant's criticism of Rosecrans is obvious in his memoirs, although at the time of the battle he seemed far more understanding of the problems of pursuit. See Simon, *Papers of Ulysses S. Grant* 6:97; and Grant, *Memoirs* 1:408–13.

into enemy territory eventually caught up with him. On December 20, the Confederate general Earl Van Dorn, who had made a swinging manuever past Grant's juggernaut, came slamming into Grant's supply base at Holly Springs. In addition to destroying Grant's supplies, Van Dorn's troopers tore up large sections of the rail line that supplied the Federal army at Oxford. Grant's advance was halted. Feeling he was out of options, Grant ordered the retreat to Memphis. He was outraged with the failure of his commander at Holly Springs to offer resistance, yet he had retained his services despite Rosecrans's denunciation of the officer's conduct at the Battle of Iuka. Grant's telegram to the Sherman expedition on the Mississippi, ordering postponement of an attack, since he could not prevent a Confederate concentration at Vicksburg, arrived belatedly thanks to enemy sabotage of the telegraph wires. Sherman, in a letter to his wife, succinctly summarized the dismal effort: "Well, we have been to Vicksburg and it was too much for us and we have backed out."[28]

December 1862 marked one of the low points in Lincoln's desire to restore the Union. There was precious little good news in the military sphere to dispel gloomy dispositions in Washington. Military commanders, themselves, had little reason to lift their glasses in holiday toasts, except to better fortune in the new year. In the East, McDowell, Pope, and McClellan had been discarded, and they left that theater for browner pastures. Burnside was essentially a spent article; he just did not know it yet. He would soon be demoted so that he could last a couple more years to experience still further indignities. Farther west, Buell had been shelved, but he did not even get an assignment to help fight the Sioux. Sherman, who was lucky enough to have survived his overworked nerves of the previous year, managed to salvage some honor from his fruitless attack at Chickasaw Bluffs by joining Adm. David Dixon Porter and Gen. John A. McClernand in subduing the Confederate fort at Arkansas Post on January 12, 1863. It was small recompense for the ill-advised assault of the month before. One of his aides put it in perspective by writing Sherman's wife that, when compared with Shiloh, Arkansas Post "was not a good

28. Grant, *Memoirs* 1:432–33, 437. Sherman is quoted in McFeely, *Grant,* 126. McPherson makes the salient point that Grant appreciated his army's ability to live off the land during his retreat to Memphis, and he and Sherman would apply the lesson with great results in the future. See McPherson, *Battle Cry of Freedom,* 579.

quail hunt." Grant, of course, was on his way back to Memphis, having aborted his campaign to assail Vicksburg from the east.[29] At about the same time, Lincoln was growing in awareness himself that offensive operations were constrained by logistical issues and the primacy of the defensive position. Having run through several generals by the end of 1862, particularly McClellan and Buell, Lincoln told his friend Carl Schurz, "I do not clearly see the prospect of any more rapid movements. I fear we shall at last find out that the difficulty is in our case rather than in particular generals."[30]

Despite the somewhat blemished performance of all these early commanders, one is struck by the fact that only two of them, Grant and Sherman, were not sacked by the end of 1862. Grant, who had his greatest victories to date under Halleck's overall command, displayed an aggressive spirit that, when contrasted to Lincoln's perceptions of other commanders, helped mitigate his setbacks. Of all the commanders in question, he fought in an area that was, though highly strategic, the greatest distance from Washington. And his seemingly rapid advances deep into enemy territory were facilitated by the region's many navigable rivers. Sherman, Grant's protege since early 1862, had survived a career-threatening crisis and enjoyed the relative obscurity of his new position.

Buell, the other western commander, faced the greatest logistical obstacles of all. Yet, he was a conspicuous failure in delivering one of Lincoln's top priorities—the liberation of East Tennessee. His repeated delays in advancing in that direction were perceived as empty excuses. Furthermore, his conservative and introspective personality and his penchant for strict discipline in the ranks did not endear him to his own troops. Whereas McClellan's hauteur came across as aristocratic, Buell's smacked of pure haughtiness.

Of the three commanders in the eastern theater, McDowell and Pope were dismissed for salutary failure on the battlefield. It is but a small wonder, then, that subsequent eastern generals thought long and hard before risking their careers on attacking the enemy. On face value, McClellan was relieved because, as Lincoln informed his own cabinet member, Montgomery Blair, he had "the slows." He had been tried twice and found wanting. McClellan would not press the enemy, so he turned

29. L. M. Dayton to Ellen E. Sherman, Jan. 14, 1863, in *Papers of William T. Sherman,* Manuscript Division, Library of Congress.

30. Lincoln to Schurz, Nov. 26, 1862, in Basler, *Collected Works* 5:509–11.

the command over to Burnside, whose subsequent actions should have quickly made Lincoln careful about what he wished for. Nevertheless, McClellan's record does not seem that much worse than Sherman's or Grant's at the time of his dismissal.

The difference may well have more to do with the fact that both Sherman and Grant were free from the pressure eastern commanders experienced. Rather than being punished for their mistakes, they were given opportunities to learn from them. It is questionable whether the Ulysses Grant who was badly surprised and unprepared at Shiloh, and who failed several times over the course of nearly a year to conquer Vicksburg, would have lived up to the expectations in the East. As for Sherman, it is doubtful that he would ever have returned from the mental crisis in Kentucky had he been an eastern commander at the time. Even granting that he might have survived that episode, he most certainly would have been more than just pilloried in the press for sharing Grant's nonchalance at Shiloh had that battle been fought on the James rather than the Tennessee River. And might he not have shared the same fate as Burnside after Fredericksburg for his suicidal assault on Chickasaw Bluffs, had that promontory been in the state of Virginia and not Mississippi?

Historians, too, occasionally reveal an understanding of the advantages held by Grant and Sherman over their counterparts in the early part of the war. Yet, they do not always keep those in mind in their summary assessments. Even T. Harry Williams, one of Grant's greatest admirers, understood that the general's initial service in the war was more fortunate in every way than the introductory experiences of McClellan and Sherman. "Unlike them," Williams admits, "he was not pushed into high command before he was ready for it or before he had been tested for it."[31]

By invoking Sherman's own words, Williams also provides a glimpse into the historical development of those generals judged as military giants and those viewed as failures, and in some way those words serve as a fitting epitaph for McClellan's Civil War career. In the early part of the war, Sherman mused that "life is a race, the end is all that is remembered by the Great World. Those, who are out at the end, will never be able to magnify the importance of intermediate actions, no matter how brilliant and important." Even at the threshold of ultimate victory, Sherman, himself, was concerned lest the adulation accorded to him by the

31. T. Harry Williams, *McClellan, Sherman, and Grant,* 86.

press for his triumph at Atlanta be swept away by a single mistake in the remaining days of the war.[32]

A careful consideration of McClellan's difficulties in waging offensive action in the early stages of the war cannot absolve him of all faults, but it does suggest that those factors need to be kept in the foreground when levying wholesale opinions on the performances of Civil War commanders. It cannot be stressed enough that McClellan was thrust into an early stage of the war when all commanders struggled with the experiment of dealing with a strange and new brand of warfare. And it would increasingly evolve into a war that both the professional training and military culture bequeathed them and left them poorly prepared to fight.[33] As Nevins saw it, the war during that period was "improvised" at best, and was fought by those McPherson deemed as rank "amateurs." Time and experience would teach both armies, North and South, the way to wage the war. Grant and Sherman were afforded both of those opportunities and had the luxury of staying around long enough to devise the strategies that have marked them for conspicuous adulation. The time, however, allotted to McClellan to learn from experience, and for his volunteer amateurs to mature as soldiers, was all too short.

Inexperience and unpreparedness were not the only issues that early Federal commanders contended with in waging a war of conquest, nor are they the only factors to consider when evaluating McClellan's overall performance. No true assessment can be made by studying the condition of the northern military establishment alone. Some consideration of the waxing and waning strength of the Confederate military during the course of the war must be taken into account. Clearly, Grant and Sherman established their reputations for prowess in the western theater of the war, and their victories at Vicksburg and Chattanooga in the latter half of 1863 vaulted them into prominence. Their situation contrasted favorably with that in the East where Burnside and Hooker had already been singed by the firepower of Robert E. Lee's army and where Meade, after his triumph at Gettysburg, was dallying across old and familiar terrain, still parrying the thrusts of the great Confederate leader. However,

---

32. Ibid., 50–51; William T. Sherman to Ellen E. Sherman, Oct. 26, 1864, in DeWolfe, *Home Letters of General Sherman*, 315–16.

33. Hagerman, "The Professionalization of George B. McClellan," 129.

Grant and Sherman did not truly ascend into the pantheon of Union hero worship until Grant brought Lee to bay at Appomattox and Sherman sliced through Georgia and South Carolina. The question that almost begs asking is, how were they able to accomplish those feats when so many before them had failed? Conversely, why was the enemy incapable of preventing those outcomes? The answers may have as much, if not more, to do with the deteriorating condition of the Confederacy and its armies than with the talents of the two generals. And the answers may well reveal why McClellan and other early Federal commanders in the East found success so elusive.

Grant's initial victories were facilitated by Federal control of the navigable rivers that sliced deep into Kentucky and Tennessee. Those rivers aided and abetted rapid and aggressive movement. The most astonishing thing about the victories at Forts Henry and Donelson was that they precipitated the entire collapse of the defensive cordon Albert Sidney Johnston had established at the beginning of the war. New Orleans had already fallen to the Federal navy, and Grant's dual victories made Confederate possession of Nashville untenable. Buell walked into the Tennessee capital virtually unmolested. Later, when Halleck took Corinth via Shiloh and the Tennessee River, Memphis was isolated and the Federal navy chalked up another triumph. Consequently, the rebel loss of Forts Henry and Donelson shoved the revised Confederate defensive line all the way back into northern Mississippi. Generally speaking, a comparable retreat by Confederate forces in the East would have permitted the Union army to march from the Potomac, whistle by Manassas or Fredericksburg, bypass Richmond, and come to a stop at the North Carolina border.

Just when it appeared that the western armies were about to drive from Corinth towards Chattanooga in the late spring of 1862, as a preliminary to piercing the deep South, Bragg and Morgan raced past them, through central and eastern Tennessee into Kentucky. That rebel force, which would soon be within striking distance of the Ohio River, drove home a painful lesson to the Federals that they had not actually secured those two states and that they should hardly be thinking in grandiose terms. Grant, Sherman, Buell, Rosecrans, and a host of subordinate generals would spend the rest of 1862, all of the following year, and the first month of 1864 before Sherman would be poised to move into the deep South. And that would be accomplished, in part, with the unwitting assistance of poor coordination and management of resources by Confederate military leadership in the region.[34]

It took two bitterly contested years to subdue the border states of Kentucky and Tennessee before Grant and Sherman parted company in search of still greater glory. It would take Grant but one year to pound Lee into submission. In the same amount of time, Sherman would drive deep into the South, effecting a wide corridor of destruction in two states on his way to a final and total victory. How is it that success was so elusive in the first scenario, yet so attainable in the latter?

One explanation comes by way of extrapolating Neely's incisive analysis of the impact of terrain in the Wilderness upon Federal campaigns in the East and applying it to the western theater. The earliest Union victories at places like Fort Henry, Fort Donelson, Memphis, Nashville, Shiloh, and Corinth profited from the manipulation of amphibious movements. After that, the victories were harder to come by, although the capture of Vicksburg and its large garrison was aided by Porter's heroics on the Mississippi and the absence of coordination between Joseph Johnston and the fortress's beleaguered commander, John C. Pemberton. The key, however, to the pacification of Tennessee and the subsequent advance into the deep South was in the interior of the state. Buell could never prevent Confederate incursions in that vast area, and he never mastered the logistical challenges of penetrating the mountainous region of East Tennessee. His successor, Rosecrans, took a long time to overcome those problems, only to find himself a victim of his success. After racing past Chattanooga, he overextended himself and suffered a stinging setback at Chickamauga. Pushed back into the city of Chat-

---

34. It is virtual consensus that Confederate military leadership in the West was vastly inferior to that exercised in Virginia by Robert E. Lee. The only variation in this theme is in the degree of ineptitude of particular generals displayed, or the degree to which Jefferson Davis was responsible for the crippling lack of coordination in the defense of that region. Among numerous studies of the issue, the greatest profit can be extracted from the following: Thomas L. Connelly, *Army of the Heartland: The Army of Tennessee, 1861–1862* (Baton Rouge: Louisiana State Univ. Press, 1967), and *Autumn of Glory: The Army of Tennessee, 1862–1865* (Baton Rouge: Louisiana State Univ. Press, 1971); Archer Jones and Thomas L. Connelly, *The Politics of Command: Factions and Ideas in Confederate Strategy* (Baton Rouge: Louisiana State Univ. Press, 1973); Grady McWhiney, *Braxton Bragg and Confederate Defeat* (New York: Columbia Univ. Press, 1969); and Steven E. Woodworth, *Jefferson Davis and His Generals* (Lawrence: Univ. of Kansas Press, 1990), and *Davis and Lee at War* (Lawrence: Univ. of Kansas Press, 1995).

tanooga, he became a virtual prisoner of his opponents perched on the mountains surrounding his army. Grant would break that grip, but as he acknowledged himself, he did so with the assistance of stupendous blundering on the part of his opposition. Once the mountains of Tennessee and northwest Georgia were breached, the sloping hills and flat plains of Georgia were ripe for Sherman's advance the following spring.[35]

The second explanation for the disparity of success in the western theater entails the corresponding fortunes of Confederate morale and resistance. The issue of the relative strength of the South's national willpower and military capabilities at any given time is perhaps one of the most controversial and unresolved. The question remains whether the Confederacy imploded upon itself, as recently asserted by the authors of *Why the South Lost the Civil War,* or whether it succumbed to the poundings delivered by the armies of Grant and Sherman, as argued by McPherson in his essay in the collection, *Why the Confederacy Lost.* Those whose arguments emphasize the internal collapse of the Confederacy cite a host of interconnecting reasons. Chiefly, the arguments point to the lack of internal cohesion, inherent in a government founded upon states' rights; the ineffective leadership of Jefferson Davis; the lack of infinite resources, both in personnel and materiel, to fight a protracted war; the impoverishment and exhaustion of the citizenry, with a corresponding sharp increase in desertion rates; the impact of the Federal blockade; the rise in class conflict between the planter and yeoman; and the absence of a moral cause to justify the carnage exacted over four years.[36]

McPherson has administered a corrective tonic to the argument that the South fell victim to shortcomings of its own device. By noting that there was a contingency to the outcome of the war from the start, he

35. According to Grant, Bragg and Davis made his victory easier for three reasons: (1) Bragg and Davis sent his "ablest corps commander," Longstreet, off to Knoxville with twenty thousand troops on a fruitless mission; (2) Bragg sent yet another division away on the eve of the battle; (3) Bragg inexplicably placed the better part of his remaining force on the "plain in front of his impregnable position." See Grant, *Memoirs* 2:85.

36. This is not an exhaustive list of the factors cited for the internal collapse of the Confederacy, nor does it reveal the sharp disagreements in specifics among those who subscribe to the overall argument. The study mentioned is useful not only for the merits of its own arguments but because it discusses a fairly comprehensive array of historical literature on the topic. See Beringer, et al., *Why the South Lost the Civil War.* McPherson rejects these arguments as paramount to the issue of the Confederacy's fall in his essay "American Victory, American Defeat," in Boritt, ed., *Why the Confederacy Lost* (New York: Oxford Univ. Press, 1992), 15–42.

argues that the South could have won. There was no preordained guarantee that they would lose. Moreover, he argues, the decline in the southern will to resist may well have had more to do with its defeat on the battlefield than with internal pressures. It was Union victory on the battlefield that destroyed Confederate resistance. And one does not have to think long and hard to figure out the Union generals who brought about the momentous victories. This view is wholeheartedly endorsed by Gary Gallagher, who claims that of all the Federal generals summoned by Lincoln to smash the rebellion, only Grant and Sherman harnessed the means and the will to accomplish it.[37]

Both arguments concerning the reasons why the South lost the Civil War have merit. At least, neither disputes that the strength of the Confederacy was rapidly eroding in the final year of the war. Why, however, are these arguments frequently cast as necessarily exclusive of one another? It seems as though the two versions, i.e., internal versus external, are indeed mutually inclusive. Confederate reverses in the field shared a mutually destructive relationship with those factors that undermined morale at home. Both processes simultaneously eroded the fabric of the nation's vitality.[38]

The Confederacy that Grant and Sherman shredded to pieces in the final year of the war was clearly not the same as the one McClellan and other early Federal commanders faced in the first two years of the war.[39] The South was on its last legs, if not by the opening of the spring campaigns in 1864, then most certainly by the fall of that year. Although Lee had taken calculated risks in his forays into Maryland in 1862 and Pennsylvania in 1863, the Army of Northern Virginia was incapable of mounting and sustaining a substantive offensive campaign by 1864.[40] The

37. Gallagher, "'Upon Their Success Hang Momentous Interests'" 79–108.

38. Beringer et al., *Why the South Lost the Civil War,* 439.

39. Escott has concluded that the Confederacy "was collapsing from within long before Federal armies managed to supply the irresistible pressure from without." See Paul D. Escott, *After Secession: Jefferson Davis and the Failure of Confederate Nationalism* (Baton Rouge: Louisiana State Univ. Press, 1978), 272.

40. McWhiney and Jamieson concluded that Lee was forced to adopt defensive tactics against Grant because prior offensives "had deprived him of the power to attack." See McWhiney and Jamieson, *Attack and Die,* 164. Reid argues that Lee had lost any hope for offensive warfare, as demonstrated in several situations between the Rapidan and Cold Harbor. Recalling Lee's remark at Fredericksburg that few realize how fragile an army could be, Reid observes that the "Army of Virginia was even more fragile in 1864." See Reid, "Another Look at Grant's Crossing the James," 315.

Confederacy had tapped out in its ability to raise new recruits for its depleted ranks. Having reached a peak of nearly five hundred thousand men on the rolls in 1863, it had less than half that number in all of its armies by 1864, and it managed that feat only by restructuring its draft to include inductees up to fifty years of age.[41] The government had all but given up assigning regulars to deal with the many coastal incursions by Federal raiders by 1863. That assignment was turned over to a motley collection of old men and young boys.[42] In many areas of the South, particularly in Alabama and Mississippi, the civil authorities waged a guerilla war with their own deserters.[43] Desertion from the armies of the South went uncontrolled throughout 1864. Letters from the demoralized families of soldiers, detailing the deprivations and the destruction they were enduring, prompted wholesale abandonment of the army. The government, riddled with the anxieties of runaway inflation, was helpless to stem the tide.[44] Talk of arming the slaves, a largely unspeakable notion in the early part of the war, seriously surfaced in January 1864. Though the idea was shelved at the time, it was acted upon in February 1865, altogether too late to have any impact. Such discussion, however, only underscored the serious manpower shortages in the South in 1864.[45]

41. Albert Burton Moore, *Conscription and Conflict in the Confederacy* (New York: Macmillan, 1927), 308–12. It is estimated that Grant suffered casualties totaling fifty thousand from the Rapidan to Cold Harbor. This was about the total number of men in Lee's army at the time. See McWhiney and Jamieson, *Attack and Die,* 165 n.62.

42. Following a successful Federal raid up the Combahee River of South Carolina in July 1863, Secretary of War James A. Seddon instructed that all volunteers were to be organized under the aegis of the central government to consolidate coastal defenses. Earlier Governor James Bonham had issued a circular to planters in the region to "remove their Negroes as far as practicable into the interior of the State as otherwise they are liable to be lost at any moment." See *OR,* vol. 28:598, 702–3.

43. William T. Blain, "Banner Unionism in Mississippi, Choctaw County, 1861–1869," *Mississippi Quarterly* 29 (Sept. 1976): 209–13; Bessie Martin, *Desertion of Alabama Troops from the Confederate Army* (New York: Macmillan, 1932), 43–51, 107–16, 150–51.

44. The standard work on desertion in both armies is Ella Lonn, *Desertion during the Civil War* (Gloucester, Mass.: Peter Smith, 1928). Lonn concluded that the "miracle is not that the Confederacy fell, but that it did not collapse in 1863." See Lonn, *Desertion,* 124.

45. The first serious discussion of that idea was introduced by Gen. Patrick Cleburne during a meeting with other general officers on January 2, 1864. After vividly portraying the poor condition of the armies and the gloomy prospects for the survival of the Confederacy, he proposed to immediately raise and train a large reserve of slave soldiers, offering freedom as an inducement. The proposal was shot down. The text of "Cleburne's Memorial" is in *OR,* vol. 52, 2:586–92.

Longstreet had surmised that the limits of Confederate military strength had been reached by May 1863. The army needed to fight a clever and more conservative style of warfare, Longstreet reckoned, since it could no longer meet force with force.[46] Though still capable of waging a concerted defensive action, the armies of Northern Virginia and Tennessee were under siege in places like Petersburg, Richmond, Atlanta, and Savannah. Streams of aimless refugees clogged the highways and added to the overall depression settling over the South in 1864.[47] Incapable of sustaining two major armies in the field, it was only a matter of time before one or the other would collapse. In time, both southern armies did.[48]

Those realities were occasionally obscured by false optimism and wishful thinking during the latter part of the war. Some continued to hope for a cataclysmic success on the battlefield. Most, however, clung to the hope that the North would grow sufficiently weary of the war and would sue for peace. Ironically, many hoped that a McClellan victory in the election of 1864 would signal an end to war and a truce on Confederate terms.[49]

But most sober-thinking Southerners were not so easily deluded. Robert E. Lee, for one, had been warning Richmond throughout 1863 that, given the enemy's undiminished ability to replace their losses, he saw little chance of the South winning the war.[50] In a letter on June 10, 1863, prior to Gettysburg, Lee commented on the fading prospects of victory in a letter to Davis. "We should not," he advised, ". . . conceal from ourselves that our resources in men are constantly dwindling." Observing that the enemy was more than capable of putting ever larger numbers on the field, the disparity in the size of the two armies "is steadily augmenting." Some

46. Longstreet, *Battles and Leaders* 3:246–47.

47. Michael B. Ballard, *A Long Shadow* (Jackson: Univ. of Mississippi Press, n.d.), 74–75.

48. Davis's refusal to yield any territory to the enemy, while understandable to a point, effectively scattered the armies and robbed them of the ability to concentrate at critical points. That was particularly the case in the western theater. See Woodworth, *Jefferson Davis and His Generals*, 316.

49. Neely, for one, believes that by the campaigns of 1864, if not earlier, "any realistic Confederate strategy for victory required the Democrats to win the presidential election in the North." See Mark E. Neely, Jr., *The Last Best Hope of Earth* (Cambridge: Harvard Univ. Press, 1993), 93.

50. *OR*, vol. 27, 3:381; Dowdy and Manarin, *Wartime Papers of Robert E. Lee*, 388–89, 843–44, 47–48.

of the disparity, which grew ever wider over the course of 1864, was the result of the immense bloodletting he initiated against McClellan on the Peninsula, against Pope at Manassas, against McClellan, again, in the Maryland campaign, and finally against Meade at Gettysburg. Lee's admonitions to Davis were probably lost to the president's ever fretful and mercurial disposition. Yet, following Lee's ejection from Maryland in 1862, Davis had confided to James Seddon that "[Our] maximum strength has been mobilized, while the enemy is just beginning to put forth his might."[51] Throughout 1864, Lee continued to voice grave doubts that his army could endure for long the pounding it was receiving from its leviathan counterpart.[52]

Most importantly, Lee's own rank and file, who abandoned him during the course of 1864, left eloquent testimony to their commander that there were many who saw the inevitability of defeat. One Confederate private stationed near Fort Fischer wrote, "iff we cant get piece as we want it we had better take it thee Best way we can get it . . . our men are going to thee yankies every night." Another soldier in Atlanta wrote his wife in June 1864 that it was "nothing but folley for our leaders to contend with the North any longer." Sentiments such as these led Reid Mitchell to conclude that "for men with clear sight, no amount of patriotism could hide the fact that the Confederacy was doomed. If Lee's army was pitifully small when he surrendered to Grant, it was still bigger than the Confederate government had any right to expect."[53]

Aside from a brief stint in the East at the beginning of the war, Joseph E. Johnston spent most of his time serving confused causes in the West, where he, too, saw the dissolution of Confederate strength, despite his valiant efforts to husband it. Considering the perpetually undersized army in the West, Johnston was crestfallen when Pemberton retired within the fortress at Vicksburg in May 1863. To him, the loss of the city was regrettable, but the surrender of twenty-six thousand troops under

51. Quoted in Hudson Strode, *Jefferson Davis, Confederate President* (New York: Harcourt, 1959), 307.

52. Dowdey and Manarin, *Wartime Papers of Robert E. Lee,* 881. Alan T. Nolan cannot condone Lee's continued vigorous prosecution of the war during 1864, given his frequently stated conviction that it was a losing cause. See Nolan, *Lee Considered,* 107–33. Jefferson Davis, while open to a negotiated settlement, was opposed to any condition that restored the South to the Union.

53. Reid Mitchell, "The Perseverance of the Soldiers," in Gabor S. Boritt, ed., *Why the Confederacy Lost,* 125–27; Mitchell, *Civil War Soldiers,* 179.

Pemberton's command was as unpardonable as it was inconsolable. John-ston knew that the South could never make good on those losses. Much like the Lee versus Longstreet debate over the wisdom of attacking at Gettysburg, little resolution is likely to be found in its western counter-part, the Johnston versus Hood approach to Sherman's march on Atlanta. However, Hood so greatly weakened the army in his attempt to defend Atlanta that it could never hope to be an effective deterrent to Sherman's subsequent ambitions. Yet, even under Johnston, the Army of the Ten-nessee was mindful of the brute strength it was up against. As one soldier put it, "[The] only fear of this army is that Grant will overwhelm Lee with superior numbers, never by skill." Notwithstanding Davis's dislike for John-ston, the president's removal of that commander in the middle of a major campaign reflected the burgeoning panic in Richmond's military circles.[54]

Perhaps no one was more acutely aware of the desperate character of the times than General John H. Winder. As provost marshal of Richmond in the first two years of the war, and later as commander of Confed-erate war prisons, Winder had to deal firsthand with the consequences of reduced manpower. Many of the horrors associated with prisons like Andersonville, Libby, Belle Isle, and Salisbury were a result of a total in-ability to handle the numbers of prisoners collected by 1864. Guarded by underpaid boys and invalids, who grew increasingly callous to the plight of their overcrowded wards, those prisons routinely featured shortages in food, clothing, medicine, and sanitation facilities. When the prisoner ex-change cartel was permanently revoked in 1864, the problems were only exacerbated. Winder tried desperately to manage the increased responsi-bilities, but the resources simply were not there. By the close of 1864 he recognized the imminent collapse of the Confederacy; consequently, he stridently argued that the only recourse remaining was to parole all pris-oners immediately, irrespective of whether the Federals reciprocated.[55]

Throughout 1864, the perspicacious Mary Chestnut of South Caro-lina, morose over the disintegration and demoralization engulfing her, emptied her weary soul into her now famous diary. Her entry for Novem-ber 6, 1864 served as a catharsis and revealed her feelings of dread over the inevitable demise of the Confederacy. Mirroring the prevailing senti-

54. Quoted in Symonds, *Joseph E. Johnston,* 317.

55. Winder receives sympathetic treatment in Arch Frederick Blakey, *General John H. Winder* (Gainesville: Univ. of Florida Press, 1990), 202–15. See also William Marvel, *Ander-sonville: The Last Depot* (Chapel Hill: Univ. of North Carolina Press, 1994).

ment in her social circles, that the battered South could not overcome the odds that irresistably favored the enemy, she wrote:

> Sherman in Atlanta has left Thomas to take care of Hood. Hood has 30,000 men–Thomas–has 40,000 now–and as many more as he wants–he has only to ring the bell and call for more. Grant can get all that he wants, both for himself and for Thomas. All the world open to them. We shut up in a Bastille. We are at sea. Our boat has sprung a leak.[56]

The gloom and doom circulating in the North during the summer of 1864, a result of Grant's inability to corner Lee in decisive combat despite the ever-mounting and frightful loss of life, belies the confidence enjoyed in Northern military circles. In recalling the last winter of the war during the siege of Petersburg, Grant noted that the enemy was losing "at least a regiment a day," and that having already robbed both "the cradle and the grave" for recruits, it was in desperate straits. When combined with the usual casualties of war and with sickness, Grant reasoned by simple "arithmetic" that the war was over. He declared that the enemy "had lost hope and become despondent." On another occasion, he wrote that the "last man in the Confederacy is now in the army." While such comments might seem the natural consequence of a bloody and punishing campaign, stretching all the way back to the start in the Wilderness, Grant had long suspected that Lee's army was beaten. Having just emerged from the Wilderness, and freshly supplied with substantial reinforcements, Grant had already apprised Halleck of the true military situation in May 1864. "Lee's army is really whipped. The prisoners we now take show it, and the action of his army shows it unmistakably. . . . [Our] men feel that they have gained the morale over the enemy, and attack him with confidence. I may be mistaken, but I feel that our success over Lee's army is already assured."[57]

In the West, Grant's more voluble protege, Sherman, despite a willingness to discourse on any subject, eschewed making any predictions.

---

56. C. Vann Woodward, ed., *Mary Chestnut's Civil War* (New Haven: Yale Univ. Press, 1981), 689. The wave of defeatism in the South can be viewed in microcosm in a study of the community of Culpepper, Virginia. See Daniel E. Sutherland, *Seasons of War: The Ordeal of a Confederate Community* (New York: The Free Press, 1995).

57. U.S. Grant to J. Russell Jones, July 5, 1864, in Simon, *Papers of Ulysses S. Grant* 11:176; Grant, *Memoirs* 2:490.

Perhaps, as he indicated in the letter to his wife regarding McClellan, he was fearful that his success was only temporary. But the relative ease with which he was able to back his opponent into Atlanta, then race to the Georgia coast, speaks volumes on southern weakness and northern power in that theater. It is one thing to have been able to win the war without fighting battles, as amply demonstrated after his departure from Atlanta. It is quite another thing, however, to acknowledge that there was no one strong enough to offer him a battle that would have put him in a position to decline.[58]

Grant and Sherman enjoyed extraordinary advantages in the spring of 1864 when they embarked on the campaigns that would end the war and cement their golden reputations. It would be unfair, however, to imply that their overwhelming numerical superiority and material strength were the only factors in their success. Sherman embarked upon a strategy that not only made Georgia "howl" but brought the entire South to its knees. It should be remembered, however, that he could only contemplate such a strategy knowing that his enemy had been worn down to the point that no effective resistance to his plans could be mustered. Grant faced a much more determined foe and a much more difficult task. To his credit, he never surrendered the initiative to the enemy. Whereas others in the past backed off after a major confrontation with Lee, Grant doggedly pushed onward, sensing, as he did, that the enemy was incapable of mounting a serious counterattack. McPherson is correct in questioning some of the sweeping judgments that the North won the war because of its staggering personnel and logistical advantages. Indeed, God has not always been "on the side of the heaviest battalions," as the American experience in war has shown.[59] Similarly, a grain of salt should be taken with Shelby Foote's colorful description that the "North fought the war with one hand tied behind its back," and his statement that had it been necessary, "The North simply would have brought that

58. T. Harry Williams demurred with Sherman's admirers, who pointed to the general's ability to achieve incredible results without much fighting as his greatest contribution to the art of war. Moreover, Williams argued, Sherman had the luxury of leaving Thomas's large army to keep tabs on the remnants of Hood's army, thus freeing Sherman to proceed undisturbed. See T. Harry Williams, *McClellan, Sherman, and Grant*, 75–77.

59. Richard Current, "God and the Strongest Battalions," in David H. Donald, ed., *Why the North Won the Civil War*, 22.

other arm out from behind its back."[60] And one should hold as circumspect the analogy, served up as verdict, that "Grant was a two-hundred pound, fully equipped boxer, who fought a half-starved, barehanded man, half his weight."[61] In and of itself, the North's advantages in the war were no guarantee of success at the beginning of the war. Foote's on-camera contention that the South never "had a chance to win that war" is overstated.[62] However, Northern advantages, in full flowering at the end of the war when the enemy was increasingly powerless to resist, were considerable ones.

The eventual triumph of Union arms in the spring of 1865, by no means guaranteed, was a reasonable outcome for a nation that possessed superior personnel and material advantages. Those factors were combined with sufficient resolve and clarity of purpose to see the process through to a successful conclusion. The North faced an opponent that had, though strong and determined in the defense of its homeland, nonetheless become progressively weakened and tapped out over a four-year period. Although the North always enjoyed a superior edge in numbers, the disparity grew greater once the South was unable to call upon its citizenry to furnish additional manpower. The North, provided it did not grow tired of the struggle, had a relatively inexhaustible supply of men, a homeland that had not experienced the ravages of war, and an expanding financial and manufacturing base to support the war effort.

It is impossible, of course, to determine how George McClellan would have fared had he remained in command to the end of the war. He needs to be evaluated on his service during his tenure in command, and his performance should be assessed within the context of the early part of the war. In that context, he does not emerge so poorly. Like Grant and Sherman, his achievements and failures in 1861–1862 are of a mixed variety. Since he never made it to the end of the war, McClellan cannot be considered a great commander, particularly when compared and contrasted to the two military goliaths, Grant and Sherman.

In attempting to evaluate McClellan's performance, one does not have to turn to Lee's alleged postwar remark that McClellan was the best

60. Foote is quoted in "Men at War: An Interview with Shelby Foote," in Geoffrey C. War with Ric Burns and Ken Burns, *The Civil War* (New York: Knopf, 1990), 272.

61. Otto Eisenschiml, *The Hidden Face of the Civil War* (Indianapolis: Bobbs-Merrill, 1961), 213.

62. Foote, "Men at War," 272.

commander he had ever faced.[63] Nor does one have to rely on McClellan's many early apologists who have passionately defended the general.[64] And one does not have to prevail upon the shrinking ranks of McClellan supporters in the post-World War II era.[65] Still, it is alluring to point to two contemporary assessments of his performance for the insight and reasonable balance and perspective they hold. Neither Francis W. Palfrey, who frequently criticized McClellan for numerous mistakes in his campaigns, nor William Swinton, a *New York Times* correspondent, turned historian at the war's end, had any particular axes to grind at the time they made their evaluations. In a remark strangely reminiscent of Sherman's opinion of McClellan, Swinton concluded that McClellan was unfortunate to have become "so prominent a figure at the commencement of the contest," and he noted that "it was inevitable that the first leaders should be sacrificed to the nation's ignorance of war."[66]

Reviewing McClellan's conduct during the battle at Antietam, Palfrey declared that "there is little to be said in the way of praise beyond the fact that he did fight it voluntarily, without having it forced upon him." The terse quality of this judgment has often scored the approbation of many subsequent critics of the campaign.[67] Yet, in coming to terms with an overall assessment of McClellan's performance, Palfrey recognized the

63. According to the story, Lee, when asked who was the best general he faced during the war, pounded his desk and emphatically declared, "McClellan by all odds!" Another anecdote reports Lee's daughter as saying, "Genl. McClellan was the only Genl. Father dreaded." Finally, Lee did write a friend after the war with the rather lukewarm endorsement: "As regards General McClellan, I have always entertained a high opinion of his capacity, and have no reason to think that he omitted to do anything that was in his power." All three of these statements are quoted in Hassler, *George B. McClellan: Shield of the Union,* 326.

64. For example, see James Havelock Campbell, *McClellan: A Vindication of the Military Career of General George B. McClellan* (New York: Scribner's, 1901); J. J. Eckenrode and Bryan Conrad, *George B. McClellan: The Man Who Saved the Union* (Chapel Hill: Univ. of North Carolina Press, 1941); and Clarence E. Macartney, *Little Mac: The Life of General George B. McClellan* (Philadelphia: Lippincott, 1940). A complete list can be found in Harsh, "On the McClellan-Go-Round," 102–3.

65. Among the few supporters, the most notable are Warren W. Hassler, Jr., Joseph L. Harsh, Rowena Reed, and Edward Hagerman. Their works have been previously cited.

66. William Swinton, *Campaigns of the Army of the Potomac,* 228.

67. See Greene, "'I Fought the Battle Splendidly,'" 56. Palfrey also criticizes McClellan's failure to fight on September 18, suggesting that McClellan "made absolutely no use of the magnificent enthusiasm which the army then felt for him." See Francis W. Palfrey, *The Antietam and Fredericksburg* (New York: Scribner's 1882), 119.

context in which McClellan fought the war. Even acknowledging that there were "strong grounds for believing that he was the best commander the Army of the Potomac ever had," Palfrey understood that McClellan fought the enemy while it was "young and fresh and rich, with blood and treasure to spare." Indeed, Lee's early successes and bold initiatives were pyrric in nature. His inability to conserve the manpower at his disposal eventually caught up with him by 1864. In this respect, it is reasonable to conclude, as Palfrey did, that "McClellan fought a good, wary, damaging, respectable fight" against the Confederates, and had he remained in command longer, "Greater things might fairly have been expected of him."[68]

Palfrey's conjecture that McClellan might have been the best commander of the Army of the Potomac obscures the importance of his subsequent remarks. Had he been killed at Antietam, as Albert Sidney Johnston was at Shiloh, or had he returned to service and vindicated himself, as did Sherman, or had he survived the improvised warfare of the early years, as Grant and Sherman did, then McClellan might be accorded such consideration. But none of those things happened. Nevertheless, while his battlefield performance left something to be desired, McClellan had engineered the strategic groundwork for the successful campaign in western Virginia. Moreover, he had developed a coherent and feasible national military strategy—consistent with the political goals of the time. He also had created a vast and well-trained army capable of assuming the offensive by late Fall 1861. He quelled complaints for the capital's defense by disciplining the army and completing the fortifications that ringed the city. His campaigns between April and September 1862 suggest a period of considerable activity. Those two major campaigns within the initial year of the war were not unqualified failures. The first fell just shy of accomplishment while the latter frustrated an enemy advance into Maryland.

68. Palfrey, *Antietam and Fredericksburg,* 134–35.

8

Bagging Bobby Lee

McClellan might have been forgiven a multitude of failures had he kept his eye on the real military target of the war–the Army of Northern Virginia–and delivered the necessary antidote to rebellion, the destruction of the Army of Northern Virginia. Above all other considerations, historians have faulted McClellan for proving to be a general who did not like to fight. Unable or unwilling to see beyond the strategic emptiness of capturing Richmond, McClellan's fixation on the Confederate capital only delayed the inevitable hard fighting that later generals, especially Grant, embraced. Then, even when handed one of the best opportunities ever presented during the war to destroy Robert E. Lee's army, he squandered it.

The interpretation that the destruction of Robert E. Lee's Army of Northern Virginia should have always been the primary northern objective in the war has become a cardinal and inviolable underpinning in Civil War history. Perhaps no one has more enshrined this perception in both scholarly and popular circles than Bruce Catton. Over the course of his prolific career, Catton bordered on hagiography when discoursing on the virtues of the humble and unassuming General Grant. "Grant considered the military problem to be basically quite simple," Catton declared. "[The] principal Confederate armies had to be destroyed." The conquest of cities and static geographical objectives was meaningless: "As long as the main Confederate armies were in the field the Confederacy lived, and as soon as they vanished the Confederacy ceased to be."[1]

T. Harry Williams had already argued this same strategic principle in similarly plaintive tones as Catton, although he credited Lincoln, and not Grant, with the insight. Williams consistently impugned the judgment of Grant's predecessors for failing to endorse their commander in chief's appreciation of Lee's army as the object of pursuit and destruction. McClellan, for Williams, was but the first of many who ignored Lincoln's strategic acumen. This is clearly seen in his initial rejection of McClellan's Urbanna plan of operations. Unable to comprehend any reason why McClellan's plan was a better guarantee of success than his own, Lincoln reiterated his conviction that the "best point of attack was the Confederate army in northern Virginia."[2] Although Lincoln eventually bowed to military expertise at that early stage of the war, he remained unconvinced that any strategy that did not uphold the destruction of Lee's army was of any value.

Contrary to Catton's estimation, Williams viewed Grant's initial designs for the campaign of 1864 as a useless rehashing of the plans laid out by his predecessors. "Like Meade, Grant was thinking of Richmond and not Lee's army as the primary objective," Williams pointed out. Halleck, who by 1864 had become so familiar with Lincoln's strategic ideas, predicted to Grant that Lincoln would veto his plan. Speaking on the president's behalf, Halleck "emphasized that Lee's army, not Richmond, should be the objective of the Potomac army." Later, upon talking to Lincoln, Grant "willingly discarded" his own plan in favor of his commander in chief's. Lincoln, according to Williams, remained the "civilian strategist who never forgot that the destruction of enemy armies was the proper objective."[3]

To varying degrees, those sentiments have filtered their way down into the writings of many Civil War historians, although their general

1. Bruce Catton, *The Civil War* (New York: American Heritage, 1960), 203.

2. T. Harry Williams, *Lincoln and His Generals*, 63. Despite this conviction, Williams believed that Lincoln should have left McClellan's army on the Peninsula rather than recalling it in August 1862. "It was only twenty-five miles from Richmond," Williams reasoned, "and on a supply line that could always be kept open. . . . it was closer to Richmond than it would be until 1864." Williams declared that the only change needed was in commanders and suggested that Pope was a possible replacement. See ibid., 163.

3. Ibid., 296.

acceptance no longer required such forceful emphasis. For McPherson, Grant was the one who came to the correct conclusion after Shiloh that the Union would be restored only when the enemy's armies were destroyed. McClellan, on the other hand, was instructed to destroy Lee's army at Antietam but failed. After recalling Lincoln's advice to Hooker before Chancellorsville that "Lee's Army and not Richmond, is your true objective," McPherson underscores Lincoln's plaintive appeal to Hooker that he destroy Lee enroute to Pennsylvania, thus making up for McClellan's earlier failure. But Hooker was not up to the task. His replacement, Meade, allowed still another opportunity to pass without crushing Lee, and when he began to contemplate ways to avoid Lee in combat, Lincoln brought in Grant, leaving Sherman to command the western theater. Finally, by 1864, McPherson maintains that Lincoln "had generals in top commands who believed in destroying enemy armies."[4]

An array of historians who respect the strategic acumen of either Lincoln or Grant have swelled the chorus of those who admire both for their singularity of purpose. Critical of McClellan's designs on the Confederate capital, Nevins minimized its strategic importance. "The mere capture of Richmond would effect little," Nevins maintained, "except the seizure of some valuable works, notably the Tredegar iron mills, and a blow to Confederate morale at home and prestige abroad." Lincoln's proposal to move against enemy forces on the way to Lynchburg, asserted Nevins, would sever Richmond's lifeline.[5] Glatthaar, too, is critical of McClellan's Urbanna Plan, although he does see some "genuine merit" in the idea. Lincoln's identification of the enemy's troops at Manassas as the primary target, however, was a better plan with concrete hopes for success. Glatthaar judges that even at that early stage of the war "Lincoln had grasped the vital need to strike the enemy armies, rather than merely occupying geographical positions."[6] Finally, Donald, in his capstone to a career of studying Lincoln, not only reiterates the strategic differences between the president and McClellan in the beginning of the war, but elaborates on the theme suggested by T. Harry Williams that Grant was

4. McPherson, "Lincoln and the Strategy of Unconditional Surrender," 44–45. In evaluating McClellan's Peninsula campaign, McPherson writes: "Like Grant, the president believed in attacking the enemy's army rather than in maneuvering to capture places." See McPherson, *Battle Cry of Freedom*, 423.

5. Nevins, *War for the Union* 2:42.

6. Glatthaar, *Partners in Command*, 69.

converted to Lincoln's strategic line of reasoning. Although initially fa-
voring a series of raids to sever communication and supply lines with
Richmond and other strategic points, Grant was persuaded by Lincoln to
reject maneuvering in favor of "assault upon assault on the Confederate
army." Moreover, Donald says, Grant was virtually hoodwinked by Lincoln into believing that he had, as Grant would later recall, authored an
entirely "new feature in war."[7]

Nonetheless, the capture of Richmond as a desirable military objective has often been underestimated. Likewise, criticism of strategies aimed
to attack the Confederate capital to the neglect of vanquishing the Army
of Northern Virginia is frequently shortsighted. Given the perceived nature of the rebellion, the reduction of Richmond emerged as an expressed
priority in war planning, for in the first year of the war, it was the firm
conviction of the vast majority in the North that a well-delivered blow
to the Confederate capital was the proper cure for secession.[8] During
the Civil War, every attempt made by the Union army, including Grant's
in 1864, to move toward Richmond invariably drew the interdicting presence of the Confederate army. Moreover, the potential significance of
Richmond's collapse eclipsed the moral symbolism inherent in the fall
of Washington. In the early part of the war, Richmond was the only industrial center in the South. The Tredegar Iron Works was the single pro-
ducer of heavy ordnance and was the leading provider of light ordnance
and ammunition. As a transportation hub for all of the southeast Atlantic
states, it served as the major supply depot and communication center for
the fledgling government. Its fall would have had dramatic consequences
for the continued viability of the Confederacy. And its vulnerability was
underscored by the absence of any extensive fortifications like those that
surrounded the Federal capital.[9]

The essential strategic underpinning of the conquest of Richmond
was political to the extent that southern rebellion, believed to be weakly
supported, would collapse by an overwhelming display of northern
strength and purpose of will. The revised Urbanna plan, now known as

7. Donald, *Lincoln*, 338, 498–99.

8. Reflecting general popular and political feeling at the beginning of McClellan's
Peninsula campaign, one paper declared: "The keys of the so-called Confederate states are
Richmond and New Orleans. When we have taken these our task will be done." See *Harper's
Weekly*, Apr. 19, 1862.

9. Clifford Dowdey, *The Seven Days: The Emergence of Lee* (Lincoln: Univ. of Nebraska
Press, 1993), 14.

the Peninsula campaign, was also motivated by sound military principles. By stealing a waterborne march on the enemy, the Army of the Potomac would obviate the need to contest the ninety miles of treacherous terrain between Washington and Richmond. Supply lines would not have to be stretched over that distance, and they would not be subjected to raids by the enemy. It would compel the menacing enemy army at Manassas, ever so close to Washington, to hastily retire to the defense of its own heartland. And if the surprise of the move did not prevent the uncontested capture of Richmond, it would force the Confederate army to fight on a site of McClellan's choosing.[10]

Unfortunately, McClellan's surprise was confounded by difficulties, some of his own invention, experienced in the reduction of Yorktown. Still, that movement struck fear in the Davis cabinet and in military circles in Richmond. On one occasion, Davis sat dumbstruck in a meeting when Joseph Johnston recommended that the army fall back in concentrated force to defend the capital. When Johnston wrote Lee, a military advisor at the time, asking what plans were being devised for the evacuation of Richmond, Davis called a meeting of the cabinet. During the session, Lee, with uncharacteristic emotion, pronounced that Richmond had to be defended to the last extremity. At least for him, the loss of his native state's capital spelled the beginning of the end for the Confederate experiment. With tears streaming down his face, he jolted his audience with the emphatic declaration: "Richmond must not be given up. It shall not be given up!"[11]

Throughout the entire course of the war, Lee consistently upheld the defense of Richmond as an absolute priority. Both at the beginning and end of the war–during McClellan's and Grant's campaigns outside of Richmond–Lee believed that the Confederacy would die the moment the capital fell. Its integrity was the foundation of his strategic and tactical outlook. His hallmark audacity and daring offensive tactics were built upon the imperative that the enemy be kept away from Richmond. He

---

10. These ideas were set forth in greater detail, including the simultaneous movement in other theaters of the war, in McClellan's lengthy letter to Stanton of February 3, 1862. See Sears, *Civil War Papers of George B. McClellan*, 162–70.

11. Steven H. Newton, *Joseph E. Johnston and the Defense of Richmond* (Ann Arbor: UMI, 1991), 242–55; Douglas Southall Freeman, *Lee's Lieutenants* 2:47-48; Walter F. McCaleb, ed., *Memoirs of John H. Reagan* (New York: Neale, 1906), 109.

abhorred any thought of abandoning the capital as much as he resisted being backed up to its gates under siege conditions. A siege would only delay the inevitable. Robert E. Lee, for one, staked his personal fortune and that of his nation upon the safety of Richmond.

When Johnston fell critically wounded at Fair Oaks on May 31, 1862, command of the Confederate defense of Richmond fell to Lee. He inherited a sorry situation, in his estimation. Johnston had ignored his advice and had retreated too close to Richmond. The formal siege of Richmond was only a matter of weeks, maybe even days, from commencing. On June 5, Lee suggested to Davis that if Jackson could be reinforced in the Shenandoah Valley, "It would change the character of the war." Lee made the suggestion, hoping the enemy would be forced to relieve pressure on the Richmond front by shuffling troops to deal with Jackson in the Valley. On a more somber note, Lee confided that McClellan was methodically preparing to commence the dreaded siege of Richmond. "McClellan will make this a battle of Posts. He will take position from position, under cover of his heavy guns, & we cannot get him without storming his works, which with our new troops is extremely hazardous. . . . It will require 100,000 men to resist the regular siege of Richmond, which perhaps would only prolong not save it."[12]

One of the more interesting strategic incongruities during the Civil War was the difference between Lee and Lincoln in their views on the best location for fighting. Lincoln consistently counseled his commanders to meet Lee in the open field, away from his source of supply and away from the cramped and confining entrenchments of Richmond. He was especially pleased on those occasions when Lee accommodated the Union army by invading northern soil, as he felt that was the best opportunity to destroy his army. Lee, on the other hand, consistently feared being pushed back into his entrenchments, feeling that the inevitable siege would be his undoing. He preferred the open field where he could employ a full range of maneuver and force the Union army to assault him.[13]

12. Douglas Southall Freeman, ed., *Lee's Dispatches: Unpublished Letters of General Robert E. Lee, C.S.A., to Jefferson Davis and the War Department of the Confederate States of America, 1862–1865* (New York: Putnam's. 1942), 5–10.

13. Samples of Lincoln's directives to destroy Lee while he was ranging into Northern territory can be found in letters to McClellan, Hooker, and Meade. See Basler, *Collected Works of Abraham Lincoln* 8: 34, 297, 9:22.

Until Grant's spring offensive of 1864, Lee guaranteed the safety of Richmond by repeatedly seizing the initiative in keeping the fighting north of the Rappahannock River and periodically spilling into the enemy's soil. Between the close of the Peninsula campaign and the spring offensive of 1864, Lee's actions were motivated, in part, by his anxiety over being backed into a siege. According to one of his division commanders, Harry Heth, Lee's decision to invade Pennsylvania in 1863 was the result of having only two options. Either he would invade the North, or he would have to "retire on Richmond and stand a siege, which must ultimately have ended in surrender."[14]

With skillful use of the terrain and his advantage of interior lines, he succeeded in thwarting Federal attempts to move on Richmond via the overland route. The resources needed to accomplish those feats, however, were eroding by the time Grant began to make his massive push through the Wilderness in 1864. Unable to seize the initiative from Grant's enormous army and concerned with Butler's concurrent invasion up the Peninsula, as well as renewed Federal offensives in the Valley, his thoughts gravitated again to the defense of Richmond. In early June, he told Jubal Early that they "had to defeat this army of Grant's before he gets to the James River." Echoing his earlier warning to Davis during the Peninsula campaign, he added, if Grant "gets there, it will become a siege, and then it will be a mere question of time."[15] At the same time, he notified his own corps commander, A. P. Hill, that he would be thoroughly defeated over time if he were "obliged to take refuge behind the works of Richmond and stand a siege."[16]

Grant would be denied his cherished hope that Lee could be outflanked and forced to assault his army as it moved closer to Richmond. He hoped to capitalize on Lee's fear that the Union army would position itself between the Confederates and their capital, thus forcing the enemy to fight for its survival. Years later, in his memoirs, Grant suggested that had he arrived at Spotsylvania before Lee, "There would have been a race between the two armies to see which would reach Richmond first." Lincoln was reported to be so gleeful with that prospect that he cavalierly

14. Henry Heth, "Causes of Lee's Defeat at Gettysburg," *Southern Historical Society Papers* 4 (Oct. 1877): 154.

15. J. William Jones, *Personal Reminiscences of Gen. Robert E. Lee* (New York: Appleton, 1875), 40.

16. *OR*, vol. 40, 2:703.

declared, "If Grant takes Richmond let him have the nomination."[17] But despite many efforts, Grant only bludgeoned himself in costly frontal assaults. When Lee beat him to the punch at Petersburg, Grant settled into a siege. Heralded for being the commander of an army always in motion, he would spend the final nine months of the war perfectly immobilized in siege warfare. Initially only a consolation prize, Grant soon came to understand the benefits of the siege and the sense of finality and closure to the war that it offered. The comfort of siege operations even allowed him on two occasions to visit his family away from the front, in Burlington, New Jersey.[18]

It seems strange in many ways that Civil War analysts have, at times, overly devalued the capture of geographical locations during the war. True, each individual conquest could not guarantee the death of the Confederacy, but they did contribute toward that end. Over the course of the war, either in and of themselves or in the natural progression of a campaign, key cities and fortifications were the objects of military, political, or psychological desire. While not of inestimable value, Buell's occupation of Nashville in early 1862 was a significant acquisition in the process of pacifying Kentucky and Tennessee. The need to control the Mississippi River alone marked the capture of New Orleans, Memphis, and Vicksburg as worthwhile goals. That Grant topped his coup at Vicksburg with the paroling of Pemberton's army was incidental to the mission and was a gratuity bestowed by inept Confederate leadership. And no one is likely to deny the strategic importance of the siege that brought Atlanta down. Despite his intention to do Grant's bidding and destroy the Army of Tennessee, Sherman followed the railway routes toward the city, with an ever-obliging Johnston giving ground before him. Johnston's replacement, Hood, after recklessly assaulting Federal entrenchments surrounding the city, precipitously evacuated Atlanta on September 2, 1864.

17. Grant, *Memoirs* 2:212. Grant also realized that Richmond's safety "would be a matter of the first consideration with the executive, legislative and judicial branches of the so-called Confederate government." See Grant, *Memoirs* 2:507. Lincoln's remark is reported in McFeely, *Grant*, 170.

18. Grant, *Memoirs* 2:426–27. Grant, who never professed to be well read in his profession, may have benefited from McClellan's study of the siege of Sevastopol, included in his report on the Crimean War. At the beginning of the war he wrote Julia, asking her to scour the house for his copy of McClellan's report. Perhaps it was one of the few books he read, and it might have come in handy for the nine-month siege he started in June 1864. See Julia D. Grant, *Personal Memoirs*, 58.

Sherman had "fairly won" Atlanta. Somewhere in the shuffle of troops in and out of Atlanta, Sherman had let Hood escape with his army. Sherman seemed unaffected by Hood's departure and was satisfied that his capture of Atlanta had earned him a great military victory. It had. The fall of that one city lifted the oppressive gloom that had settled over the nation from Grant's sanguinary stalemate with Lee in Virginia. Incidentally, the fall of Atlanta also resuscitated the flagging spirits of Lincoln's reelection campaign and assured him of success at the polls in November. Otherwise, the next president would have been George B. McClellan.[19]

Richmond, then, was the top prize of them all. The final siege of Petersburg destroyed Robert E. Lee's army. Richmond fell the day after the lines at Petersburg were abandoned. Lee's ragged, half-starved army was quickly nabbed in its vain attempt to flee to the southwest. The war was effectively over. Lee's worst fears had been realized. As the war progressed, the capture of Richmond and the destruction of Lee's army were not such distinct and separate entities; the terms, or the objectives in that case, were nearly synonymous. The way to get at Lee's army in the most advantageous way was to harness the general's brilliant open-field maneuvering, forcing him to shrink back into the confining strictures of Richmond's defenses.[20]

As suggested in the introduction to this study, a consensus has emerged over the last fifty years that George B. McClellan was a general who could not deliver the death blow to the enemy. On this basis, Catton, while admiring some of McClellan's qualities, concluded that "he did not like to fight." T. Harry Williams also found him a "bad general" for the very same reason. It is easy to see these opinions as they have trickled down into more recent assessments of McClellan's abilities. Sears endorses Lincoln's decision to sack McClellan because his post-Antietam campaign

19. At the beginning of the campaign, Sherman assured Grant that Johnston's army alone was the primary target, particularly so that Lee would receive no reinforcement from that theater. See OR, vol. 32, 3:245–46, 312–14, 465–66. On September 15, Sherman explained to Halleck that since he had already achieved his goals, it was useless to pursue Hood's army any further. See OR, vol. 38, 1:82–83.

20. Grant's language underscores the ambivalence in military objectives in the East. Almost apologizing for Sherman's failure to destroy Johnston's army during the Atlanta campaign, Grant reasoned that it "would not produce so immediate and decisive a result in closing the rebellion as would the possession of Richmond, Lee and his army." See Grant, *Memoirs* 2:423.

cemented the opinion that he was too sluggish in moving against the enemy; it seemed that he did not want to inflict a stinging defeat upon Lee's army, and he had failed to mature in his role as commander. Glatthaar sympathizes with a weary Lincoln who did everything in his power to aid his general. He could not, however, make McClellan "advance vigorously or fight aggressively." Even those whose works are focused upon entirely different subjects establish perspectives in their own studies by marring McClellan's fighting reputation by inference or outright comparison. So it is that Mitchell, in his study of the Union soldiers' perseverance, might applaud the general's "strategic brilliance" in the Peninsula campaign, only to conclude that his "gutless" nature sabotaged those plans. Then there are those who employ other military figures as measuring sticks against McClellan. "[It] is a pity he was no Winfield Scott," Russell Weigley declared, particularly "when it came to the execution of his strategy in the cash payoff of battle."[21]

Critiques of McClellan's failure to destroy the Confederate army are sprinkled throughout the pages of studies of the Peninsula and Antietam campaigns. "More than anybody," T. Harry Williams intoned, "he [McClellan] was responsible for the collapse of the Peninsula campaign." Noting the general's relish for siege warfare, Williams writes that McClellan "undoubtedly . . . could have broken through" the defenders of Yorktown and "driven up the Peninsula." Williams sympathizes with a frustrated Lincoln begging his general to "strike a blow" and urging him to "act." For Williams, then, McClellan's Harrison Landing letter of July 7, at the denouement of the campaign, is not so much impertinent, as others have maintained, as it was inappropriate. "Only generals who win great victories," Williams trumpeted, "should presume to counsel their political superiors about policy." Sears has reached similar conclusions. He observed that Lincoln, after surveying "the ruins of the Peninsula campaign . . . concluded that there was nothing indispensable about General McClellan. . . . [He] had failed the test the president was now applying to all his generals—did they know how to win on the battlefield?"[22]

It was at Antietam, however, where the criticism of McClellan's failure to deliver the knockout punch to Lee's army reached its zenith. In his

21. Sears, *George B. McClellan: The Young Napoleon,* 338–39; Glatthaar, *Partners in Command,* 52; Mitchell, "The Perseverance of the Soldiers," 118; Weigley, *The American Way of War,* 135.

22. T. Harry Williams, *Lincoln and His Generals,* 83–84, 133; Sears, "Lincoln and McClellan," 38–39.

narrative of the Antietam campaign, Sears finds consistent fault in Mc-Clellan's excessive caution, particularly in his failure to renew the battle on the second day and to organize an effective pursuit of the retreating enemy. "Dame Fortune smiled on General McClellan," writes Sears. "He was presented with not just one, but six highly favorable opportunities to crush the rebellion's principal army." A. Wilson Greene's coverage of the battle itself is a scathing attack upon McClellan's military management that concludes with the assessment that "George B. McClellan discarded the best opportunity ever offered to destroy the Confederacy's principal field army." This verdict is readily endorsed by Gallagher, who observes that the "salient feature of the Maryland campaign . . . was McClellan's opportunity to inflict a catastrophic defeat on Lee's army." Moreover, that defeat "would have uncovered Richmond and crippled Southern morale; it might have ended the war." Since McClellan chose "not to force the issue," Gallagher concludes that "his military performance in Maryland must be judged harshly." Jeffry Wert echoes these sentiments in his defense of Lee having taken such unprecedented risks in the Maryland campaign. Lee "was certain he could beat McClellan in battle," Wert offers. "And he was correct. . . . [T]he Union commander squandered the finest opportunity given a Federal general to destroy the Army of Northern Virginia."[23]

The lingering and indelible impression is that Lee bested McClellan on the Peninsula and that only blunders committed by his subordinates there prevented Lee from destroying the Army of the Potomac. Again, at Antietam, historians conclude that Lee, having taken the measure of his antagonist, decided he could risk battle even in an undesirable location with the Potomac river at his back. In the battle that ensued, Lee stands up to the superior enemy force, mostly because its commander is a moral coward who cannot make appropriate decisions or accept the risks associated with committing an army in battle. Lee's own army is again saved from total destruction during its withdrawal from the field by a timid, vacillating, and demoralized George McClellan.

In isolation, the substantial indictments of McClellan's failure to destroy Lee's army both on the Peninsula and at Antietam might appear as conclusive evidence of his limited military abilities. In a much broader and

23. Sears, *Landscape Turned Red,* 298; Greene, "'I Fought the Battle Splendidly,'" 83; Gallagher, "The Maryland Campaign in Perspective," 88–89; Wert, *General James Longstreet,* 202.

comprehensive view of the conduct of Civil War battles, however, these judgments lose a great deal of their impact. The most singular anomaly in a war thought to be guided by grand Napoleonic-inspired strategies is that only one major battle resulted in the utter rout and destruction of an army. Moreover, in an age where technological means of fighting had outstripped the tactical applications, the assaulting armies were placed at a distinct disadvantage over an entrenched foe. Furthermore, it should be noted that the one truly decisive and complete victory in the war came at the very end, against a thoroughly exhausted and used-up army. Practically on its last legs, after desperately and recklessly allowing itself to fall upon fortified entrenchments at the battle of Franklin, Hood's army was not able to absorb the shock of Thomas's attack at Nashville. Finally, by what comparative standard do we judge McClellan as an abject failure in field command? Presuming that there actually were opportunities to destroy enemy armies in the Civil War, were there not any other commanders who failed in that endeavor? If so, should that inability necessarily consign them to the ranks of flawed generals along with McClellan?

Even at Nashville, the destruction of Hood's army was not the result of Thomas's hammering blows or the two-week pursuit that ensued. Confederate battlefield casualties were comparatively low at Nashville because Hood's army fought on the defensive. At Franklin, where Hood's army attacked Schofield's entrenched lines, the losses were frightful, particularly in the loss of seasoned line officers. At Nashville, Thomas was able to use his seasoned veterans to flank and overrun Hood's left, even though part of his own line was anchored by seven thousand erstwhile quartermaster employees. Even green units could fight well when entrenched behind fortifications. Hood's army, demoralized at Atlanta, shot to pieces at Franklin, and overwhelmed at Nashville, melted away to nothing with all the deserting and straggling that happened en route to their encampment at Tupelo, Mississippi.[24]

Although it is the closest thing to a totally annihilative victory in the Civil War, the battle of Nashville only underscores the difficulties inherent in producing the destruction of the foe. No one has illustrated the reasons why this was so difficult as have Grady McWhiney and Perry D. Jamieson in their oft-quoted work, *Attack and Die* (1982). The introduction of rifled muzzle-loaders and the minié ball had nullified the advantage of offensive shock tactics in the Napoleonic tradition, long revered by West Point

24. Hattaway and Jones, *How the North Won*, 643–54.

graduates. The technology of war had shifted the tactical advantage to the defender. The standard for Civil War engagements now called for three attackers against a single defender. If the defenders were supported by entrenchments, breastworks, and artillery, the ratio increased to five to one. A number of professional officers understood that tactical reality from the outset; others paid dearly for their education in the early part of the war. Yet, many officers could not be shaken from the conviction that assaulting entrenched lines was still the order of the day. The popular clamor for spectacular victories forced many commanders to needlessly bleed their armies in inconclusive assaults against enemy lines. Poor communications exacerbated the bloodbath by compelling the attacking force to concentrate troops in close order against a fixed point in the enemy line. It should surprise no one that smashing victories remained elusive.[25]

On those occasions when an army was routed from the field, pursuit with the intent to destroy was always thwarted. Again, after the first day at Nashville, Grant, who never overtook any army himself, wired Thomas to "push the enemy now and give him no rest until he is entirely destroyed. . . . [It] will break up Hood's army and render it useless for future operations." Thomas was fortunate in that Hood obliged him by hanging around another day. Nevertheless, the Confederates managed to cover their retreat and ward off Thomas's cavalry. It was the haste in which the retreat was conducted that led to the straggling and desertion that rendered that army useless for future operations.[26]

Effective pursuit was hampered by many factors. Often the costs of field victory were almost as staggering as the wages of defeat. Adrenalin alone could not compensate for the fatigue and shock that settled over an army after a battle. Disorder in the ranks of the victor was usually as pervasive as that which afflicted the retreating foe. Regiments, all mixed

25. The overall thesis of the study is that the South was fonder than the North of employing offensive shock tactics, and this fondness led it to ultimate defeat. See McWhiney and Jamieson, *Attack and Die*, 3–139; Barney, *Flawed Victory*, 8–9. Grant endorsed the concept of the primacy of the defensive by suggesting that "one man inside to defend was more than equal to five outside besieging and assaulting." See Grant, *Memoirs* 2:419. In his defense of Meade's cautious pursuit of Lee, A. Wilson Greene asserts that although the Federal commander enjoyed a five to three manpower advantage over Lee, these were "sufficiently short odds to justify some caution even had Lee's actual strength been universally understood." See A. Wilson Greene, "Meade's Pursuit of Lee," in Gary W. Gallagher, ed., *The Third Day at Gettysburg and Beyond* (Chapel Hill: Univ. of North Carolina Press, 1994), 188.

26. Grant to Thomas, Dec. 15, 1864, in *OR*, vol. 55, 2:195.

together during the course of battle had to be sorted out in order to organize and execute a pursuit. In many locations, pursuit was feasible to the extent that supply lines could be established to sustain forward movement. Most importantly, however, pursuit was more dangerous than frequently imagined. Retreating armies were capable of fighting vicious rearguard actions. Moreover, the tactical advantage passed over to the army in retreat since it was able to reestablish defensive lines to meet the oncoming pursuers.

A general overview of the Peninsula and Maryland campaigns is instructive as to how difficult it was to destroy an opponent's army. McClellan's first significant obstacle on the Peninsula was the Confederate fortifications at Yorktown. Among his shortcomings during that campaign, his decision to delay there was probably the greatest mistake. The time it took to prepare for the siege that never happened might have enabled him to maximize the surprise element of the expedition and deny Johnston the opportunity to concentrate his forces. But he was beguiled by his theatrical opponent, John B. Magruder, whose ruses and disguises confused Union intelligence gatherers into believing that Yorktown was both well manned and fortified. Without an organized staff system, information gathering was doled out to civilian amateurs whose methods were ineptly informal and whose sources were of dubious quality. In the early years of the war it was not unusual for commanders to have little or no idea of the strength of their opposition.[27] As for McClellan's overestimation of enemy strength, it should be noted that he was not the only Federal commander to doodle with arithmetic when it came to gauging numbers. In addition to his wildly inflated estimate of Confederate strength in Kentucky in 1861, Sherman, during the lumbering advance toward Corinth, shared Halleck's apprehension that Beauregard's force numbered one hundred thirty thousand when only sixty-six thousand were present. Much has been said of McClellan's susceptibility in believing inflated information fed to him by Allan Pinkerton, yet he was not inordinately worse than many others in obtaining reliable information from conventional sources.[28]

27. Joseph E. Johnston: *Narrative of Military Operations* (New York: Appleton, 1874), 31.

28. For Sherman's overestimation of enemy strength, see Marszalek, *Sherman: A Soldier's Passion for Order,* 182; Fishel, "Pinkerton and McClellan," 115–42; Harsh, "McClellan-Go-Round," 115. Even after the battering Lee endured at Gettysburg, Meade's two corps commanders, Wright and Sedgwick, still believed Lee's forces numbered near eighty thousand. See Greene, "Meade's Pursuit of Lee," 188.

McClellan's tightly reasoned strategy of deploying overwhelming strength came increasingly unravelled as he drew to within six miles of Richmond. Studied caution gave way to excessive caution. In tying tactics employed to the strategy devised, the withholding of nearly a third of his invasion force has been dismissed too readily by McClellan's critics.[29] Alternately promised and denied the use of McDowell's First Corps, McClellan was deprived of the means to implement his strategy of stepping up the pressure on Richmond's defenses. Worse, his hope to link Porter's Fifth Corps with McDowell's forty thousand-man force that never came actually exposed his right wing to Confederate assault. Once Johnston left the scene, Lee seized the initiative by doing precisely that.

On one point some of the critics of McClellan's campaign on the Peninsula are correct. Even had McDowell's force arrived as promised, McClellan was not about to rush the Confederate entrenchments with his larger army. Having moved to within view of the church spires of Richmond, he was about to move in his heavy siege guns. With the possible exception of Sherman, who made a career after Chickasaw Bluffs of avoiding frontal assaults, McClellan was the most astute of Federal commanders in recognizing the advantages possessed by an entrenched force. All along, that stark reality had fashioned his strategy that only an overwhelming force maneuvered along the correct lines of operation would have any chance of success. For McClellan to have successfully stormed the defenses of Richmond, he would have needed a force considerably larger than even he had imagined. He did what any reasonable commander would have done; he closed in on Richmond as much as he dared, ordered up the big guns, and prepared for a siege.[30]

Lincoln had envisioned that McClellan's preference for a waterborne strategy would only transfer the hard fighting from the Manassas line to the Peninsula. Even had McClellan not been delayed at Yorktown, it was unlikely he could have taken Richmond in a sweeping coup de main. Johnston would eventually have figured out McClellan's intentions and concentrated his army to intercept the enemy's approach to Richmond.

29. Sears, for example, criticizes McClellan's myopic view of the situation by suggesting that he might have turned Jackson's departure from the lines at Richmond to his own advantage. See Sears, *George B. McClellan: The Young Napoleon*, 199.

30. McPherson surmises that McClellan would not have moved with any more speed or boldness in capturing Richmond even if he had McDowell's force. See McPherson, *Battle Cry of Freedom*, 460.

Nonetheless, McClellan was prepared, as Lee divined, to conduct a traditional siege, digging switchback trenches to protect his engineers until the big guns he had on hand began the systematic destruction of the Confederate defenses. McClellan had every right to believe that he could win a contest between his artillery and that of his opponents. It was the one recognized advantage of the North from the very beginning of the war. As already discussed, Lee expected to lose such a match. Moreover, as he had pointed out to Lincoln in his defense of the Urbanna plan, McClellan correctly anticipated that the enemy would have no alternative but to attempt to disrupt a methodical siege by resorting to the tactical offensive. While that did not ensure the destruction of Lee's army, it offered the promise of inflicting staggering casualties upon that army. With an army the size he had hoped to have under his command, McClellan was within reason to believe the enemy would have been repulsed with heavy losses, and he would experience no significant interruption in the momentum of his siege.[31]

That is precisely why the retention of McDowell's corps from McClellan's right wing was a "strategic error—perhaps even the colossal blunder that McClellan considered it," as McPherson admits.[32] Irrespective of whether McClellan would have used that forty-thousand-man force appropriately or not, its very absence allowed Lee an opportunity to change the complexion of Richmond's dire straits. Just as McClellan was beginning to implement the formal siege of Richmond, Lee, with Jackson's force retrieved from the Valley, slammed into the vulnerable right flank of McClellan's army. To Lee's credit, he never surrendered the initiative to McClellan. Alarmed, McClellan gave up all thoughts of resuming the offensive and pulled his army into a full-scale retreat to Harrison's Landing.

Now it was Lee's turn to attempt the destruction of McClellan's army. Between the incredible bungling of his own lieutenants' performance and the skillful retreat conducted by the Federal army, Lee was to be denied his objective. From the initial action at Mechanicsville, things continually went awry. No one would have anticipated the trustworthy Jackson to miss a moment of a bloodletting, but he was inexplicably caught dozing through the opening hours of the action, and then he lost his way and wandered away from the battlefield. At each of the battles comprising

31. Beringer, et al., *Why the South Lost the Civil War,* 143–44.
32. McPherson, *Battle Cry of Freedom,* 460.

the battle of The Seven Days, one or the other Confederate unit disappointed Lee. At Glendale, for instance, Lee's future chief artillerist, E. Porter Alexander, later mused that the Confederate army had missed its best chance to end the war.[33] If it wasn't Jackson on the first day, then it was Longstreet on another day, or Magruder, Theophilus Holmes, and A. P. Hill the following day. With the exception of Magruder and Holmes, all those commanders would go on to serve with distinction in later battles, but in The Seven Days, they showed how inexperienced they were in handling and coordinating large numbers of troops.[34]

The final and most costly of Lee's blunders occurred at the last of the battles—Malvern Hill. There, Lee, who had become alternately obsessed and frustrated in his attempts to destroy the retreating Federal army, ordered a suicidal assault on the entrenched and heavily fortified Union positions atop the hill with less than adequate knowledge of the situation. On that day, Lee had lost control of his army. Waves of Confederate assault lines were mowed down by well-trained artillery in the Federal ranks. In the words of one of Lee's own generals, D. H. Hill, "It was not war, it was murder." Lee finally called an end to the carnage. McClellan moved his army to the James under the protection of Union gunboats. While satisfied with the deliverance of Richmond, Davis glumly informed his wife that had all of his orders been executed as planned, "There would have been a general dispersion" of the enemy army. Lee was unequivocal in his belief that the "Federal army should have been destroyed."[35]

Because of the immense moral victory he gained during the Seven Days' Battle, Lee's foibles are largely overlooked. He had saved Richmond from certain capture and had neutralized the largest army ever assembled on the continent. His failure to destroy McClellan's retreating army is understandable. An army in retreat is capable of meting out a great deal

---

33. Gary W. Gallagher, ed., *Fighting for the Confederacy: The Recollections of General Edward Porter Alexander* (Chapel Hill: Univ. of North Carolina Press, 1989), 109–10.

34. In spite of its near beatification of Robert E. Lee's prowess, and occasional factual errors, Dowdey's narrative of the Seven Days remains the most lively account of Confederate blunders. See Dowdey, *The Seven Days.* Also cataloging the list of Confederate errors during the campaign is Sears, *To the Gates of Richmond;* see also, Wert, *General James Longstreet,* 111–50.

35. Daniel Harvey Hill, "McClellan's Change of Base and Malvern Hill," in *Battles and Leaders* 2:394; Jefferson Davis to Varina Davis, July 6, 1862, in Dunbar Rowland, ed., *Jefferson Davis, Constitutionalist: His Letters, Papers, and Speeches,* 10 vols. (Jackson: Mississippi Department of Archives and History, 1923), 5:290–91; *OR,* vol. 11, 2:497.

of punishment, especially when drawn up behind impressive fortifications like Malvern Hill. Like McClellan's, Lee's troops were inexperienced and were officered by men who had not yet proven their abilities. Lee would exile those officers, like Holmes and Magruder, who demonstrated they were unfit to command. The movement and coordination required in bringing disparate units of the army to the right place and time were prevented by what military historians are fond of calling the "fog of war."[36]

McClellan, on the other hand, had suffered a shocking setback to his grand campaign, although his opportunities were not irretrievably lost. In many respects, McClellan had scored a tactical triumph. Fighting on the defensive during the Seven Days battle, he inflicted twice as many casualties on Lee's army as he himself sustained. Lee lost 21 percent of his engaged force.[37] At that pace, Lee would eventually drain his limited manpower pool. Harvey Hill put it more succinctly: "The attacks on the Beaver Dam intrenchments, on the heights of Malvern Hill, at Gettysburg, etc., were all grand, but of exactly the kind of grandeur which the South could not afford." Again, he bitterly recalled, "[We] were lavish of blood in those days."[38]

Although any remaining sinews of confidence in McClellan had been severed by the outcome of the Seven Days' Battle, Lincoln still recognized the advantages gained by the fierce fighting on the Peninsula. Because of the intense public scrutiny of the eastern theater, Lincoln was perplexed how Shiloh, which was, after all, a half-victory and near defeat, drew negligible attention when compared to McClellan's setback. Lincoln bemoaned the fact that the political and moral implications of the Seven Days' Battle would far outweigh any positive results. He understood that the Army of the Potomac had won a tactical victory to the extent that the "enemy suffered more than we" in both "men and material," and they were "less able to bear it." He was frustrated that a "half-defeat should hurt us so much" in "moral effect."[39]

* * *

36. McClellan was equally dissatisfied with a number of his corps and divisional commanders, such as Erasmus Keyes and Silas Casey. Edwin "Bull" Sumner was a more difficult case. As Sumner was the senior general on the field he would assume command of the army in the event McClellan was disabled or killed. Consequently, McClellan kept a tight rein on Sumner's movements. See Sears, *To the Gates of Richmond*, 159–60.

37. McWhiney and Jamieson, *Attack and Die*, 8.

38. Hill, "McClellan's Change of Base," 352.

39. Basler, *Collected Works of Abraham Lincoln* 5:355–56.

If, in the eyes of McClellan's detractors, the Peninsula campaign ended up as the biggest fizzle of the war, his management of the battle at Antietam and his failure to renew fighting the next day are unforgivable mistakes. His inability to utterly and completely destroy Lee's army as it evacuated the battlefield to cross the Potomac is but the icing on the proverbial cake—a stirring testimony to a career that was flawed from the beginning of the war. For some, he not only wasted the best chance ever presented the Federal army to destroy Lee's army, but he bears the responsibility for prolonging the war until 1865.

Attempting to catalog in the historical literature the impressive array of McClellan's mistakes, either of commission or omission, is a daunting task itself. Many narratives of the Antietam campaign reach back to Manassas where needless delays on McClellan's part assured that Pope would not get out of his "scrape."[40] He was restored to command the defense of Washington on September 2 only because Lincoln appreciated the general's organizational skills and realized that he enjoyed the confidence of the army. When information suggested that Lee might well be on his way towards Maryland and Pennsylvania, Lincoln reluctantly ordered McClellan to move the army to meet the threat. He moved northward, in the opinion of many, at the "glacial pace" that had characterized his advances on the Peninsula.[41]

According to historians, McClellan's first major mistake occurred when he failed to act with all possible dispatch against Lee's army after obtaining a copy of that general's "lost orders" on September 13. His ambiguous instructions to his subordinate, William Franklin, allowed valuable daylight hours to be wasted that could have been used to push through the gaps in the South Mountains and fall upon Lee's divided army. The resulting delay also resulted in the loss of the besieged Federal garrison at Harpers Ferry. After a leisurely advance to the banks of the

40. In a recommendation to Halleck upon hearing news of reverses at the front in Manassas, McClellan urged either an immediate juncture of his army with Pope's or concentration of the army for the defense of Washington, leaving Pope "to get out of his scrape." Irrespective of the logical quality of that advice, it was a poorly selected phrase to employ and obviously revealed McClellan's satisfaction that his earlier prediction about Pope receiving the comeuppance he deserved was coming true. See Sears, *Landscape Turned Red*, 7–8; Kenneth P. Williams, *Lincoln Finds a General* 2:359–60; T. Harry Williams, *Lincoln and His Generals*, 157; Glatthaar, *Partners in Command*, 84.

41. Dennis Frye, "Drama Between the Rivers," in Gallagher, ed., *Antietam: Essays on the 1862 Maryland Campaign*, 15; Kenneth P. Williams, *Lincoln Finds a General* 2:364.

Antietam, many critics of the northern campaign believe that McClellan wasted an entire day (September 16) in which he should have hurled his army against the incompletely united rebel army.[42]

As for the battle itself, most historians disparage the plan of attack and its implementation. Instead of pressuring Lee's entire line simultaneously, McClellan committed his troops in driblets and in piecemeal fashion. He yielded control of the initiative by permitting attacks that looked promising to be inexplicably curtailed. Reserves that might have been used to good effect were left idly standing by. Joseph Hooker's First Corps assault was left initially unassisted by Joseph Mansfield's Twelfth Corps until its fighting strength had been spent. The center thrust under Edwin Sumner's direction was likewise poorly orchestrated. Then, at the moment when a breakthrough was within grasp, McClellan refused to override Sumner's misgivings to resume the drive, even though Franklin's troops were available for support. McClellan frittered away the final chance to cave in Lee's right flank by failing to issue timely orders to his left wing commander, Burnside, to cross the Antietam near the lower bridge. Once Burnside did get across, McClellan failed to sustain the drive, allowing it to stall at the edge of Sharpsburg, only to be shattered by the arrival of A. P. Hill's force from Harpers Ferry.[43]

In spite of those shortcomings, McClellan's reputation was still salvageable, in the view of some analysts of the campaign, up to the point where he forfeited the option to resume the assault the following day. Reserve levels in the Federal army had been buoyed by the constant arrival of fresh troops from Washington since the battle began on September 17. Yet, McClellan elected to sit tight and ponder what his enemy, whom he supposed was likewise reinforced, planned to do. Finally, he failed to destroy Lee's army during its retreat across the Potomac. It was the most incommodious and unenviable position any Federal army would find its opponent in during the war.[44]

42. Murfin, *Gleam of Bayonets*, 184, 205; T. Harry Williams, *Lincoln and His Generals*, 166–67; Nevins, *War For the Union* 2:223–24.

43. Murfin, *Gleam of Bayonets*, 208, 223, 226–27, 264; Greene, "'I Fought the Battle Splendidly,'" 69–70, 72–75; McPherson, *Battle Cry of Freedom*, 539–44.

44. Donald, *Lincoln*, 385–86; Nevin, *War for the Union* 2:226–27; Sears, *Landscape Turned Red*, 298, 303, 306–8; Sears, *George B. McClellan: The Young Napoleon*, 319–22; Greene, "'I Fought the Battle Splendidly,'" 80–83; Gallagher, "The Maryland Campaign in Perspective," 89–90.

A microscopic analysis of that campaign does indeed point to a number of critical errors that substantially subtract from its baseline success. In many ways, those mistakes were being made by all commanders and in all theaters to a greater and lesser extent. Surely, McClellan passed up opportunities for greater success. Nonetheless, when one considers that the whereabouts of the enemy was consistently in doubt during the march to Frederick, Maryland, he had moved with commendable alacrity. However, upon coming across the copy of the "lost orders," he should have moved with greater urgency in forcing his way through the gaps of South Mountain. Moreover, his instructions to William B. Franklin, assigned to push through Crampton's Gap in order to assist in the relief of Harpers Ferry, allowed too much individual discretion. In granting Franklin the latitude "to change any of the details of this order as circumstances may change," he obscured his more urgent directive to his subordinate. Instead of asking Franklin to summon "all your intellect and the utmost activity that a general can exercise," he should have commanded him to move immediately with all possible dispatch. Better phraseology would have conveyed his sense of urgency and might have rescued Harpers Ferry, as well as exploited the opportunity created by Lee's having divided his army. Then, again, Sears is quite right in his criticism of McClellan's rather languid movement toward the battlefield. He should have been prepared to launch his attack a full day earlier and not have permitted Lee to collect his scattered forces.[45]

A fair amount of ambivalence surrounds the merit of McClellan's tactical assault plans. In his detailed examination of the campaign, Sears quickly glosses over that aspect. In his biographical study of the general, Sears reserves most of his criticism for McClellan's vague ideas of the role Burnside's army would play in the unfolding battle. Given Sears's unabashed disdain for McClellan's leadership, one could almost consider this a reverse of the old bromide—praising by faint damnation.[46] Greene sees a lack of clarity in McClellan's plans but believes that "any plausible scheme" should have been a guarantee of success.[47] McPherson compli-

45. George B. McClellan, *Report on the Organization of the Army of the Potomac, and Its Campaigns in Virginia and Maryland* (Washington, D.C.: GPO, 1864), 191–92; also in *OR*, vol. 51, 1:826–27; Sears, *Landscape Turned Red,* 155–63.

46. Sears, *Landscape Turned Red,* 160–74, and *George B. McClellan: The Young Napoleon,* 297–303.

47. Greene, "'I Fought the Battle Splendidly,'" 65–67.

ments McClellan by judging it a "good battle plan."[48] McClellan's principal failure on September 17 was when he yielded control of its execution at three critical points. First, he was tardy in pushing Sumner's corps, assigned the center of the field, into the fray at the same time Hooker was engaged on the Federal right. Then, he sided with Sumner in that general's dispute with the normally cautious Franklin over making a final concerted push at the Confederate center. Franklin believed that one more effort in that arena would push through the line. Sumner, normally an aggressive, though unimaginative soldier, begged off, citing exhaustion and the poor prospects for success. Finally, McClellan failed to exploit an opportunity to support Burnside's tardy advance over the creek on the Federal left by committing Porter's reserve force. At one point, McClellan seemed tempted to do so, but he was discouraged by Porter's sober reminder that he commanded the "last reserve of the last army of the Republic." Unfortunately, McClellan would not gamble when the stakes were articulated in that manner.[49]

Up to a point, campaign analysts are justified in condemning McClellan for his failure to renew fighting on September 18 and for his timid pursuit of Lee's retreating army the day after. Earlier in the campaign, McClellan had spoken euphorically about bagging Bobby Lee and had promised the president that he would be forwarding battle trophies. Lincoln was a bit more understated in his response and expressed only his wish that McClellan not allow Lee to get away "without being hurt."[50] The carnage and devastation unleashed on September 17 at Antietam convulsed the sensibilities of both armies. In one of the war's most perverse ironies, it was George B. McClellan, reviled as the most reluctant of warriors, who presided over the bloodiest day in the nation's military history. McClellan was staggered by the destruction and decided to wait and see what Lee planned for the next day. According to one study of the remaining battle strength of both armies on the morning of September 18, McClellan had sixty-two thousand serviceable troops on hand

48. McPherson, *Battle Cry of Freedom*, 539.

49. A tidy summary of McClellan's lack of control during the battle itself is found in Greene, "'I Fought the Battle Splendidly," 72–80. Porter denied making the comment that was reported by Capt. Thomas M. Anderson in Johnson and *Battles and Leaders* 2:656.

50. George B. McClellan Papers, Manuscript Division, Library of Congress. McClellan's dispatch is in *OR*, vol. 19, 2:281.

while Lee had half that number. Without reinforcements, McClellan did not want to resume the offensive.[51]

Critics are partially accurate in their assessment that McClellan lost his final and golden opportunity to make a vigorous pursuit of Lee's defeated army. It was almost certain that he could have inflicted greater punishment on Lee by forcing him to abandon larger numbers of ordnance and material. A more concerted follow-up might well have scooped up the invariable scores of stragglers and might have induced greater desertion. It would have gone a long way in fulfilling Lincoln's request not to allow Lee to get away "without being hurt." McClellan's critics, however, have long erred in their categorical and unequivocal assertion that he should have destroyed Lee's army. Even in effecting a river crossing, Lee was not incapable of mounting a punishing defense. In fact, McClellan sent Porter with a detachment of the Fifth Corps to harass the Confederate withdrawal. That force succeeded in capturing four artillery pieces before the enemy rear guard under A. P. Hill counterattacked and drove it back across the Potomac. It was a particularly sharp engagement that saw one Union regiment, the 118th Pennsylvania, more commonly known as the Corn Exchange Regiment, go into action for the first time. Their initiation was marked by having just received newly issued Enfields that proved totally defective as they straddled the Potomac fighting off Hill's attack. In Hill's own words, it was "the most terrible slaughter" he had witnessed to date and provided "a wholesale lesson to the enemy, and taught them to know it may be dangerous sometimes to press a retreating army."[52]

Criticisms of other aspects of the Maryland campaign are considerably off the mark and quite unwarranted. The most egregious charge is that of McClellan's slowness in moving out of Washington to meet Lee in Maryland. The Confederate army only began its march into Maryland

51. Greene, "'I Fought the Battle Splendidly,'" 81.

52. The Corn Exchange Regiment's dilemma is detailed in Murfin, *Gleam of Bayonets*, 305. Hill's report is in *OR*, vol. 19, 1:982. Meade's chief of artillery at Gettysburg exonerated his superior for not attacking Lee at the Potomac crossing, despite the fact that the Confederate army was pinned against a raging current of flood waters and lacked a suitable bridge. "As to bagging Lee—bah!" Henry Hunt exclaimed. "How many instances of bagging can you find in history?" he asked. Quoted in Greene, "Meade's Pursuit of Lee," 192. Greene is demonstrably sympathetic with Meade's admission of physical and mental exhaustion following the Battle at Gettysburg, standing in sharp contrast to his analysis of McClellan following the battle at Antietam.

between September 4 and 7, enroute to Frederick. The Army of Northern Virginia, despite its bedraggled appearance, was in fine spirits, having just pounded John Pope at Second Manassas. Lee recognized that the Federal army under any circumstances would need time to reorganize to contend with his own movements. In a conversation with Gen. John G. Walker, who had just arrived in camp with reinforcements from Richmond, Lee repaid McClellan for his gaffe in earlier describing Lee as a timid soldier.[53] After pointing to Harrisburg on a map and noting it as his objective, Lee turned to an astonished Walker and asked if he knew McClellan. "He is an able general but a very cautious one," Lee remarked. He continued. "His enemies among his own people think him too much so. His army is in a very demoralized and chaotic condition, and will not be prepared for offensive operations—or he will not think so—for three or four weeks. Before that time, I hope to be on the Susquehanna."[54]

For a change of pace, Lee had greatly underestimated McClellan. Although Lee's whereabouts and intentions were great mysteries, McClellan proved his resourcefulness in reorganizing the demoralized units of Pope's army with his own army just arrived from the Peninsula. The recruiting stations, unfortunately closed at the beginning of the Peninsula campaign, where they might have supplied the reinforcements that McClellan requested, had resumed operations and were forwarding freshly minted volunteer regiments to Washington. Those units were integrated with the army that promptly moved out on September 9. Throughout the march, McClellan was besieged by intelligence reports that the rebel army numbered anywhere between sixty thousand and two hundred thousand. His cavalry commander, Alfred Pleasonton, consistently reported an average of one hundred twenty thousand. Moreover, Halleck remained convinced that Lee's real purpose was to lure McClellan northward in order to strike at Washington from northern Virginia. Even on the very day that Lee's lost orders were discovered, Halleck was admonishing McClellan for leaving the capital uncovered, even though three army corps under the command of Nathaniel Banks remained there for that purpose. All things

53. Upon hearing that Lee had replaced Johnston after the Battle of Fair Oaks, McClellan remarked that Lee was "too cautious and weak under grave responsibility . . . wanting in moral firmness . . . & is likely to be timid and irresolute in action." Sears has correctly suggested that McClellan was fortunate that that appraisal was never made public in his lifetime. See Sears, *To the Gates of Richmond*, 57.

54. John G. Walker, "Jackson's Capture of Harper's Ferry," in *Battles and Leaders* 2:605–6.

considered, McClellan moved rapidly. And it was surely fast enough to abruptly derail Lee's timetable for reaching the Susquehanna.[55]

Some have argued that McClellan may have moved faster than he was accustomed to doing, but not fast enough to save the garrison at Harper's Ferry. The loss of those troops added 12,500 casualties to the Federal loss column on the Maryland campaign.[56] To be sure, Franklin's delay at South Mountain permitted the Confederates a little additional time to prompt the surrender of Federal troops under the command of Gen. Dixon S. Miles. Miles, on the other hand, put up a mediocre defense and all but assured the garrison's capitulation when his troops abandoned Maryland Heights, the key to controlling Harpers Ferry.[57] McClellan had argued from the outset of the campaign that the garrison should have been evacuated before Lee's army arrived. In a discussion with Seward he revealed that he "regarded the arrangements there as exceedingly dangerous." The garrison should be removed, he argued, and attached to his own army. Otherwise, McClellan suggested, the force should be moved to Maryland Heights, and once there should "hold out to the last." Impressed with McClellan's logic, Seward took McClellan to Halleck to discuss what to do with Harpers Ferry, where, according to McClellan, his ideas were icily rebuffed by the general in chief. Again, on September 10, McClellan suggested to Halleck that Miles's force was powerless to do anything at Harpers Ferry and should be joined with his army. That suggestion was also rejected.[58] Even the faintest familiarity with the geography of Harpers Ferry would have suggested the impracticality of holding out. Crowned by three heights, at the confluence of the Shenandoah and Potomac Rivers, the town was at the bottom of a huge bowl. A Gibraltar it was not. It vied with Winchester as the spot most frequently captured and recaptured during the war. Miles's own adjutant, Lieutenant Henry Binney, described Harpers Ferry as a "complete slaughter pen—a small triangular position, contracted between two rivers and surrounded on all sides by bluffs and hills." Stonewall Jackson was reported as saying

---

55. The varying estimates of Confederate troop strength are in *OR*, vol. 19, 2:193–230, 354–55. Sifting through these reports, McClellan settled on a figure of approximately 120,000. See "McClellan to Halleck, September 8 and 9, 1862," *OR*, vol. 19, 2:211, 219. Note that Alfred Pleasanton's reports are found in McClellan Papers, Manuscript Division, Library of Congress.

56. Frye, "Drama Between the Rivers," 25, 34.

57. Ibid., 18–22.

58. McClellan, *McClellan's Own Story*, 549–50, 559.

that his army "would had rather take it fifty times than undertake to defend it once." While it was unfortunate that Franklin was not a few hours quicker on September 14 to prevent the garrison's surrender on the morning of the 15th, McClellan does not deserve any censure for the loss of Harpers Ferry. That fault lies with Miles in Harpers Ferry and Halleck in Washington.[59]

McClellan's battle plan at Antietam was not as disjointed as frequently portrayed. Pressure was to be exerted on Lee's flanks by both the Federal left and right. The concerted push was to come through the center of the line. As in so many Civil War battle plans, the execution left much to be desired. Unforseen events reshape battle plans. Certainly Grant, who was the architect of the battles that broke the rebel stranglehold on Chattanooga, did not envision Thomas and Hooker to be the ones to produce the victories at Missionary Ridge and Lookout Mountain. In his plan, Sherman's assault was expected to carry the day. At Antietam, the impression that McClellan fought the battle in "driblets" was in large measure the result of delays in getting the Federal left into action. The story of what happened on Burnside's front has been rehashed so often that it has become a quagmire in which historians get bogged down. Critics of McClellan's handling of the battle are correct in assigning him partial blame for the confusion surrounding the orders designed to unleash Burnside's assault on the Confederate right. Burnside, who was at the ready early in the morning, should have been engaged at the same time Hooker was wading through the cornfields on the Confederate left.

Disputes over the hour Burnside's orders arrived cite evidence suggesting the time to be anywhere between 8:00 and 10:00 in the morning. Even assuming that those infamous orders reached Burnside shortly before 10:00 A.M., an immediate assault would have had desirable effects. Moreover, an inexcusable delay of two hours to requisition ammunition that should have been on hand added another two hours before Burnside advanced towards Sharpsburg at 3:00 P.M. A timely advance might have undermined Confederate efforts to reinforce their center lines, allowing Federal assaults underway there to be more productive. It would also have moved up four hours Burnside's timetable for advancing towards Sharpsburg. That would have enabled McClellan to exploit

---

59. Frank Moore, ed., *The Rebellion Record*, 11 vols. and supplement (New York: Putnam's, 1861–63; Van Nostrand's 1864–68), 5:443.

Burnside's having turned Lee's right flank and would have negated A. P. Hill's late afternoon heroics.[60]

As it was, Burnside took three hours to storm the lower bridge and establish himself on the embankment above the Antietam, and then he took another two to regroup before he moved towards Sharpsburg. In attempting to disparage McClellan's management of the battlefield, inordinate efforts have been made to stress Burnside's difficult assignment to storm the bridge and ascend the heights beyond. Alternate assault positions were available, and although McClellan had not used the cavalry to discover all of them, Burnside, who was assigned that single phase of the attack, displayed little imagination and initiative in probing for them. Moreover, the Confederate detail at the bridge crossing, despite its envious defensive position, numbered a mere 500 to 600 men. Burnside made unconcerted efforts to storm the bridge and needlessly exposed his assault teams to enfilading fire by marching them parallel to the creek in their approach to the bridge. In the end, two regiments, the 51st New York and the 51st Pennsylvania, the latter whose courage was fortified by its colonel's promise to restore the regiment's whiskey ration, crashed the bridge and scurried up the ravine on the other side.[61]

In the end, flawless execution on McClellan's part would have led to a more serious maiming, perhaps even the elusive destruction, of Robert E. Lee's army. In several instances, McClellan's errors and oversights marred that execution. In other ways, he was poorly served by his corps commanders, particularly Sumner and Burnside. Not unlike Lee in the Seven Days' Battle, complete success eluded McClellan on September 17. Yet,

60. "The culpability for not capturing the Lower Bridge until 1:00 P.M. rests less with Burnside's conduct of the operation than with McClellan's delay in unleashing it," writes Greene in "'I Fought the Battle Splendidly,'" 75. Additional support for this claim can be found in Marvel, *Burnside,* 127–48.

61. Both Greene and Sears posit that McClellan's decision not to reinforce Burnside's drive toward the town was a result of his obsession with defending against an imagined counterattack by Lee. See Greene, "'I Fought the Battle Splendidly,'" 75–77; and Sears, *Landscape Turned Red,* 280. From the evidence they marshal for this argument, they appear correct to a point. By midafternoon, McClellan was awaiting a possible Confederate counterattack and had lost his desire to commit reserves to support Burnside's advance. On the other hand, had Burnside not delayed so long at the Rohrbach Bridge and had he been ready to advance anytime before noon, McClellan might have been willing to support that move. The whiskey ration story is recounted in Sears, *Landscape Turned Red,* 265. A good case can be made for the advantages of having ladled out that ration sometime earlier in the morning.

where in the Civil War did battle plans come off exactly as planned, and when did vigorous pursuits assure the destruction of the fleeing foe? That kind of unqualified success eluded McClellan's chief antagonist Robert E. Lee on several occasions during the war, just as it frequently did McClellan's greatly acclaimed compatriots, Grant and Sherman.

The Seven Days' Battle was not the first and only time Lee believed he had lost a precious opportunity to destroy his opponent in battle. It is, of course, to Lee's credit that we can even speak of the possibility of a small army as missing opportunities in crushing the larger Federal armies. However, when Pope and McDowell mismanaged the defense of their left flank against Longstreet's oncoming corps, Lee believed the chance existed to defeat that "miscreant" Pope. He was not content with his signal victory over Pope on August 30. Pope's army, though demoralized and shaken, remained intact and had established a defensive perimeter at Centreville. With Longstreet positioned in front of Pope's main force, Lee ordered Jackson on a flanking maneuver around Pope's right. In a fierce action, punctuated by claps of thunder and bursts of rain, Lee's attempt to destroy Pope came to a climactic end at the Battle of Chantilly.[62]

Fredericksburg presented Lee with yet another opportunity to inflict significant damage upon the Army of the Potomac. After allowing Burnside to impale his army upon his impressive fortifications, Lee waited for two days for the next Federal advance. With their backs to the deep and forbidding Rappahannock, and compelled to retreat across the river on pontoon bridges, Burnside's army crossed unmolested. British military historian J. F. C. Fuller concluded that Lee forfeited "his one and only opportunity for ending the war."[63]

In what most historians consider to be Lee's masterpiece campaign, the battle of Chancellorsville, Lee was again frustrated in his attempt to destroy the larger part of Hooker's army that was stranded at U.S. Ford on the Rappahannock. Taking a force half the size of the enemy's, Lee had divided his force twice in the face of the enemy to bring an end to any thoughts Hooker entertained about marching into Richmond. Yet, despite

---

62. Hennessy, *Return to Bull Run*, 439–51.

63. J. F. C. Fuller, *Grant and Lee: A Study in Personality and Generalship* (Bloomington: Indiana Univ. Press, 1957), 174. A useful review of critiques of Lee's performance at Fredericksburg can be found in Gary W. Gallagher, "Confederates Evaluate the Battle," *The Fredericksburg Campaign: Decision on the Rappahannock* (Chapel Hill: Univ. of North Carolina Press, 1995), 113–16.

that enormous triumph, Lee was disappointed when his army failed to destroy Sedgwick's relief column coming out from Fredericksburg. Meanwhile, fifty thousand soldiers of Hooker's main army were undertaking a perilous nighttime evacuation over pontoon bridges during a raging storm that swelled the river to a torrent, right in front of Lee's army. The next morning, May 6, Lee awoke to find that the Yankees had skedaddled. When General Dorsey Pender reported that finding to Lee, the commander was furious. "Why General Pender!" he lashed out, "That's the way you young men always do. You allow those people to get away. I tell you what to do, but you don't do it! Go after them! Damage them all you can!" It was too late. Lee would have to be content with the victory he had already earned.[64]

Upon Grant's reassignment to the Army of the Potomac in 1864, William T. Sherman assumed control of the armies that were poised to descend into Georgia to do some hard fighting and destroy Joe Johnston's enemy army. A close examination of his career prior to that time does not suggest that Sherman possessed an inherent knack for war, and he might not have been able to handle an independent command in 1864 had Grant not trained and sustained him. His approach to Atlanta suggests that he was less inclined even than McClellan to order frontal assaults. From the very outset in Dalton, he preferred maneuvering Johnston back into Atlanta. He considered his one attack on Kennesaw Mountain a mistake; and despite the strategic effectiveness of his subsequent march to the sea, he opted for marching over fighting. Albert Castel's examination of the Atlanta campaign led him to the conclusion, usually levelled at McClellan, that Sherman was a "general who did not like to fight." Even by his own admission, Sherman chose not to pursue Hood's army as it fled from Atlanta. Hood would eventually be left for Thomas to handle.[65]

The terminus for Sherman's march to the sea was Savannah. There a force of roughly ten thousand Confederates under William J. Hardee served as the city's garrison. Sherman determined to soften up Hardee's

64. Lee is quoted in Freeman, *R. E. Lee: A Biography* 2:557. See also, Thomas, *Robert E. Lee: A Biography,* 285–86; and Ernest Ferguson, *Chancellorsville, 1863* (New York: Knopf, 1992), 311–18. Later, Lee declared that despite widespread jubilation in the South for the victory at Chancellorsville, he was disappointed by its barren results. "I, on the contrary, was more depressed than after Fredericksburg," he claimed. "Our loss was severe, and again we had gained not an inch of ground and the enemy could not be pursued." Quoted in Gallagher, "Confederates Evaluate the Battle," 133.

65. Castel, *Decision in the West,* 565; Sherman, *Memoirs* 2:108.

defenses by bombarding them with siege guns as a prelude to ordering a general assault. In an attempt to avoid bloodshed, he formally asked Hardee to consider surrender terms, which the Confederate commander quickly declined. Hoping to avoid another "Balls Bluff," Sherman ordered the cordon surrounding the city to be completed. Taking leave of his force, Sherman retired to meet with Adm. John A. Dahlgren about future operations. The one escape route available to Hardee over the Savannah River remained open for several days. While Sherman was gone, Hardee took advantage of that route and escaped over a pontoon bridge made up of thirty rice flats. One Union officer was puzzled about why the route had not been sealed, and he noted that it had been left open "for at least nine days." Another officer with keener insight observed that "General Sherman wanted the enemy to leave and not make a fight necessary." Although the Confederate army remained incapable of stemming Sherman's advance through the Carolinas, Hardee's troops participated in the surprising attack at Bentonville, North Carolina, where, again, Sherman refused even to consider the opportunity to crush Johnston's army.[66]

Sherman, it would seem, was the most reluctant of warriors. While his plundering of the deep South proved a most valuable contribution to the cause of Union victory, he was not a destroyer of Southern armies. Increasingly, Confederate armies in the West lost the ability to seriously derail Sherman's ambitions. In the Atlanta campaign, he made no serious attempt to trap and destroy Hood's army. Leaving Hood behind on his march to the sea, he was free to leave his "bummers" to their own devices without the slightest threat of interruption. At Savannah, he found Hardee's army backed into a corner and ripe for the picking, yet almost nonchalantly he allowed it to escape. In fact, he seemed to want it to get away. The swath of destruction he cut through the Carolinas was uncontested except for Johnston's desperate attempt at Bentonville. It can be said that Sherman had no interest in destroying rebel armies; he was pleased not to fight. After all, he could win without fighting.[67]

Unlike Sherman, Grant looked forward to destroying Confederate armies, but he was denied the pleasure. "I wanted to pursue," recalling his counterattack at Shiloh, "but had not the heart to order the men who had

66. Marszalek, *Sherman: A Soldier's Passion for Order*, 307–8, 330.
67. Fellman suggests that "Uncle Billy not only charmed his men, he seemed to spare their lives, and they loved him for that as much as for the glory." See Fellman, *Citizen Sherman*, 194.

fought desperately for two days, lying in the mud and rain whenever not fighting." In a scene strangely similar to that enacted by McClellan at Antietam, Grant advised Buell that the general fatigue of the men after the battle "would preclude an advance tonight." Yet Grant acknowledged all the same that an "immediate pursuit must have resulted in the capture of a considerable number of prisoners and probably some guns." When the smoke cleared at Shiloh, the scene looked strikingly familiar. Everything appeared pretty much the same as before the battle, except that a quarter of the soldiers who struggled there had become battlefield casualties. His brilliant campaign at Vicksburg, aided by Pemberton's and Johnston's folly, ended in a successful siege and produced the surrender of the garrison there. As effective as that technique proved to be, Grant had been frustrated in his attempts to destroy Pemberton's army outside of the fortress. At the battle of Champion's Hill, Grant blamed McClernand for failing to "come up with reasonable promptness." He added that had he known the lay of the land, "I cannot see how Pemberton could have escaped with any organized force." In fact, Grant admitted that neither he nor Logan "knew that we had cut off the retreat of the enemy." Later at Chattanooga, where Bragg and Jefferson Davis made his work easier by a series of compounding errors, Grant was able to break the stranglehold on that city but failed to organize any effective pursuit. Sherman, who had been denied the taste of battlefield victory by the amazing successes of Thomas and Hooker, was denied the live trophies of pursuit, as the only Confederates remaining on his front were of the dead variety.[68]

Despite his opinion that "Lee's army is really whipped," Grant's campaign from the Wilderness to Petersburg is a mixed record of triumph and frustration. Any discussion of Grant's difficulties in demolishing Lee's army can begin and end with an examination of his own memoirs. While acknowledging that they are a true literary *tour-de-force,* his memoirs are also a veritable novena to the conjunction "if " and the past participle "had." A virtual litany to these words is enshrined therein. Sprinkled throughout his memoirs of the campaign of 1864 are explanations of the conditions that prevented complete success. Had Burnside done this, or if Hancock had only been here or there, things would have ended quite differently. Try as he would, he was not able to destroy Lee's army.

68. Grant, *Memoirs* 1:519–20, 2:84, 385; McFeely, *Grant,* 115. The normally loquacious Sherman dedicates but two paragraphs to his efforts in the battle at Chattanooga. See Sherman, *Memoirs* 1:364.

In the opening action in the Wilderness on May 4, Grant firmly believed that "if the country had been such that Hancock and his command could have seen the confusion and panic in the lines of the enemy," he would have exploited the opportunity to such an extent that "Lee would not have made another stand outside of his Richmond defences." Again, later the same day, Grant discerned that "Lee was now in great distress." That fact, however, was not realized at the time, Grant declared, "or we would have taken advantage of his condition and no doubt gained a decisive success." His drive towards Spotsylvania was also a catastrophe. He hoped to turn Lee's right at that location, so he could race toward Richmond and force Lee to fight a battle in a site of Grant's choosing. Yet the race to Spotsylvania was won by Lee. Grant ascribed the failure to his army's inability to follow up "the success gained over Hill's corps on the morning of the 6th" and on the fires in the woods that forced the enemy to march hours before it was scheduled. "But accident," Grant sighed, "often decides the fate of battle."[69]

Grant assumed some of the responsibility for the failure at Spotsylvania. "Had I ordered the movement for the night of the 7th," he offered, "it would have put Hancock in the lead." That would have enabled Hancock to destroy the small enemy force that had first arrived near the Court House. Nonetheless, Burnside's force presently arrived at the Court House and completely turned Lee's right. It was unfortunate, Grant explained, that Burnside "was not aware of the importance of the advantage he had gained." Nor did Grant possess that knowledge at the time, and he was willing to shoulder the responsibility for not assigning a staff officer with Burnside to report the situation. The ensuing struggle for control at Spotsylvania was fierce, and both Federal and Confederate fortunes waxed and waned there many times. Neither side appeared to be getting the better of the other despite the launching of several promising initiatives. In his tactical orders to Meade on May 11, Grant expressed disappointment that an earlier assault "would have proved entirely successful if it had commenced one hour earlier and had been heartily entered into by Mott's division and the 9th corps." The following day ended with yet more frustration. Better results "might have been obtained," Grant

69. Grant, *Memoirs* 2:197, 199, 213–14. Wert relates that many Confederates believed that had Longstreet not been wounded, Lee's army "would have swept the Army of the Potomac back across the Rapidan." See Wert, *General James Longstreet*, 388.

recalled, "if the 5th corps, or rather if Warren, had been as prompt as Wright was with the 6th corps."[70]

Two of his final initiatives before settling in for the long siege at Petersburg were also marred by poor execution, in his opinion. The massacre at Cold Harbor, Grant believed, would have been skipped had Federal columns converged at that location according to timetable. But Wright's force was tardy by three hours, and William F. Smith's column, "by some blunder," was inadvertently ordered to Newcastle instead of Cold Harbor. By the time the Federal army was concentrated, Lee was well entrenched. Cold Harbor was cause for sober thinking on Grant's part. He had come to realize that Lee was waging a wily battle. He would not come forth from his entrenchments and offer the great battle Grant yearned for. In his report to Halleck on June 5, Grant admitted as much, noting that he was not willing any longer to order "a greater sacrifice of human life" to effect that which he had "designed outside of the city." Grant proposed to cross the James River and move south of Richmond in hopes of strangling Lee's lifelines. Grant ably managed his crossing of the James, and advance units were flying to the weakly fortified defenses of Petersburg. Again, Grant was denied the fruits of success. Smith, however, moved with "so much delay" that the enemy was able to muster a stout defense. "I believed then, and still believe," Grant wrote, "that Petersburg could have been easily captured at that time." Regrettably, Grant's hopes were dashed and subordinates failed him yet again. That failure was particularly hard on Grant, for he strongly believed that "Petersburg itself could have been carried without much loss." It would have given him immediate control of the Weldon and South Side railroads. Moreover, in Grant's opinion, it would have "saved an immense amount of hard fighting from the 15th to 18th, and would have given us greatly the advantage in the long siege which ensued."[71]

In the light shed by a wider focus on the Civil War, McClellan's mistakes and lost opportunities on the Peninsula and at Antietam are both more understandable and less magnified than many historians have suggested. When we look at the larger perspective, we can determine that not a single commander from either side produced the total destruc-

---

70. Grant, *Memoirs* 2:215–16, 232. For the adverse affect these failures were having upon Northern opinion, see Donald, *Lincoln,* 512–17.

71. Grant, *Memoirs* 2:264–65, 276–77, 279–80, 297–99.

tion of an opposing army. We can also understand why it was so difficult to pursue and demolish an army on the run. When we take those factors into consideration, we are still able to admit that McClellan did not prove to be an exceptional field commander. Even in that earlier stage of the war, facing a fresh and audacious opponent, McClellan's performance rated as average, fair at best, mediocre at worst. He was not, however, the unredeemable and pathetic commander that is portrayed in Civil War literature.

Undoubtedly, McClellan did fail to inflict greater punishment on Lee's retreating army after the battle at Antietam. His defensive posturing, no doubt enhanced by Halleck's frequent telegraphic fulminations on safeguarding routes to the capital, caused McClellan to forfeit a chance to rough up Lee's army as it crossed the river. Given the other lost opportunities to destroy the enemy's army during the Civil War, it seems somewhat unfair to categorically expect McClellan to have done that which was never accomplished elsewhere. Participants at the battle of Antietam had mixed feelings over McClellan's failure to pursue Lee across the Antietam. Most likely, Philadelphia's Corn Exchange regiment would have had a decided opinion on that subject. Of course, using quotes from those who witnessed the battle itself is similar to quoting from the scriptures: anyone can assemble a host of support or denunciation to suit a particular bias. Soldiers felt it their prerogative to criticize those who led them into battle, but as Reid Mitchell contends, they resented it when civilians told them what could or should have been done. In their opinion, the public did not know the difficulties of soldiering. After the battle of Antietam, one Pennsylvania lieutenant, who resented the implication that McClellan had allowed Lee to escape unharmed, wrote home protesting the public's ignorance. He complained that if the men at home "think the Rebble army can be Bagged let them come and bagg them. . . . Bagging an army is easy to talk about."[72]

The intense scrutiny of McClellan's shortcomings at the battle of Antietam frequently obscures the fact that it was a Union victory that bore significant fruit. Murfin is one who at least acknowledges McClellan's accomplishment. Noting that in less than three weeks of being placed in command of Washington's defenses, McClellan "had brought some semblance of order to the Federal army, fought two hotly contested battles, forced Lee to withdraw from Maryland soil, and effectively established a

72. Quoted in Mitchell, *Civil War Soldiers*, 67.

blockade against a Confederate re-entry." Indeed, McClellan checked Lee's dangerous mission of dealing a demoralizing blow on northern soil and evened the score after the dismal rout at Second Manassas. Between the Peninsula campaign and the end of the Maryland campaign, McClellan inflicted over forty-seven thousand casualties in Lee's army. That was a figure greater than the entire Confederate Army of Tennessee at the time. Those were irreplaceable losses that over time would prove the undoing of the Army of Northern Virginia. He succeeded in his primary task, which was to repel the invader and secure the safety of Washington, although it was to his discredit that he never truly contemplated doing more than that. The victory at Antietam also dampened whatever support European capitals were giving to officially recognizing the existence of the Confederate States of America. And although McClellan never would have wanted the accolade for that association, it was his victory, after all, that gave Lincoln the opportunity to issue the Emancipation Proclamation. Assessments of McClellan's performance at Antietam should be tempered in the light of those achievements.[73]

73. Murfin, *Gleam of Bayonets*, 306; Wert, *General James Longstreet*, 207; McWhiney and Jamieson, *Attack and Die*, 8–11. Sears notes that it became clear even to Lee that the "Army of Northern Virginia had been wounded in spirit as well as in body at Sharpsburg . . . [and] now could be driven no more." See Sears, *Landscape Turned Red*, 308.

9

Emerging from the Shadows

THE OPINION OF GEORGE B. McCLELLAN THAT HAS dominated contemporary historiography has been molded by the collapse of the Confederacy and the triumph and vindication of Abraham Lincoln in 1865. In coming to terms with this opinion, Unionist historians have tried to explain why success proved so elusive for four long years. Seeing success incarnated in the persons of Grant and Sherman, they discerned that their predecessors were all pathetic failures. In retrospect, it became easy to dismiss McDowell, Pope, Burnside, Hooker, and even Meade as unequal to the task. McClellan could not be dismissed as peremptorily; he and his actions needed to be explained. Believing that decisive victory was feasible in 1862 and that the mettle of Federal soldiering was not found wanting, then it necessarily followed that McClellan was the problem. His critics have been indulgent in applying every psychological impediment imaginable in their attempts to explain his otherwise unexplainable failure.

The psychological argument is the first thing that has to be considered in arriving at a more balanced and realistic understanding of McClellan's place in Civil War history. The argument is plagued by faulty reasoning, a skewed standard of evaluation, and a failure to consider the social and cultural milieu of the period. Any comparison with his peers reveals that McClellan's psychological baggage was not remarkable, and it most certainly was not the reason he failed. His personality flaws may well have had an impact upon his decision making. Under the stressful and anxiety-provoking conditions that a command position entails, certain people react better than others. Those were, after all, times in which Gary W. Gallagher recognized that "momentous interests" were held in the balance.[1] Not only was the preservation of the Union at stake, but one's military career depended upon being successful. In that situation one might be prone to excessive caution, racked with indecision, or suddenly become sullen and belligerent. McClellan does not compare well with Grant under such stressful situations. But he does not seem that much worse than a mentally unhinged Sherman in Kentucky or a distraught Burnside at Fredericksburg who was prepared to lead a final suicidal charge up Mayre's Heights. Nor does he seem particularly worse than Hooker, who became so paralyzed with fear and indecision that he failed at Chancellorsville. It is grossly unfair and considerably unobjective if we cannot get past the clinical issue with McClellan. It means that we cannot ignore Grant's alcoholism and view his drinking as somehow ennobling. Nor can we chuckle at Sherman's fits of excited anxiety and view his morbid fatalism and depression as the mere consequence of a nimble intellect. And, if psychosis becomes the basis for explaining McClellan's poor generalship, then we might well be compelled by consistency to argue that psychosis had to be the basis of success for men like Grant and Sherman, and that Lincoln's clinical depression was the reason for his successful presidency.

The quality of generalship was only one factor among many that explain why Union efforts in the East were stymied until Grant arrived in 1864. It was not so much that Grant's predecessors in the East were incompetent commanders; rather, it was that they proved incapable of overcoming the significant obstacles and handicaps of securing victory in the early part of the war. To a great degree, early commanders like McClellan fell victim to the fixed idea that a quick victory was a distinct possibility in 1861 and 1862. In much the same way, they suffered from being among the first to command in the East, the most important and intensely scrutinized theater of the war. Advantages like numerical superiority and logistical largesse were but raw potential in the early years of the war and were not effectively harnessed until later. Conversely, the Confederate opponent, with all the advantages of interior lines, was capable of maximizing and husbanding its more meager resources until the

1. Gary W. Gallagher, "'Upon Their Success Hang Momentous Interests,'" 79–108.

strain of prolonged warfare in 1864 exhausted them. Moreover, eastern commanders were constrained in their efforts to devise offensive campaigns by the imposed requirement of safeguarding Washington at their backs. Western commanders were not afflicted by that constraint and could afford to take greater risks. Unlike in the East, generals who came up short in the Western theater were not guaranteed reassignment into military exile and oblivion. Nor does it seem especially fair that eastern commanders should be faulted for failing to do what every one else failed to do during the war–destroy an enemy army. Grant had not achieved it at Shiloh or Chattanooga, and when all is said and done, Grant's campaign in the Wilderness, designed to smash Lee's army, was no more successful than Hooker's had been. It would seem, then, that the length of the war had far more to do with the challenges posed by geography and the difficulties of maintaining the offensive in enemy territory than it did with the presumed superiority of Southern generalship or the abject incompetence of Northern commanders. Consequently, it seems like a much more valid question to ask why anyone would have expected a Northern triumph in 1862, rather than why McClellan and others failed to deliver it.

It does not become necessary, then, to tarnish gratuitously McClellan's reputation as a Civil War commander in order to sustain high regard for Grant and Sherman. In many respects, the Civil War was essentially two wars within one. Particularly in the East, the realities of 1861–62 were a world apart from those of 1864–65. The profound differences in waging war in those periods were reflected in all echelons of the Union war effort. The rank and file, who had rushed to enlist with boyish, amateurish enthusiasm and gilded notions of courage and gallantry in 1861, had the scales lifted from their eyes by 1864, provided, of course, they were still alive by that time. Most certainly, the men of Chamberlain's 20th Maine regiment considered themselves grizzled veterans by the time Grant commenced his spring campaign of 1864, even though they had only begun their service at Antietam, which, of course, was George McClellan's swan song. By 1864, if not well before, veterans like the soldiers of the 20th Maine had long become disillusioned with heroic visions of the struggle and viewed the war with a grim, almost fatalistic, resolution. Nothing etches that realization in the memory of the war more than Horace Porter's recollection of the "deliberate and desperate courage of the men" at Cold Harbor. There, Union soldiers knew they were

Selected to honor a handful of Northern war heroes, McClellan's Gate at Arlington National Cemetery serves as a memorial to those who fought and died to preserve the Union.

Photo courtesy of William E. Kotwas.

being ordered to their deaths, and rather than sulk or balk, they calmly wrote their names and addresses on slips of paper that they sewed onto their coats.[2]

For its part, the Lincoln administration, though never totally abandoning hopes for a decisive campaign, at least adopted a more patient and understanding attitude toward those in command. It, too, had come to learn that a titanic triumph in arms was most likely not in the offing and that the implementation of a relentless, grinding pressure upon the enemy's logistics was the required ingredient for victory. Confidence in Grant's abilities was most certainly a factor in Lincoln's newly acquired patience. Still, Lincoln was keenly aware that his history of interference had played a part in the disruption of earlier campaigns.

Perhaps the significant difference between the early and later periods of the war was the way in which the styles of military leadership had been transformed. McClellan's dramatic proclamations about sharing soldiers' dangers at the front or Pope's boast that he had only seen the backs of his enemies, entertaining and inspiring in 1861 and 1862, would have appeared ludicrously theatrical in the later years of the war. Federal generals, like their government leaders, had become disabused of the idea that a quick and painless victory would be obtained. War had become a dirty, grimy business.[3]

McClellan's strategy, though reflective of the unrealistic war aims of the years 1861–62, was cogent, reasoned, and consistent with conventional military wisdom and his personal views of the nature of the conflict. It was not hallucinatory or deranged; it mirrored the views of the administration and of a sizeable, if not shrinking, majority. He exited the war at a time when more radical views had become ascendant. That attitudinal shift supported a change in strategy that permitted Grant time to grind out the final year of the war. McClellan can scarcely be elevated to the ranks of the great captains of war, but he was hardly the worst that the conflict dragged onto center stage. For his many accomplishments during a difficult period of the war, McClellan's reputation needs to be guided out of the shadows of Grant and Sherman and accorded both the balanced criticism and recognition it deserves.

2. Linderman, *Embattled Courage,* 265; Porter, *Campaigning with Grant,* 174.

3. McClellan, *McClellan's Report,* 22–23; *OR,* vol. 12, 1:473–74. Hyperbole was not entirely eliminated by 1864, as seen in Grant's inspired claim that the "Army of the Potomac is in splendid condition and evidently feels like whipping somebody." Quoted in John S. Bowman, ed., *The Civil War Almanac* (New York: Almanac Publications, 1983), 195.

NOTE ON SOURCES

THE UNDERLYING THESIS OF THIS BOOK HAS DETERMINED THE nature of the source material employed in the research. It has required a survey of numerous secondary books and articles concerned with McClellan, Grant, and Sherman and the Civil War in general.

Nevertheless, certain primary source materials, both published and archival, are indispensable in any study of the persons mentioned above. Foremost among them are the letters and papers of George B. McClellan that are housed in the Manuscript Division of the Library of Congress. Stephen B. Sears's edited selection of the *Civil War Papers of George B. McClellan* (New York: Da Capo Press, 1989) were useful in targeting pertinent correspondence during the war years. The Library of Congress also houses important manuscripts of other Civil War participants that were occasionally consulted in the course of this study. Among them are the papers of William T. Sherman and his brother, John; Samuel P. Chase; Edwin M. Stanton; Fitz John Porter; and the journal of Samuel P. Heintzelman. Chase's papers can also be found in John Niven, ed., *The Salmon P. Chase Papers,* 3 vols. to date (Kent: Kent State Univ. Press, 1996).

Published sources also yielded great insights into the personalities and affairs of the subjects in this work. On Sherman, see Rachel Sherman Thorndike, ed., *The Sherman Letters* (New York: Scribner's, 1894), and Mark DeWolfe Howe, ed., *Home Letters of General Sherman* (New York: Scribner's, 1909). Grant's papers are thoroughly documented in John Y. Simon, ed., *Papers of Ulysses S. Grant,* 19 vols. to date (Carbondale: Southern Illinois Univ. Press, 1967). The basic source for any of Lincoln's writings is Roy P. Basler, ed., *The Collected Works of Abraham Lincoln,* 8 vols. (New Brunswick: Rutgers Univ. Press, 1953).

The most important of all published sources, and indispensable to any study of field operations during the Civil War, is *The War of the Rebellion: A Compilation of the Official Records of the Union and Confederate Armies,* 128 vols. (Washington, D.C.: GPO, 1880–1901). Also useful is the U.S. Congress, *Joint Committee on the Conduct of the War, Reports,* 3 vols. (Washington, D.C.: GPO, 1865).

Perhaps the most valuable and revealing sources for the objectives of this study were the memoirs of the principals involved. McClellan's posthumous memoirs are found in *McClellan's Own Story* (New York: Charles L. Webster, 1887). See also, William T. Sherman, *Memoirs of William T. Sherman*, 1st ed., 2 vols. (New York: D. Appleton, 1875), and Ulysses S. Grant, *Personal Memoirs*, 2 vols. (New York: Charles L. Webster, 1885–86). Additional reminiscences by Grant can be found in John Russell Young, *Tour Around the World with General Grant*, 2 vols. (New York: American News Company, 1879). A variety of other primary source materials, particularly diaries, journals, and memoirs, are cited in the text and the reader is encouraged to consult them.

Central to an understanding of the Unionist interpretation of the war and the quality of Federal military leadership during it are the works of Bruce Catton, T. Harry Williams, and Kenneth P. Williams. Catton was a prolific writer, and many similar themes regarding Federal leadership, as well as his glowing admiration for Grant, can be found in nearly all his works. Of particular use, however, are *Grant Moves South* (Boston: Little, Brown, 1960), *U.S. Grant and the American Military Tradition* (Boston: Little, Brown, 1954), and *Grant Takes Command* (Boston: Little, Brown, 1968). T. Harry Williams agreed with many of Catton's analyses of Federal military leadership, but his *Lincoln and His Generals* (New York: Knopf, 1952) argues that Lincoln emerged as the architect of Union military triumphs and that Grant was largely the instrument. His *McClellan, Sherman and Grant* (New Brunswick: Rutgers Univ. Press, 1962) is invaluable for its outright comparisons of the three commanders reviewed in this study. Kenneth P. Williams's *Lincoln Finds A General: A Military Study of the Civil War*, 5 vols. (New York: Macmillan, 1949–1959) is an elaborate review of how Lincoln searched in vain for the correct strategy and commander to win the war until Grant arrived in 1864.

The Unionist interpretation of Civil War command leadership has been perpetuated in scores of studies in more recent years; these are altogether too numerous to cite. Several, however, are worth mentioning since they have played a prominent role in the course of this study. Stephen Sears has emerged as the indisputable authority on the life and career of George B. McClellan. His *George B. McClellan: The Young Napoleon* (New York: Ticknor and Fields, 1988) is the paramount study of the man's life and military career. *Landscape Turned Red: The Battle of Antietam* (New York: Ticknor and Fields, 1983) is Sears's well-written study of McClellan's handling of the Antietam campaign. In much the same way, Sears's *To the Gates of Richmond: The Peninsula Campaign* (New York: Ticknor and Fields, 1992) is an attack on McClellan's management of the Federal offensive towards Richmond in 1862. A classic study of the Civil War that contains judicious assessments of military commanders is James B. McPherson's *Battle Cry of Freedom* (New York: Oxford Univ. Press, 1988). A most engaging and provocative study of Civil War command relationships is Joseph T. Glatthaar's *Partners in Command: The Relationship Between Leaders in the Civil War* (New York: Free Press, 1994). It is especially useful in that it makes decided comparisons on the quality of military leadership of all of the major principals involved in this study. Finally, Gary W. Gallagher's edited volume, *Antietam: Essays on the 1862 Maryland Campaign* (Kent: Kent State Univ. Press, 1989) is useful for the unequivocal verdicts leveled at McClellan's command capabilities.

A number of studies serve as a counterpoise to the prevailing interpretation of McClellan's military leadership and are worthy of mentioning. Joseph L. Harsh's "On the McClellan-Go-Round," *Civil War History* 19 (June 1973), 101–21 provides both an excellent review of the McClellan historiography and a context in which to understand how the Unionist interpretation has come to dominate assessments of Civil War military history. Edward Hagerman's *The American Civil War and the Origins of Modern Warfare* (Bloomington: Indiana Univ. Press, 1988) is an absolute necessity for an understanding of how commanders in the early part of the war tried to come to grips with fighting a modern war. An unusual and perceptive study that hails McClellan as the war's most imaginative commander is Rowena Reed's *Combined Operations in the Civil War* (Annapolis: United States Naval Institute, 1978).

Biographical works were also of great benefit in the course of this study. William S. McFeely's *Grant: A Biography* (New York: Norton, 1981) takes its subject to task for many shortcomings as a commander, but it should be balanced by Brooks D. Simpson's *Let Us Have Peace: Ulysses S. Grant and the Politics of War and Reconstruction* (Chapel Hill: Univ. of North Carolina Press, 1991). The best full biography of William T. Sherman appears to be John Marszalek's *Sherman: A Soldier's Passion for Order* (New York: Free Press, 1993). However, a more critical and provocative work is that of Michael Fellman, *Citizen Sherman* (New York: Random House, 1995). Other than Sears, Warren W. Hassler, Jr., provides the only other modern biography of George B. McClellan in *George B. McClellan:*

The Shield of the Union (Baton Rouge: Louisiana State Univ. Press, 1957). See also Hassler's *Commanders of the Army of the Potomac* (Baton Rouge: Louisiana State Univ. Press, 1962).

Both general and specific studies of the Civil War abound, and several have been invaluable in their application to this study. Mark Grimsley's *The Hard Hand of War: Union Military Policy toward Southern Civilians* (New York: Cambridge Univ. Press, 1995) provides an excellent insight into the very gradual application of hard war aimed at civilian populations in the South during the war. Useful in coming to terms with the advance of technology and its tactical implications is Grady McWhiney and Perry D. Jamieson, *Attack and Die: Civil War Military Tactics and the Southern Heritage* (Tuscaloosa: Univ. of Alabama Press, 1982). The edited works of Gabor S. Boritt, namely, *Why the Confederacy Lost* (New York: Oxford Univ. Press, 1992), and *Lincoln's Generals* (New York: Oxford Univ. Press, 1994) proved interesting and challenging. Any understanding of military tactics and strategy would be incomplete without a thorough reading of Herman Hattaway and Archer Jones, *How the North Won: A Military History of the Civil War* (Urbana: Univ. of Illinois Press, 1983). Phillip Shaw Paludan's *"A People's Contest": The Union and Civil War, 1861–1865* (New York: Harper, 1988), and Charles Royster's *The Destructive War: William Tecumseh Sherman, Stonewall Jackson, and the Americans* (New York: Knopf, 1991) merely highlight a long list of secondary works employed in this study. The reader is advised to consult the notes for specific citations.

INDEX

Adams, Michael C. C., 71–72
Alexander, E. Porter, 214
American Revolution, 131, 136
Anaconda Plan, 83, 137
Anderson, Robert, Gen. USA, 155, 160–61
Antietam campaign, 67, 68, 71, 96, 175–77, 196–97, 208, 216–23, 219–20, 223–25, 231–32
Atlanta campaign, 64, 192, 193, 194, 205–6, 226–27
Attack and Die, 209–10

Baker, Edward, Col. USA, 66, 142
Ball's Bluff, Battle of, 66, 142
Banks, Nathaniel P., Maj. Gen. USA, 104, 109, 110–11, 113–14, 117
Barlow, Samuel, 25, 78, 104
Barnard, John G., Gen. USA, 140–41
Bates, Edward, 82
Beauregard, P. G. T., Gen. USA, 55, 64, 69, 137, 138
Belmont, Augustus, 25
Belmont, Battle of, 178
Binney, Henry, Lt. USA, 222
Blair, Montgomery, 83, 182
Blenker, Louis, Gen. USA, 104–5
Boritt, Gabor S., 6–7
Bragg, Braxton, Gen. CSA, 80, 157–58, 185
Brewerton, Henry, 17
Buchanan, Robert Christie, 40, 58
Buckingham, Charles P., Brig. Gen. USA, 177
Buckner, Simon Bolivar, Gen. CSA, 38, 172, 179
Buell, Don Carlos, Gen. USA, 54, 57, 155, 161, 182, 185, 186, 205; on civil policy, 86; delay of active campaigning, 145; logistical problems of, 172–73; pressure for quick victory, 156–58
Bull Run, Battle of. *See* Manassas

"Bull run syndrome," 143
Burnside, Ambrose, Gen. USA, 8, 61, 145, 183, 229, 234; aggressive strategy of, 150, 152–53; at Antietam, 223–24; demotion of, 153, 181; and Lincoln, 159; logistical problems of, 177n.21; and McClellan, 67; at Petersburg, 68–69
Burns, Ken, 10–11
Butler, Benjamin F., Maj. Gen. USA, 61, 64
Butterfield, Daniel, Maj. Gen. USA, 54

Cameron, Simon, 38, 51, 89, 148
Carter, Hill, 93
Castel, Albert, 226
Catton, Bruce, 4, 7, 8, 33, 160n.55, 198–99, 206
Champion's Hill, Battle of, 228
Chancellorsville campaign, 29, 154–55, 225–26
Chase, Salmon P., 38, 136
Chattanooga campaign, 228
Chestnut, Mary, 192–93
Chickasaw Bluffs, Battle of, 161–62, 181, 212
Civil policy, 92–95, 100, 101
Civil War: and annihilative victory, 209–10, 230–31; early and later periods of, 235, 237; expectation of quick victory, 130–36, 163–64, 234, 237; pursuit in, 210–11
"Civil War Journal," 11
"The Civil War," documentary, 10–11
Clinton, William, 10
Cold Harbor, First Battle of, 70; Second Battle of, 230, 235, 237
Confederacy: erosion of strength, 188–93, 209; internal collapse of, 187; prisons of, 192; secession of, 78–83. *See also* Lee, Robert E., Gen. CSA
Confiscation law, 92, 94

Cooling, Benjamin F., 126
Corinth, Battle of, 69, 157, 162, 163, 173, 180, 185
Corn Exchange Regiment, 220, 231
Cornwallis, Lord, 131
Crater, Battle of the, 68–69, 73n.39
Crimean War, 205n.18
Crittenden, John, 82, 83
Custer, George Armstrong, 41n.37

Dabney, Robert L., 29
Dahlgren, John A., Adm. USA, 227
Dana, Charles, 41, 42
Davis, Jefferson, 55, 111, 116, 187, 190, 191, 214
Delafield, Richard, Maj. USA, 58–59
Diagnostic and Statistical Manual-IV (DSM-IV), 19–20
Donald, 200–201

Early, Jubal A., Gen. CSA, 88, 126–27, 145, 167, 204
Emancipation Proclamation, 96
Ewel, Richard, 31

Fair Oaks, Battle of, 76n.2, 115, 203
Fellman, 56
Floyd, John, 179
Foote, Andrew Hull, 162, 178–79
Foote, Shelby, 128, 194–95
Forrest, Nathan Bedford, Gen. CSA, 29, 180
Fort Sumter, bombardment of, 81–83
Forts Henry and Donelson campaign, 51, 69, 156, 162, 173, 178–80, 185
Fox, Gustavus V., 126
Franklin, William B., Gen. USA, 107, 167, 216, 218, 219, 222, 223
Franklin, Battle of, 209
Fredericksburg, First Battle of, 153, 183, 225, 234
Freeman, Douglas Southall, 31
Frémont, John C., Gen. USA, 87, 104, 117; abolition proclamation of, 88–89; in Shenandoah Valley campaign, 105, 110–11
French and Indian War, 131
Fuller, J. F. C., 225

Galena, USS, 66, 67
Gallagher, Gary W., 7, 188, 208, 234

Gardner, William, 25
Gentleman and the Tiger, 36
Gettysburg, Battle of, 30, 155
Gibbon, John, 25
Glatthaar, Joseph T., 7, 12, 18, 24, 27, 49, 159, 200, 207
Goldsborough, Louis M., 106, 107
Gordon, John B., Gen. CSA, 54
Grant, Ulysses S., Gen. USA: civilian career of, 13; on commanders, 61–62; and conciliatory policy, 98–99, 100–101; confidence of, 72–74; at Corinth, 156, 157; on decline of Confederacy, 193; defense of Washington, 124–27, 128–29, 167; delay of active campaigning, 147; and delegation of authority, 64; drinking habits of, 40–41, 42, 58, 234; and embarrassments and mistakes, 68–70; factors in success of, 194–95; failures as field commander, 161, 162–63, 227–30; and Halleck, 158; and hard war policy, 101; heroic reputation of, 6, 13, 184–85; historical assessment of, 6–7, 11, 43, 183; and Lincoln, 125, 128, 148, 182, 204–5, 237; logistical problems of, 177–81; and McClellan, 13, 53, 59–61, 166–67; memorial to, 3; military career of, antebellum, 58; moral courage of, 70, 71; Peninsula strategy of, 118–19; psychological profiling of, 40–42; reinforcement of, 127–28; in Richmond siege, 204–5; on secession, 79; secrecy of, 65, 148; and Sherman, 39; on Stanton, 50; strategic thinking of, 77, 85, 87–88, 198–99, 200–201; success in western theater, 73–74, 185–87
Grant's Tomb, 3
Greeley, Horace, 51, 137n.10
Greene, A. Wilson, 208, 218
Greenhow, Rose, 64–65
Grimsley, Mark, 99n.45, 101

Hagerman, Edward, 7, 23, 165
Halleck, Henry, Gen. USA, 13, 40, 55, 61, 65, 69, 87, 145, 153, 167, 173, 185, 199; and civil policy, 94; at Corinth, 157; and defense of Washington, 122–24, 125, 126, 221, 231; and Sherman, 38–39, 56–58
Hamilton, Charles S., Brig. Gen. CSA, 104
Hanover Court House, Va., 113

Hardee, William J., Gen. CSA, 226–27
Harpers Ferry, 216, 218, 222–23
Harper's Weekly, 108
Harrison's Landing letter, 77n.5, 89n.27, 93, 207
Harsh, Joseph L., 5, 23, 44, 86, 97
Hassler, Warren W., 4–5, 7
Hay, John, 46, 47–48
Heintzelman, Samuel P., Gen. USA, 47, 108
Herblock, 10
Heth, Harry, 204
Hewitt, Abram, 25
Hill, A. P., Gen. CSA, 25, 204, 217, 220
Hill, D. H., Gen. CSA, 214
Hill, Harvey, 215
Hitchcock, Ethan Allen, Maj. Gen. USA, 52
Holly Springs, Miss., 69–70, 163,
Holzer, Harold, 18
Hood, John Bell, Gen. CSA, 192, 193, 205, 206, 209, 210, 227
Hooker, Joseph, Gen. USA, 41n.37, 58, 145, 146, 150, 200; at Chancellorsville, 29, 154–55; Grant on, 61; and Lincoln, 32, 153–55; personality flaws of, 54; religious beliefs of, 30
Howard, Oliver O., Gen. USA, 30
Hunter, David, Gen. USA, 89, 126

Inman, Bobby Ray, 10
Iuka, Battle of, 163, 180, 181

Jackson, Thomas J. (Stonewall), Maj. Gen. CSA: 55, 213, 222–23; historical assessment of, 43; at Second Manassas, 151; religious beliefs of, 31; in Shenandoah Valley, 104, 108, 110, 111, 115, 117, 127
Jamieson, Perry D., 7, 209–10
Johnston, Albert Sidney, Gen. CSA, 185, 197
Johnston, Joseph E., Gen. CSA: 25, 50, 55, 186, 191–92; in Peninsula campaign, 103, 111, 112, 203
Jomini, Henri, 5

Kelley, D. C., Maj. CSA, 29
Keyes, Erasmus, 34
Kirby Smith, Edmund, Maj. Gen. CSA, 157

Ledlie, James H., 68, 69
Lee, Robert E., Gen. CSA: at Antietam, 176, 216; at Chancellorsville, 154, 225–26; civil policy of, 91n.30, 93–94; at Cold Harbor, 70; defense of Richmond, 202–4, 206, 214; failures in field command, 213–15, 225–26; at Fredericksburg, 153; historical assessment of, 14, 43; on inevitability of defeat, 190; "Lost Orders" of, 123, 216, 221; on McClellan, 4, 177, 195–96, 221; in Peninsula, 115–17, 208, 213–15; religious beliefs of, 30–31; reputation with Northern commanders, 72–73
Lincoln, Abraham: and Burnside, 159; and defense of Washington, 103–4, 109, 110–11, 114, 125, 126, 127, 144; Emancipation Proclamation of, 96; and Grant, 125, 128, 148, 182, 204–5, 237; heroic reputation of, 6, 45–46; and Hooker, 32, 153–55; and McDowell, 138, 139; and Meade, 155; psychological profiling of, 43; on secession, 79, 81–82, 83 ; selection of command, 168–70; and Sherman, 160n.56; and slavery issue, 88–90; strategic thinking of, 77, 88, 137, 199, 200–201, 203
Lincoln-McClellan relationship: contemporary analogies to, 9–10; and delay in active campaigning, 144, 145, 147; Harrison's Landing letter, 77n.5, 89n.27, 93, 207; historical view of, 12–13; lack of frankness in, 49–50, 147–48; and Peninsula campaign, 49, 103–5, 107–8, 109, 113–14, 118, 121, 207; psychological analysis of, 18; McClellan's rudeness toward Lincoln, 46–49, 53, 147; Stanton's role in, 50–53
Logan, John S., Gen. USA, 58
Longstreet, James, Gen. CSA, 8, 14–15, 151, 153, 177, 190, 225
Ludendorff, Erich von, 134
Lyon, Nathaniel, Gen. USA, 146

MacArthur, Douglas, 9
McCall, George A., Brig. Gen. USA, 116
McClellan, Ellen Marcy (wife), 48; correspondence with GBM, 22–24, 25–26, 36, 57; courtship and marriage, 27, 36; religious influence on GBM, 27

McClellan, George B., Gen. USA:
achievements of, 197, 237; at Antietam,
196–97, 216, 219–20, 223–25, 231;
boyhood of, 35n.27; and Buell, 156;
caution of, 71–72, 74–75, 129, 143–44,
149–50; civilian career of, 35–36, 37;
civil policy of, 90–94, 95; comparison
to Grant and Sherman, viii–ix, 6, 11,
182–83, 234, 235; conciliation strategy
of, 76–77, 84–87, 88, 90–99, 101–2; delay
of active campaigning, 145–48, 149;
and delegation of authority, 62–63,
141–42; demotion of, 49, 177, 182–83;
distrustfulness of, 62–63; embarrassments and mistakes of, 65–66, 67;
estimates of enemy strength, 20–21,
71–72; failures as field commander, ix,
13–14, 159–60, 206–9, 216–24; family
life of, 36; friendships of, 24–25, 36;
historical assessment of, viii–x, 3–11, 15,
43–44, 62, 143, 149–50, 159–60, 183–84,
196–97, 206–8; and inquiry into Ball's
Bluff, 66, 142–43; later years of, 37;
letters of, 6n.7, 22–24, 25–26, 36, 42;
logistical problems of, 173–77; marriage
of, 22, 27, 36; in Maryland campaign,
175–77, 216–23, 231–32; memorial to,
1–3, 8–9, 236; military career of,
antebellum, 35; mission to save Union,
25–26, 31–34; moral courage of, 66–67,
70–71; organization of army, 71, 139–41,
144, 171, 175; and problems of early
command, 165, 171, 174, 184, 234–35;
psychological profiling of, ix–x, 7, 16–25,
37, 233–34; religious beliefs of, 25–28;
respected by soldiers/officer corps, 54;
rudeness of, 46–48, 53, 58–59; on
secession, 78; secrecy of, 63, 64, 147–49;
selection for command, 170; and
Stanton, 51–52, 54; vanity of, 4, 17,
33–34, 53–54; at West Point, 17, 25, 34.
See also Grant Ulysses S.; Lee, Robert E.;
Lincoln-McClellan relationship;
Peninsula campaign; Sherman, William
T.; Slavery issue; Washington, D.C.
McClellan, Max (son), 36
McClellan, May (daughter), 36
"McClellan's Way," 11
McClernand, John A., Gen. USA, 58, 61,
64, 69, 163, 181
McCullough, David, 9

McDowell, Irvin, Gen. USA, 37, 54, 61, 64,
151, 182, 225; and McClellan, 114–15; at
First Manassas, 83, 84, 136–39, 140, 168;
at Second Manassas, 158; recall from
Peninsula, 52, 107, 108, 109, 113–14, 115,
116–18, 212, 213; selection for command,
169–71; in Shenandoah Valley, 111, 116
McFeely, William, 43, 59, 69, 163
McPherson, James B., 6, 21, 77n.5, 160n.55,
184, 187–88, 194, 200, 218–19
McWhiney, Grady, 209–10
Magruder, John B., Gen. CSA, 106, 107,
112, 120
Malvern Hill, Battle of 66–67, 119, 214, 215
Manassas: First Battle of, 37, 65, 83, 84,
136–39, 140, 160; Second Battle of 54,
96, 139n.14, 144, 151–52, 158
Mansfield, Joseph, 170
Marble, Manton, 25
Marszalek, John F., 39, 68n.32, 100
Marvel, William, 8, 67
Maryland campaign. See Antietam
campaign
Mason, R. B., Col. USA, 56
Maury, Dabney, 25
Meade, George C., Gen. USA, 55, 145,
146, 149, 200, 229; and conciliatory
strategy, 82; at Gettysburg, 155; and
Grant, 61; at Holly Springs, 69–70
Meigs, Montgomery C., 176
Memphis, Battle of, 99, 185, 205
Mexican War, 35, 40, 132–33
Miles, Dixon S., Gen. USA, 222, 223
Mill Springs, Battle of, 156, 172–73
Missroon, J. F., Capt. USA, 107
Mitchell, Reid, 231
Moore, Thomas O., 80
Mordecai, Alfred, Maj. USA, 58–59

Napoleonic Wars, 131–32, 163
Nashville, Battle of, 156, 173, 185, 205,
209–10
Neely, Mark, Jr., 99n.45, 100, 186
Nevins, Allan, 17, 26, 143, 173, 200
New Orleans, 205
Nicolay, John, 46

Palfrey, Francis W., 196–97
Paludan, Phillip S., 49–50
Patrick, Marsena, Gen. USA, 94–95
Patterson, Robert, Gen. USA, 138, 170

Pemberton, John C., Gen. CSA, 186, 191–92, 205
Pender, Dorsey, Gen. CSA, 226
Pendleton, William Nelson, 29
Peninsula campaign: 4–5; conciliation policy in, 90–95; enemy strength assessments in, 20–21, 120, 211; evacuation from, 95, 119; landing in, 103–4, 106–7; Lincoln-McClellan relations during, 49, 103–5, 107–8, 109, 118, 121, 207; logistical problems in, 174–75; reduction of campaign force, 52, 104–5, 107–8, 114–18, 129, 212, 213; responsibility for failure in, 119–24, 129, 175, 211–15; siege of Richmond, 202–3, 212–13; Stanton's blunders in, 52–53, 105–6, 107, 113, 120, 121; strategic thinking in, 90, 96–98, 103–4, 200–202, 213; supply base in, 112, 173–74
Perryville, Battle of, 157, 173
Petersburg campaign, 68, 119, 205, 206, 230;
Pickett, George, 31
Pillow, Gideon, Gen. CSA, 179
Pinkerton, Allan, 65, 211
Pleasonton, Alfred, 221
Polk, James K., 132
Polk, Leonidas, Maj. Gen. CSA, 29
Pope, John, Gen. USA, 76, 225, 237; aggressive strategy of, 150–52; civil policy of, 92–93, 94, 95; at Second Manassas, 96, 145, 151–52, 158; in Virginia command, 91–92
Porter, Andrew, Brig. Gen. USA, 140
Porter, David Dixon, Adm. USA, 181
Porter, Fitz John, Gen. USA, 24, 25, 113, 118, 158
Porter, Horace, 72, 235
Powell, Colin, 10
Prime, William, 25
Psychohistorians, 19n.6

Randall, James G., 4–5, 23
Rawlins, John, 41–42
Reed, Rowena, 23
Religious beliefs: of commanders, 29–30; force in society, 28; of McClellan, 25–28; military ecclesiastics, 29; moral framework for war, 28–29
Resaca, Battle of, 67, 68n.32;

Richmond, Va., 98, 200–205, 206, 212–13
Rodgers, John, 66
Rosecrans, William S., Gen. USA, 29–30, 32, 61, 67, 150, 163, 181, 186–87
Royster, Charles, 100
Ruffin, Edmund, 90

Santa Anna, Antonio Lopez de, 132
Schimmelfennig, Alexander, 169
Schurz, Carl, 78, 182
Scott, Thomas W., 38
Scott, Winfield, Gen. USA, 54n.12, 84, 86, 96, 97, 117, 136; liabilities as commander, 170; in Mexican War, 132–33; strategic plan of, 82–83, 137
Sears, Stephen W., 7, 8, 11, 17, 18, 22, 35n.27, 63, 86, 143, 159, 206–7, 208, 218
Secession: Northern beliefs on causes of, 78–81; strategic options in, 81–83
Seddon, James, 191
Sevastopol, siege of, 205n.18
Seven Days' campaign, 64, 66, 70, 91, 106, 119, 214, 215, 225
Seward, William H., 47, 48, 82, 91, 106
Shea, William, 8
Sheridan, Philip H., Gen. USA, 6, 42, 50
Sherman, John, 80
Sherman, Thomas W., Gen. USA, 86, 99n.46
Sherman, William T., Gen. USA: in Atlanta campaign, 192, 193, 194, 205–6, 226–27; civilian career of, 13; civil policy of, 100, 101; and conciliatory policy, 98–100; death of son, 18n.3; delay of active campaigning, 146–47; and delegation of authority, 63–64; enemy strength estimates of, 211; failure to pursue, 205–6, 226–27; failures as field commander, 160–62; heroic reputation of, 6, 13, 43, 184–85; in Kentucky, 155–56, 168, 171, 172; and Lincoln, 160n.56; logistical problems of, 180, 181–82; on McClellan, 167; memorial to, 3; personality flaws of, 55–58; and problems of early command, 167–68, 171, 172; psychological profiling of, 37–40; religious beliefs of, 30; on secession, 79–81; secrecy of, 65, 148;

Sherman, William T., Gen. USA (*cont.*)
  selection for command, 169–70; and
  slavery issue, 80; and Stanton, 50, 56
Shiloh, Battle of, 69, 100, 156–57, 158, 161,
  162, 173, 180, 183, 215, 227–28
Sigel, Franz, Gen. USA, 8, 118, 126–27
Slavery issue: as cause of secession, 78–81;
  and confiscation law, 92, 94; and
  Lincoln's policy, 88–90; McClellan on,
  90, 91, 94; Sherman on, 80
"Smithsonian's Great Battles of the Civil
  War," 11
Smith, W. F. "Baldy," 25
Spanish-American War, 132
Spotsylvania Court House campaign,
  229–30
Stanton, Edwin M., 33, 54, 61, 90, 109,
  177; blunders in Peninsula campaign,
  52–53, 105–6, 107, 113, 120, 121; and
  defense of Washington, 126; dislike
  of McClellan, 51–52; relations with
  commanders, 50, 55; and Sherman,
  50, 56
Stevens, Isaac I., 35
Stewart, Charles, 34
Stille, Charles Janaway, 163
Stone, Charles P., Gen. USA, 66, 142
Stuart, James, 25
Stuart, J. E. B., Gen. CSA, 66, 117
Sumner, Edwin, 170, 215n.36, 217, 219
Swinton, William, 196

Taylor, Richard, 80
Taylor, Zachary, 170
Thomas, George H., Gen. USA, 57, 58, 61,
  172–73, 209, 210
Tredegar Iron Works, 200, 201
Truman, Harry, 9

Urbanna Plan, 103, 200, 201–2, 213

Van Dorn, Earl, Gen. CSA, 181
Vicksburg campaigns: First, 64–65, 161,
  163, 180–81, 183; Second, 101, 191–92,
  205, 228
Vietnam War, 135, 136
Virginia, CSS, 112

Wadsworth, James, Brig. Gen. USA,
  109
Walker, John G., Gen. CSA, 221
Wallace, Lew, Gen. USA, 126
War of 1812, 132
Washington, Martha Custis, 90
Washington, D.C.: Grant's defense of,
  124–27, 128–29, 167; McClellan's
  defense of, 52, 103–4, 108–12, 121–24,
  140–41, 144–45, 171, 198
Weigley, Russell, 207
Wert, Jeffry, 8, 208
West Point, 17, 25, 34
Wilcox, Cadmus, 25
Wilderness, Battle of the, 72, 125, 128, 204,
  229, 235
Will, George F., 8–9
Williams, Kenneth P., 4, 5, 6, 7, 8, 17, 86,
  143, 159
Williams, T. Harry, 4, 6, 7, 8, 12, 13, 17,
  76n.1, 77n.3, 86, 104, 143, 156, 160, 183,
  199, 206, 207
Wilson's Creek, Battle of, 87, 146
Winder, John H., Gen. CSA, 192
Wool, John, 170
World War I, 133–34
World War II, 134, 135
Wright, Horatio, Gen. USA, 127

Yorktown, Va., 65, 107, 211
Young, John Russell, 166

Zollicoffer, Felix, Gen. CSA, 172–73

George B. McClellan and Civil War History
was designed by Gary Gore;
composed in 10½/13 Caslon Book with Birch display
on a Power Macintosh using QuarkXPress
by The Book Page, Inc.; printed
by sheet-fed offset lithography
on 50-pound Turin Book natural stock
(an acid-free, totally chlorine-free paper),
Smyth sewn and bound over binder's boards
in Arrestox B cloth, and wrapped with dust jackets
printed in four colors on 100-pound enamel
stock coated with polypropylene
matt film lamination
by Thomson-Shore, Inc.;
and published by
The Kent State University Press
KENT, OHIO 44242 USA